P9-DJK-225

Methodological Approaches to Community-Based Research

Methodological Approaches to Community-Based Research

Edited By

Leonard A. Jason and David S. Glenwick

American Psychological Association • Washington, DC

Copyright © 2012 by the American Psychological Association. All rights reserved. Except as permitted under the United States Copyright Act of 1976, no part of this publication may be reproduced or distributed in any form or by any means, including, but not limited to, the process of scanning and digitization, or stored in a database or retrieval system, without the prior written permission of the publisher.

Published by
American Psychological Association
750 First Street, NE
Washington, DC 20002
www.apa.org

To order
APA Order Department
P.O. Box 92984
Washington, DC 20090-2984
Tel: (800) 374-2721; Direct: (202) 336-5510
Fax: (202) 336-5502; TDD/TTY: (202) 336-6123
Online: www.apa.org/pubs/books
E-mail: order@apa.org

In the U.K., Europe, Africa, and the Middle East, copies may be ordered from
American Psychological Association
3 Henrietta Street
Covent Garden, London
WC2E 8LU England

Typeset in Goudy by Circle Graphics, Inc., Columbia, MD

Printer: Edwards Brothers, Inc., Ann Arbor, MI
Cover Designer: Mercury Publishing Services, Rockville, MD

The opinions and statements published are the responsibility of the authors, and such opinions and statements do not necessarily represent the policies of the American Psychological Association.

Library of Congress Cataloging-in-Publication Data

Methodological approaches to community-based research / edited by Leonard A. Jason and David S. Glenwick. —1st ed.
    p. cm.
  Includes bibliographical references and index.
  ISBN-13: 978-1-4338-1115-9
  ISBN-10: 1-4338-1115-4
  1. Community psychology—Research—Methodology. 2. Community mental health services—Research—Methodology. 3. Community-based social services—Research—Methodology. 4. Public health—Research—Methodology. I. Jason, Leonard. II. Glenwick, David.
  RA790.55.M48 2012
  362.196'890072—dc23

                              2011036626

British Library Cataloguing-in-Publication Data

A CIP record is available from the British Library.

Printed in the United States of America
First Edition

DOI: 10.1037/13492-000

To our students, with whom we have shared our knowledge and from whom we have learned even more.
—*Leonard A. Jason and David S. Glenwick*

CONTENTS

CONTRIBUTORS

Nicole E. Allen, PhD, Department of Psychology, University of Illinois at Urbana–Champaign

Chris Barker, PhD, Department of Clinical, Educational, and Health Psychology, University College London, London, England

G. Anne Bogat, PhD, Department of Psychology, Michigan State University, East Lansing

Deborah Bybee, PhD, Department of Psychology, Michigan State University, East Lansing

Rebecca Campbell, PhD, Department of Psychology, Michigan State University, East Lansing

Christian M. Connell, PhD, Yale University School of Medicine, New Haven, CT

Joseph A. Durlak, PhD, Department of Psychology, Loyola University, Chicago, IL

Allison B. Dymnicki, PhD, Institute for Health Research and Policy, University of Illinois at Chicago, and American Institutes of Research, Washington, DC

David S. Glenwick, PhD, Department of Psychology, Fordham University, New York, NY

Katie A. Gregory, PhD, Department of Psychology, Michigan State University, East Lansing

David B. Henry, PhD, Institute for Health Research and Policy, University of Illinois at Chicago

Bettina B. Hoeppner, PhD, Center for Addiction Medicine, Psychiatry Department, Massachusetts General Hospital, Harvard Medical School, Boston

Joseph Hughey, PhD, Department of Architecture, Urban Planning, and Design, University of Missouri–Kansas City

Leonard A. Jason, PhD, Department of Psychology, DePaul University, Chicago, IL

Shabnam Javdani, MA, Department of Psychology, University of Illinois at Urbana–Champaign

James G. Kelly, PhD, Emeritus, Department of Psychology, University of Illinois at Chicago

Raymond P. Lorion, PhD, School of Education, Towson University, Towson, MD

Anthony T. Lo Sasso, PhD, Division of Health Policy and Administration, School of Public Health, University of Illinois at Chicago

Cory M. Morton, PhD, School of Social Work, Rutgers, The State University of New Jersey, New Brunswick

Molly Pachan, PhD, Illinois Institute of Technology, Chicago

Debra Patterson, PhD, School of Social Work, Wayne State University, Detroit, MI

Stephen C. Peck, PhD, Institute for Social Research, University of Michigan, Ann Arbor

N. Andrew Peterson, PhD, School of Social Work, Rutgers, The State University of New Jersey, New Brunswick

Nancy Pistrang, PhD, Department of Clinical, Educational, and Health Psychology, University College London, London, England

Nicole Porter, PhD, Center for Community Research, DePaul University, Chicago, IL

Rae Jean Proeschold-Bell, PhD, Center for Health Policy, Duke University, Durham, NC

Alfred Rademaker, PhD, Northwestern University, Evanston, IL

Robert J. Reid, PhD, Department of Family and Child Studies, Montclair State University, Montclair, NJ

Paul W. Speer, PhD, Department of Human and Organizational Development, Vanderbilt University, Nashville, TN

Jacob Kraemer Tebes, PhD, Division of Prevention and Community Research and the Consultation Center, Yale University School of Medicine, New Haven, CT

Nathan R. Todd, PhD, Department of Psychology, DePaul University, Chicago, IL

Alexander von Eye, PhD, Department of Psychology, Michigan State University, East Lansing

Nicole Zarrett, PhD, Department of Psychology, University of South Carolina, Columbia

FOREWORD

RAYMOND P. LORION

The purpose of a foreword varies somewhat depending on the contents of the volume that it opens. In some cases it provides an overview of what lies ahead. In the case of the present volume, that responsibility has been met at the outset within the editors' Introduction. In the pages that follow, I attempt to meet the other responsibility of a foreword, that is, to prepare readers for what lies ahead, not so much in terms of content as in terms of effort and the attendant reward.

Many readers may find the contents of chapters in this volume somewhat unfamiliar. I expect that those community psychologists of my generation who have not kept up with methodological advances may feel unprepared for the quantitative sophistication of the approaches herein. Younger readers may be quite comfortable with some chapters but find others unfamiliar and challenging. Few readers will complete this volume without considerable thought, effort, and consequent benefit. Those who read the chapters carefully, consider what they have read, and in all likelihood, reread several of them will be richly rewarded for that effort. They will learn much and benefit from then on as consumers as well as producers of studies relevant to the interests of their discipline, whatever it may be, as long as it focuses on the lives of people in the contexts of their life experiences.

As noted, readers should proceed with some degree of caution—but they should also be buoyed by scholarly curiosity and professional enthusiasm—for I would predict that if read carefully, the contents of this volume are very likely to change the questions that readers ask and the solutions that they seek. As a consequence, the discipline's rigor will be enhanced, along with its heuristic contributions to readers' understanding of human behavior within real-life settings and under real-life circumstances. The methods described in this volume add substantially to the tools readers will have available to understand, predict, and ultimately influence the healthy development of individuals, groups, and communities. Readers will complete the volume with a broadened sense of community psychology's impact on and relationships with multiple other disciplines. With methodological pluralism will come disciplinary pluralism!

The latter prediction is based on my long-standing belief in the seemingly age-old adage—also known as Maslow's hammer or the law of the instrument[1]—that when the only tool one has is a hammer, every problem begins to resemble a nail. Community psychology's development as an applied human science reflects its continued reliance on a series of hammers, each of which determined its selection of questions and its pursuit of answers. Reliance on parametric and nonparametric statistical procedures such as *t* tests, analyses of variance, and a variety of bivariate correlational analyses heavily impacted early forays into community studies. Those methods shaped the questions psychologists asked and their sense of what answers they found.

Because many of the variables we as psychologists sought to examine had never before been studied, we invested time and energy in the development of scales and measures whose structures we unraveled through the application of orthogonal and oblique factor analyses. All too often we relied on measures of internal reliability as meeting that psychometric requirement and glanced over the all-important requirement that the appropriate evidence of reliability was important only when accompanied by substantive evidence of validity. Subsequently, we expanded our statistical toolkits to include multivariate procedures, thereby allowing expanded consideration of the complexity of the phenomena focused upon by our discipline. Psychologists' forays into preventive interventions required measures and methods that could monitor pathogenic trajectories and allow for the comparison of influences on the pathways to health, dysfunction, and pathology. Our studies in prevention and health promotion made evident that such pathways often

---

[1]Maslow, A. (1966). *The psychology of science: A reconnaissance*. New York, NY: Harper & Row.

represent group rather than individual journeys and that the resulting complexity of influences, albeit conceptually modeled, could not be rigorously studied in light of limitations in our analytical methods.

Those impasses may now be confronted! Pluralistic methods have long been endorsed by community psychologists. In reality, however, the pluralism was limited to qualitative and quantitative methods, occasionally applied in the same study but rarely conceptually integrated. More often, qualitative methods have served as the "scouting party" to open a pathway into uncharted territory and unstudied phenomena. Although frequently justified as a necessary initial step in the programmatic study of the chosen phenomena, too often one qualitative study has been followed by another qualitative study leading to yet another qualitative study. Too rarely have those applying qualitative methods consolidated their findings in ways that informed the design of psychometrically and ecologically valid quantitative methods that moved from the generation to the testing of theory-based hypotheses. Similar criticism can be applied to those whose only view of research has been quantitative investigations within randomized controlled trials or their nearest quasi-experimental kin.

Too often these investigators viewed scientific findings as built solely on statistical significance without applying qualitative methods such as interviews, focus groups, Delphi techniques, and the like to unravel the clinical, practical, and ecological significance of their "discovery." Granted that their intervention resulted in a change in one or more dependent measures at or beyond even the most rigorous alpha level. Sadly, however, the reality is that in many cases, the participants were only slightly better off than they had been before the intervention. Everyone has been in traffic jams in which inch by inch one moves forward and must acknowledge progress, all the time knowing that the event one needs to reach (or the level of reading or math ability necessary to succeed in high school or college) remains beyond one's grasp, closer perhaps but still out of range within the time available.

The chapters within this volume offer substantive hope for coming markedly closer to true methodological pluralism in the design of psychologists' studies and, most important, in the conceptualization of their research programs. Presented herein are the pieces necessary for community psychologists to appreciate, adapt, and integrate methods from other fields within psychology (e.g., developmental psychopathology, neuroscience), educational science, sociology, anthropology, economics and economic forecasting, and especially for those interested in prevention and health promotion, public health and its biostatistical allies. The messages herein, however, extend beyond borrowing methods from others and encourages genuine collaboration with others from these various disciplines.

These messages also urge us to understand the potential for understanding human phenomena of interest when we approach and invite those who display or experience those phenomena to join our studies not simply as participants but also as coinvestigators. Methodological pluralism assumes a deep appreciation of the limits of our perspective and our reliance on others to broaden and inform that perspective. Across the chapters in this volume, readers are repeatedly advised to shed the mantle of the academy and enter and experience, insofar as possible, the communities and populations that we seek to study. Our interpretation of the meaning of findings becomes grounded when viewed and refined from the eyes and minds of their targets.

As readers begin to engage such methods as cluster analysis, meta-analysis, time-series analysis, cost–benefit analysis, geographic information systems analytic methods, and a host of epidemiological designs, the work of moving through this volume will intensify. Familiarity with the terms is not the same as the in-depth knowledge necessary for their application and interpretation. Again, collaboration with others who use these methods with regularity will both inform and broaden psychologists' work. In the process, we will sustain and expand a characteristic of community psychology's development that is insufficiently acknowledged yet highly important. Many of our early efforts in cutting previously unexplored paths as we struggled to understand persons in context, the evolution of health and pathology, and the potential to expand service availability and acceptability—all within the context of, and reaping the benefits of, genuinely interacting with the subjects of our studies as active and engaged participants—have been admired and adopted by the very disciplines whose sophisticated methods we are now recognizing and adopting.

Such openness may cloud the distinctiveness of psychologists' discipline, but it will clarify our ability to understand, predict, and ultimately shape behavioral outcomes. That, after all, is the defining purpose of science! Readers, prepare to grow as you proceed through this most important volume!

PREFACE

The past 30 years have seen a dramatic increase in the number of professionals involved in community-based research. Their work includes applied interventions and program evaluation as well as basic research on social problems. During this period, however, the methodologies used in such activities have not kept pace with the development of theory and techniques pertaining to data collection and analysis. Unfortunately, few research methods textbooks take an applied focus, and none of them focus specifically on aiding the community researcher in learning about and actually using relevant cutting-edge methodologies.

A number of excellent edited books have been published in the last decade or so on methodological issues in psychology. None, though, have had as their focus methodologies for analyzing community-level data or, most important, included practical step-by-step illustrations of how to carry out such analyses. In contrast, the aim of Leonard A. Jason, David S. Glenwick, and the other contributors to this volume is to present a range of innovative methodologies relevant to community-based research as well as illustrations of the applicability of these methodologies to specific social problems and projects.

xix

In this volume, we also highlight the increasing collaboration that is occurring between psychologists and professionals from a variety of disciplines, such as epidemiology, public health, and economics. Furthermore, we point to the benefits that ensue when community theorists, interventionists, and methodologists from these disciplines work together to better understand complex person–environment systems, the transactions that characterize them, and the change processes within communities.

Our intended audience for the present work comprises several groups: The first includes researchers across the social and behavioral sciences involved in the empirical investigation of contemporary social problems. The second group consists of researchers in related fields, such as social work, education, public health, nursing, and communications, engaged in similar social analyses and change efforts. The third group includes advanced graduate students seeking to become familiar with methodologies that, although innovative today, are likely (we believe) to become increasingly commonplace. The fourth group consists of mental health and other community-based professionals charged with designing, implementing, and/or evaluating intervention programs at the community level. Each, we hope, will find much that is heuristically (and professionally) valuable in the following pages.

The chapters in this book provide an introduction to the theory behind, the procedures involved in, and the application of each of the methodologies presented. However, often the most valuable learning occurs by doing. Thus special features of the methodology chapters in Parts II through IV of *Methodological Approaches to Community-Based Research* are web appendices that include specific applications (e.g., SPSS, SAS, GIS) and detailed guidelines on how to run the applications for analyzing the accompanying data sets. We encourage readers to explore these web appendices, thereby learning firsthand how to use the innovative methodologies explored in Parts II through IV of this volume.[1]

---

[1] There are a number of excellent online qualitative data analysis websites. For example, one at http://onlineqda.hud.ac.uk/Introduction/index.php includes a collection of learning tools and materials that address common issues when conducting qualitative data analysis.

ACKNOWLEDGMENTS

A number of people have, at various stages, facilitated bringing this work to fruition. We are deeply appreciative of our many current and former students who have helped us think through many of the issues considered here, including Darrin Aase, Monica Adams, Josefina Alvarez, Christopher Beasley, Abby Brown, Molly Brown, Richard Contreras, Margaret I. Davis, Julia DiGangi, Meredyth Evans, Ron Harvey, Jean Hill, Bronwyn Hunter, Elias Kithuri, Cecile Lardon, John M. Majer, Susan McMahon, Steven Pokorny, Olya Rabin-Belyaev, Karina Reyes, Jean Rhodes, Doreen Salina, Sharon Song, Edward B. Stevens, Renee Taylor, Susan Torres-Harding, and Lynn Wagner. Our thanks, too, to many colleagues for their input related to the concepts and approaches discussed in this book, including Steven Everett, Joseph R. Ferrari, Fred Friedberg, Daryl Isenberg, Christopher Keys, Ray Legler, John Moritsugu, David Mueller, Bradley Olson, LaVome Robinson, and Lisa Walt.

We are also indebted to Raymond Lorion and James Kelly, whose writings and perspectives, as reflected in the insightful Foreword and Afterword, respectively, which they have contributed, have constituted an important part of the theoretical underpinnings of this volume.

The overall idea for this book emerged out of a series of informal discussions with Anne Bogat over several years, and we are grateful for her encouragement and intellectual stimulation.

In addition, the editors appreciate financial support received from the National Institute on Alcohol Abuse and Alcoholism, the National Institute on Drug Abuse, the National Center on Minority Health and Health Disparities, the National Cancer Institute, the National Institute of Allergy and Infectious Diseases, and the National Institute of Nursing Research.

Finally, we express our thanks to the editorial staff of the American Psychological Association and especially to Linda Malnasi McCarter, Peter Pavilionis, and Neelima Charya for the continuous support and invaluable guidance that they have provided us.

Methodological Approaches to Community-Based Research

1

INTRODUCTION: AN OVERVIEW OF METHODOLOGICAL INNOVATIONS IN COMMUNITY RESEARCH

LEONARD A. JASON AND DAVID S. GLENWICK

Until recently, the vast majority of community-based programs have been health and clinical interventions targeting individual change. However, with the growing awareness of the limitations of this approach, (Lorion, Iscoe, DeLeon, & VandenBos, 1996; Tolan, Keys, Chertok, & Jason, 1990), a more encompassing social change perspective (Jason & Glenwick, 2002; Lorion, 1990) has achieved increasing prominence. This perspective as indicated by Jason et al. (2004), which conceptualizes individual behavior as embedded within communities, has given rise to a new generation of social problem analyses and interventions based on the transactions between persons and community-based structures. Such an orientation, which is both more nuanced and broader, requires more sophisticated methodologies to be able to simultaneously analyze community-level and individual-level phenomena and their mutual impact. These methodologies are the focus of the present volume.

One paradigm that has captured the attention of many prevention practitioners is an ecological model (Kelly, 1985, 1990, 2006), which attempts to explicate how people adapt to and become effective in diverse social environments. An ecological analysis seeks to understand behavior in

3

the context of individual, family, peer, and community influences (Bronfen-brenner, 1979). This ecological paradigm underlies—sometimes explicitly, at other times implicitly—the application of the methodological approaches described to the analysis of community-level data and the amelioration of social ills.

In Part I of this volume, authors focus on the importance of pluralism and mixed methods (i.e., the use of both quantitative and qualitative approaches) in community research. In so doing, the authors of the three chapters in this section provide the theoretical and conceptual underpinnings for the more methodological sections that follow. In Chapter 2, Jacob Krae-mer Tebes, from a philosophy of science perspective, provides philosophical bases for the use of multiple methods in community research. He discusses two positions in particular—pragmatism and perspectivism—that offer philo-sophical underpinnings for the use of both quantitative and qualitative meth-ods. Tebes shows how these positions have significant implications both for how community researchers carry out their work and for the knowledge that is arrived at through this process.

In Chapter 3, Chris Barker and Nancy Pistrang review four guiding principles of community psychology that affirm a belief in research using multiple methodologies. Yet, despite their endorsement of methodological pluralism, community researchers rarely pause to reflect on exactly what such a stance actually entails in practice. Therefore, Barker and Pistrang consider the implications of a pluralist stance for both the producers and the consumers of community research. They address the question of how research using multiple methodologies is to be evaluated: Does adopting a stance of pluralism mean that there are no longer any solid central criteria against which to judge the quality of research? The authors argue that there is a central core of principles, some methodological and some values oriented, that can be applied to all community research and that there are additional more genre-specific criteria that can be articulated for vari-ous discrete research orientations. Barker and Pistang also differentiate among several levels at which pluralism can be incorporated, namely, within individual studies, within a research program, and within the field as a whole.

In Chapter 4, Rebecca Campbell, Katie A. Gregory, Debra Patterson, and Deborah Bybee offer a detailed illustration of the integration of qualitative and quantitative approaches. They highlight methodological issues in a 12-year longitudinal analysis of legal case prosecution outcomes for adult sex-ual assault cases before and after the implementation of a community-level intervention for sexual assault survivors. To evaluate the intervention's effec-tiveness, the authors used a mixed methods design involving the sequential collection and analysis of quantitative and qualitative data. The quantitative component revealed a significant increase in the successful prosecution of reported rapes after the program's implementation, and the qualitative component (primarily qualitative interviewing) identified the mediating mechanisms of this system change.

In Parts II through IV, authors present chapters on methodologies that involve the grouping of data (e.g., cluster analysis, meta-analysis), change over time (e.g., time series analysis, survival analysis), and the context of behavior and community-wide interventions (e.g., multilevel modeling, epidemiologic approaches, geographic information systems). To provide consistency in format, the majority of the chapters include two sections. The initial section is a review of that chapter's methodological approach, including the theory underlying the approach and a summary of the steps involved in using it. This section also considers the approach's benefits and drawbacks for community-based research. The second section then presents either an investigation of a social problem or an evaluation of a community intervention, demonstrating for the reader how to analyze relevant data in this area from the perspective of the chapter's methodological approach.

The case studies described include concrete, detailed procedures to guide the reader through the analysis of the data. Online examples of relevant statistical applications, available in the web appendices to the respective chapters (http://pubs.apa.org/books/supp/Jason-Glenwick), include the data and instructions for the applications used by the contributors.

In Part II of the book, authors present methods that involve the grouping of data in various ways, including cluster analysis, within-person analysis, and meta-analysis. In Chapter 5, Allison B. Dymnicki and David B. Henry consider methods for delineating natural groups, or clusters, in data sets. These involve sorting cases or variables according to their similarity on one or more dimensions, thereby creating groups that maximize within-group similarity and minimize between-groups similarity. This process facilitates the uncovering of diversity and heterogeneity within data (e.g., types of neighborhoods). As an example, Dymnicki and Henry describe a study involving the clustering of community (e.g., concentrated poverty) and family (e.g., cohesion) characteristics to help explain youth delinquent behavior, with different patterns of clustering having different relationships with the criterion variable.

G. Anne Bogat, Nicole Zarrrett, Stephen C. Peck, and Alexander von Eye, in Chapter 6, describe a person-oriented approach that enables the exploration of patterns that exist between an individual and his or her behavioral contexts. This perspective is in contrast to variable-oriented approaches that are used to compare groups (rather than individuals) and that aggregate data across individuals, thereby minimizing, often inappropriately, interindividual differences. A person-oriented approach permits the researcher to detect possible subgroups within larger groups (i.e., different patterns or profiles varying in subgroup size). As an example, the authors describe a study that uncovered several patterns in the relationship between adolescent out-of-school activities and later college attendance.

In Chapter 7, Joseph A. Durlak and Molly Pachan outline the components of meta-analysis, an increasingly popular technique that allows the researcher to combine and analyze data from multiple studies in a research area (e.g., the effects of a preventive intervention on at-risk youth) to quantitatively evaluate the literature. This technique complements narrative approaches to research reviews. Besides evaluating the impact of interventions, meta-analysis is a valuable tool for investigating what features of an intervention are crucial in influencing outcomes as well as potential moderators of such impact.

The authors of the chapters that make up Part III consider methodologies that examine change over time, including time series analysis and survival analysis. Bettina B. Hoeppner and Rae Jean Proeschold-Bell, in Chapter 8, describe how time series analysis, through the collection of information at regular intervals, allows the monitoring of trends over time, particularly with respect to whether the unit of interest is changing in a systematic fashion and how such change may be impacted by specific events. As an example, they discuss the effects of a multilevel (i.e., intrapersonal, interpersonal, and community) intervention on hepatitis C knowledge across time among people with HIV.

Survival analysis, the approach considered by Christian M. Connell in Chapter 9, encompasses a range of strategies for studying the likelihood and timing of a target event (e.g., the initiation of substance use) as well as factors that increase or decrease the likelihood of that event occurring for individuals. Community-based programs often are aimed at delaying or reducing the rate of the occurrence of negative events (e.g., the recurrence of child maltreatment) or expediting the occurrence of positive outcomes (e.g., obtaining employment), and survival analysis is particularly suited for addressing the degree to which such goals are attained. To highlight the contributions that survival analysis can make, Connell shows how the approach can be applied in evaluating an intervention aimed at reducing recidivism rates among first-time juvenile offenders.

In the book's last section, Part IV, authors discuss approaches that take into account the context of behavior and of community interventions. The contextual factors addressed include space (multilevel modeling, epidemiologic approaches, geographic information systems) and available resources (economic cost analysis). Multilevel modeling, as Nathan R. Todd, Nicole E. Allen, and Shabnam Javdani elucidate in Chapter 10, can be extremely useful for analyzing data involving either space (i.e., settings), time, or both. Also known as hierarchical linear modeling, multilevel modeling is a method that examines simultaneously how characteristics of the individual (e.g., a participant's socioeconomic status) and the setting (e.g., the average socioeconomic status of a classroom) may predict individual attitudes and behavior (e.g., academic achievement). Settings also can include organizations and communities. This analytic technique permits the examination of multiple levels of analysis beyond the individual and is extremely helpful in delineating specific intervention effects over time (i.e., longitudinal research). A study conducted by the authors on the influence of religious settings on social justice engagement highlights the value of and the issues involved in using multilevel modeling.

Epidemiologic approaches to community research are considered by Leonard A. Jason, Nicole Porter, and Alfred Rademaker in Chapter 11. Through the use of such approaches, researchers can uncover associations between possible risk factors and various social and health conditions (e.g., homelessness, teenage smoking) within a population of interest. Illustratively, the authors present the use of epidemiologic approaches for calculating the extent of one particular disorder, chronic fatigue syndrome, and discuss issues involved in attempting to gather valid data.

In Chapter 12, Cory M. Morton, N. Andrew Peterson, Paul W. Speer, Robert J. Reid, and Joseph Hughey detail how geographic information systems greatly facilitate the analysis of spatial or geographic data. These systems, the authors demonstrate, enable the researcher to examine how physical (e.g., the number and type of buildings in an area) and socioeconomic (e.g., the demographic characteristics of persons in a particular zip code) factors are related to and may influence individual and group behavior such as child abuse and alcohol and tobacco retailing. Such systems, by enabling the creation of maps depicting the variables of interest, vividly communicate the relationships existing among these variables.

In Chapter 13, in the final approach presented, Anthony T. Lo Sasso and Leonard A. Jason show how economic cost analysis enables the assessment of whether a program's benefits exceed its costs. The various types of economic analyses delineated by the authors allow the computation of the relative costs and benefits of a community-based intervention, either by itself or in relation to other interventions for that social or health problem. Lo Sasso and Jason demonstrate the value of such analyses for determining the benefits of self-help recovery homes for persons with a history of substance abuse problems.

In reflecting on the extant state of methodological sophistication in community-based research, we also have observed that the quality of information presented in many published articles in the field is quite inconsistent, with sometimes only minimal information presented. Are there minimum types and threshold levels of information concerning the reporting of sociodemographic features of samples, characteristics of the environments and settings where data were collected, and data collection methods so that others have a better chance of both understanding and replicating findings? In fact, there is already a growing consensus within scientific communities with respect to the creation of minimal reporting guidelines for published research (American Psychological Association, Publications and Communications Board Working Group on Journal Article Reporting Standards, 2008; Taylor et al., 2008). Such standards might profitably be considered by community researchers.

Furthermore, there are many novel ways in which researchers are collaborating and interacting with each other across various institutional settings, and many of these innovations will allow community researchers to share promising instruments, data sets, and new methods of exchanging and pooling data. For example, REDCap (research electronic data capture) is an open-access online database at http://project-redcap.org/ that allows researchers to submit their own instruments and scales as well as to use a large number that already have been inventoried. In addition, investigators can share data across settings in databases, thus enlarging communication lines and enhancing standardization procedures across sites. This is a free service and requires only that a given university sign up as a participating site. We believe that community researchers will increasingly use such websites to provide greater consensus regarding instruments and methods used in multisite studies.

This book provides profiles of only some of the more promising community-level methods, and because of space considerations, there are several other approaches that we were not able to include, such as social network analysis (Bohnert, German, Knowlton, & Latkin, 2010; Borgatti & Everett, 2000; Entwisle, Faust, Rindfuss, & Kaneda, 2007; Snijders, 2011), dynamic modeling (Hirsch, Levine, & Miller, 2007; Westaby, 2011), and multilevel structural equation modeling (Preacher, Zhang, & Zyphur, 2011). Still, we hope that this volume will stimulate its readers to contribute to the further maturation of community-oriented research by using a wide array of contemporary research methods that are theoretically sound, empirically valid, and creative, thereby addressing in a fresh and innovative manner questions of import for the communities in which they work. The results, we believe, will be (a) social problem analyses that are more holistic and culturally valid and (b) preventive and social change efforts that are more contextually grounded, far-reaching, and impactful.

REFERENCES

American Psychological Association, Publications and Communications Board Working Group on Journal Article Reporting Standards. (2008). Reporting standards for research in psychology. *American Psychologist, 63,* 839–851. doi:10.1037/0003-066X.63.9.839

Bohnert, A. S. B., German, D., Knowlton, A. R., & Latkin, C. A. (2010). Friendship networks of inner-city adults: A latent class analysis and multi-level regression of supporter types and the association of supporter latent class membership with supporter and recipient drug use. *Drug and Alcohol Dependence, 107*(2–3), 134–140. doi:10.1016/j.drugalcdep.2009.09.012

Borgatti, S. P., & Everett, M. G. (2000). Models of core/periphery structures. *Social Networks, 21,* 375–395. doi:10.1016/S0378-8733(99)00019-2

Bronfenbrenner, U. (1979). *The ecology of human development: Experiments by nature and design.* Cambridge, MA: Harvard University Press.

Entwisle, B., Faust, K., Rindfuss, R. R., & Kaneda, T. (2007). Networks and contexts: Variation in the structure of social ties. *American Journal of Sociology, 112,* 1495–1533. doi:10.1086/511803

Hirsch, G. B., Levine, R. L., & Miller, R. L. (2007). Using system dynamics modeling to understand the impact of social change initiatives. *American Journal of Community Psychology, 39,* 239–253. doi:10.1007/s10464-007-9114-3

Jason, L. A., & Glenwick, D. S. (Eds.). (2002). *Innovative strategies for promoting health and mental health across the lifespan.* New York, NY: Springer.

Jason, L. A., Keys, C. B., Suarez-Balcazar, Y., Taylor, R. R., Davis, M., Durlak, J., & Isenberg, D. (Eds.). (2004). *Participatory community research: Theories and methods in action.* Washington, DC: American Psychological Association.

Kelly, J. G. (1985). The concept of primary prevention: Creating new paradigms. *The Journal of Primary Prevention, 5,* 269–272. doi:10.1007/BF01324551

Kelly, J. G. (1990). Changing contexts and the field of community psychology. *American Journal of Community Psychology, 18,* 769–792. doi:10.1007/BF00938064

Kelly, J. G. (2006). *Becoming ecological: An exploration into community psychology.* Oxford, England: Oxford University Press.

Lorion, R. P. (1990). Developmental analyses of community phenomena. In P. Tolan, C. Keys, F. Chertok, & L. A. Jason (Eds.), *Researching community psychology: Issues of theories and methods* (pp. 32–41). Washington, DC: American Psychological Association.

Lorion, R. P., Iscoe, I., DeLeon, P. H., & VandenBos, G. R. (Eds.). (1996). *Psychology and public policy: Balancing public service and professional need.* Washington, DC: American Psychological Association. doi:10.1037/10194-000

Preacher, K. J., Zhang, Z., & Zyphur, M. J. (2011). Alternative methods for assessing mediation in multilevel data: The advantages of multilevel SEM. *Structural Equation Modeling, 18,* 161–182. doi:10.1080/10705511.2011.557329

Snijders, T. A. B. (2011). Statistical models for social networks. *Annual Review of Sociology, 37*, 131–153. doi:10.1146/annurev.soc.012809.102709

Taylor, C. F., Field, D., Sansone, S., Aerts, J., Apweiler, R., Ashburner, M., . . . Wiemann, S. (2008). Promoting coherent minimum reporting guidelines for biological and biomedical investigations: The MIBBI project. *Nature Biotechnology, 26*, 889–896. doi:10.1038/nbt.1411

Tolan, P., Keys, C., Chertok, F., & Jason, L. A. (Eds.). (1990). *Researching community psychology: Issues of theories and methods.* Washington, DC: American Psychological Association. doi:10.1037/10073-000

Westaby, J. D. (2011). *Dynamic network theory: How social networks influence goal pursuit.* Washington, DC: American Psychological Association.

I

PLURALISM AND MIXED METHODS IN COMMUNITY RESEARCH

2

PHILOSOPHICAL FOUNDATIONS OF MIXED METHODS RESEARCH: IMPLICATIONS FOR RESEARCH PRACTICE

JACOB KRAEMER TEBES

Mixed methods research combines qualitative and quantitative inquiry in a given study or program of research (Teddlie & Tashakkori, 2009). The most common type of qualitative and quantitative mixing that takes place is at the levels of data (mixing numbers and text) and methods (mixing data collection or data analysis; Biesta, 2010; Creswell & Plano Clark, 2007; Greene, 2007; Morse & Niehaus, 2009).

From a practical perspective, mixing qualitative and quantitative approaches in the same study or program of research has several advantages. As various authors (e.g., Creswell & Plano Clark, 2007; Teddlie & Tashakkori, 2009) have noted, these include (a) being able to draw on each approach when neither is adequate to address a given research question; (b) dealing with both confirmatory and exploratory questions within the same study; (c) making stronger and more valid inferences from data; (d) using one approach to tailor the study design, data collection, or data analyses for the other approach; and (e) bringing more diverse voices into the research process.

Importantly, mixed methods research also addresses fundamental philosophical challenges to scientific inquiry, such as the relationship between subjective and objective reality and the nature of truth. The two main philosophical positions that form the foundation for mixed methods research,

13

pragmatism and perspectivism, address these types of challenges. By doing so, they provide a more comprehensive and integrative basis for scientific inquiry than is offered by the philosophical foundations for either qualitative or quantitative research alone.

A central assumption of this chapter is that mixed methods research refers not only to a way of conducting research but also to a philosophical orientation to inquiry. The former is covered ably in Chapter 4 of this volume and in numerous recent books on this growing approach to inquiry (Creswell & Plano Clark, 2007; Greene, 2007; Teddlie & Tashakkori, 2009, 2010); the latter is the subject of this chapter. In the next sections, I summarize pragmatism and perspectivism as philosophical foundations for mixed methods research. I then discuss their implications for research practice, with an emphasis on community-based research, in five areas: (a) intersubjectivity and the research process, (b) theoretical and methodological pluralism, (c) culturally situated inquiry, (d) interdisciplinarity and heterarchy in research, and (e) truth as a research objective.

PRAGMATISM AND PERSPECTIVISM AS FOUNDATIONS FOR MIXED METHODS RESEARCH

As noted earlier, *pragmatism* and *perspectivism*, two contemporary philosophical positions, provide a foundation for mixed methods research. Each offers a unique justification on philosophical grounds and has been previously linked to mixed methods research. Pragmatism has been explicitly tied to mixed methods research by a number of scholars (e.g., Biesta, 2010; Greene, 2007; Greene & Hall, 2010; Morgan, 2007), whereas perspectivism's link has been more implicit, based mostly on its implications for research practice (McGuire, 1986, 1989; Tebes, 2005; Tebes, Kaufman, & Connell, 2003). Before describing how each position provides a foundation for mixed methods research, I present some relevant background.

Within philosophy, the discussion here involves questions of epistemology and ontology. *Epistemology* concerns itself with how one knows the world (i.e., reality), whereas *ontology* focuses on the nature of the world itself. Thus, consideration of knowledge claims or the different types of knowing involves epistemological questions, whereas consideration of the nature, quality, or content of reality involves ontological questions. The distinction between epistemology and ontology is important because a common fallacy is the failure to distinguish between reality itself and one's ability to know it (Bhaskar, 1975; Tebes, 2005).

Another background issue is the distinction between *objectivism* and *subjectivism*. Although in ancient philosophy Plato noted this distinction, it was not until the 17th century that it was crystallized by Rene Descartes in his famous postulate "Cogito, ergo sum" (I think, therefore I am). For Descartes, all that he knew with certainty was that he is capable of doubt, or mind. Through this statement, he drew the distinction between the subjective world (mind) and the corporeal world (body) that exists in a mind–body duality. This dualism has troubled philosophers ever since because it yields an apparently irreconcilable dichotomy between subjective knowledge (mind) and objective reality (body). Philosophers and scientists have implicitly wrestled with this distinction by developing parallel epistemological tracks—one that seeks knowledge about the subjective world and another that seeks knowledge about objective reality. Both pragmatism and perspectivism address this dichotomy, and their respective solutions to it provide the philosophical basis for mixed methods research.

Pragmatism

Pragmatism is a distinctly American philosophy that emerged near the turn of the 19th century. Its leading proponents were William James, Charles Sanders Pierce, and John Dewey. Initially, James and Pierce described pragmatism as an approach for clarifying concepts or ideas to understand their practical consequences. Dewey extended their thinking by emphasizing the utility of this perspective as a basis for practical problem solving (Hookway, 2008). In so doing, he emphasized common features among various forms of inquiry, including scientific inquiry (Dewey, 1903).

Dewey's pragmatism informed modern epistemology by dismantling some troublesome features of the mind–body problem (Biesta, 2010). He considered this problem impossible to solve and so approached it from a different perspective. For Dewey, living organisms engage in dynamic interactions with their environment (Dewey, 1905). These interactions, which he later termed *transactions*, make up experience. Experience does not constitute knowledge, but rather, simply is (Dewey, 1905); for human beings, experience represents a by-product of one's transactions with the environment (Biesta, 2010). Knowledge emerges out of those transactions because human action results in consequences that inform subsequent, more effective, and more purposeful action. As Dewey showed in his classic paper on the reflex arc (Dewey, 1896), a young child's actions on touching a burning candle yield knowledge that will guide future, more effective action when confronted with a similar circumstance (Hickman, 2009).

The coupling of knowledge with individual action represented a critical departure from previous epistemological thinking because it showed that knowledge is constructed through unique transactions with one's environment (Vanderstraeten, 2002). Thus, what I know to be real may differ from

Foundations, tools, ref. → students, scholar pract.
commty psy c impl. for relat disc (social

what someone else knows to be real because each of us has unique transactions with the world (Biesta, 2010). As a result, individual knowledge is inextricably linked to one's position in the world; that is, it is *situated knowledge* (Tebes, 2005), which is a central tenet in both feminist theory (Anderson, 2010; Lather, 1991; Longino, 2002) and critical theory (Lather, 1991; Webb, 1993). It is in this sense that Dewey's philosophical position is consistent with the epistemologies of feminism (Siegfried, 2002) and constructivism (Vanderstraeten, 2002).

Dewey's epistemology, that is, his views on how one knows the world, also has important implications for social science research. Because human knowledge is fallible, it is no longer possible to achieve objective truth through inquiry; one can only establish warranted assertions about the world through specific transactions in specific contexts (Biesta, 2010; Morgan, 2007). Thus, truth is not fixed or absolute, as is implied by moral or scientific laws. Rather, in lieu of such laws, Dewey argued that there are only regulative principles, which represent assertions that have been carefully refined over time as useful guides for action and the generation of knowledge (Hickman, 2009). Exceptions for moral laws are inevitably dictated by circumstance, and new regulative principles eventually come to replace established scientific "laws." This explains why it is morally justifiable to kill others when defending ourselves or others, and why it makes scientific sense to supplant Newtonian physics with relativistic physics (although the former is still useful in many contexts).

Dewey's discarding of objective truth has another important implication for research, one that directly addresses the subjectivism–objectivism dichotomy rooted in Descartes' mind–body duality. Because human knowledge depends on one's transactions with the world and those transactions are shaped by specific contexts, factors such as culture and one's history of past experiences are central to inquiry of all kinds (Dewey, 1925). Research that seeks to understand human behavior must therefore examine the factors that shape knowledge as it is constructed. The implication of this for research is that all knowledge is ultimately subjective and that objectivism is impossible (Biesta, 2010). Dewey also considered what this means in a transactional context. According to Biesta (2010), the multiple subjective worlds of individual human experience themselves require "interaction, cooperation, coordination, and communication" (p. 112) across individuals, thus creating the conditions for an intersubjective world to guide action and, thus, knowledge. This *intersubjectivity* effectively avoids the subjectivism–objectivism dichotomy by emphasizing shared meanings about reality that make action possible. At first glance, Dewey's resolution of the subjectivism–objectivism dichotomy appears rather facile. However, his distinctions among one's subjective knowledge about reality, reality itself, and the intersubjectivity that emerges in one's transactions with others offer a pragmatic remedy to this dichotomy and provide an ingenious alternative way forward in this debate.

Although Dewey's pragmatic response to the subjectivism–objectivism dichotomy was eventually overshadowed at the time by the emergence of logical empiricism in science (discussed in the section that follows), it began to find favor once again in the latter half of the 20th century as a guiding framework for social science, in part because it offered an intriguing alternative to the subjectivism–objectivism dichotomy (Biesta, 2010, Hookway, 2008). In more recent years, Dewey's position, as well as pragmatism more generally, has been advanced as the basis for a more comprehensive approach to research (Biesta, 2010; Greene & Hall, 2010; Morgan, 2007). In addition, Dewey's pragmatism has implications for the value given to one type of research over another. If all knowledge depends on how one engages the world and transactions are unique, many different approaches to research are justified (Biesta, 2010; Morgan, 2007). The choice among these various approaches (i.e., among the specific methods for doing research) is determined by the types of questions able to be addressed by a given approach. Pragmatism is agnostic about the use of particular methods for generating knowledge, as different methods yield different answers from research depending on one's engagement with the world (Greene & Hall, 2010).

Finally, Dewey's pragmatism offers an intriguing way of thinking about transactions among scientists. Just as individuals develop a workable intersubjectivity among one another to guide "interaction, cooperation, coordination, and communication" (Biesta, 2010, p.112), so too do scientists develop shared meanings and joint action as a community of scholars (Morgan, 2007). As Laudan (1996) noted, the scholarly community develops distinctive norms, values, and practices that further the scientific enterprise. As mixed methods researchers develop shared meanings, joint action, and workable solutions to research challenges, their transactions embody a pragmatist intersubjectivity that circumnavigates the subjectivism–objectivism dichotomy.

Perspectivism

A second philosophical position that provides a foundation for mixed methods research is perspectivism. Writing about the emerging field of community science, Tebes (2005) argues that perspectivism serves as a philosophical foundation for research that integrates qualitative and quantitative approaches, the hallmark of mixed methods research. Like pragmatism, perspectivism also addresses the subjectivism–objectivism dichotomy but takes as its point of departure the actual practice of research—what scientists do—rather than philosophical principles per se (Brante, 2010; Giere, 2006). Ronald Giere is the leading contemporary proponent of perspectivism (Giere,

2006, 2009, 2010), which the late William McGuire (1986, 1989) also discussed in relation to social and behavioral science research. I focus here on Giere's (2006) well-developed formulation of scientific perspectivism but begin with background about key developments in the philosophy of science from Dewey's era to Giere's.

20th-Century Developments in the Philosophy of Science Before Perspectivism

By the early 1900s, the dominant orientation in science was logical positivism. As noted by Tebes (2005), positivism emphasized (a) application of a common scientific method to the study of all phenomena, including human behavior, (b) observation and careful measurement carried out through rigorous research operations, (c) establishment of an objective and value-free stance for scientific inquiry, (d) development of theories that could be falsified through the testing of hypotheses derived from theory, (e) promotion of the use of statistics for hypothesis testing, and (f) devaluation of meaning and human subjectivity as a legitimate part of scientific inquiry. Logical empiricism emerged as the practical extension of logical positivism to become the dominant approach to scientific inquiry from the 1920s to the 1960s (and continuing, in some degree, to the present). It offered an unambiguous method for deducing hypothesizes from empirically supported theory (an a priori phase) and then subjecting those hypotheses to empirical test (an a posteriori phase; McGuire, 1999).

However, when Karl Popper (1935/1959), an adherent of logical empiricism, showed that all observation in science was ultimately guided by theory, the philosophical foundations of logical empiricism began to crumble. Thomas Kuhn (1962/1970) built on Popper's contention that observations were theory laden to argue that scientific revolutions had less to do with rigorous empirical tests that reveal the underlying objective truth embedded in theory than with social, cultural, and normative interactions among scientists. As is now widely known, Kuhn's analysis was seminal in ushering in a reconceptualization of scientific inquiry and practice. Kuhn's work also encouraged a number of subsequent scholars (e.g., Feyerabend, 1965, 1975; Lakatos, 1970, 1978) to challenge the prevailing view of science and replace it with a vision that science was, at root, a human construction that did not always address the nature of objective truth about the world.

Kuhn's (1962/1970) analysis was also consistent with the constructivist scholarship that was gaining ascendance at the time. Constructivism had its roots in the work of the 18th-century philosopher Immanuel Kant, and early 20th-century adherents included John Dewey and Jean Piaget (Beilin, 1992). As noted earlier in describing Dewey's philosophy, constructivism's central feature is the belief that human knowledge emerges out of an active process of engagement with the world, one that is shaped by each individual's unique experiences. Thus, reality is not given but is constructed on the basis of each individual's unique background and circumstances. A form of constructivism that first emerged in the 1960s, known as *social constructionism*, pointed out the importance of social interactions in the construction of human knowledge, including science (Berger & Luckmann, 1966; Gergen, 1985; Knorr-Cetina, 1981).

Advocates of the constructivist position—including adherents of contextualism, who argue that context alone determines knowledge (Rosnow & Georgoudi, 1986)—face a dilemma similar to the one encountered by Dewey, that is, how to reconcile one's subjective world with objective reality. As several scholars have noted, constructivism in its purest form eventually devolves into relativism because there is no clear basis beyond subjective discernment for accepting one knowledge claim over another (Capaldi & Proctor, 1994; Tebes, 2005).

This brief history captures the relevant state of affairs in the philosophy of science predating Giere's (2006) scientific perspectivism. Logical empiricism as a philosophical position had been discredited (even though it still has a hold on much of current scientific practice), and social constructivism had been found wanting (despite its appeal in legitimizing many more forms of scientific inquiry). Giere (2006) advanced scientific perspectivism to fill this void and in doing so provided an additional philosophical foundation for mixed methods research.

Scientific Perspectivism

Giere (2006) begins by accepting two fundamental assumptions underlying scientific perspectivism: *naturalism* and *realism*. Naturalism refers to the belief that one need not resort to supernatural or metaphysical explanations to account for reality; rather, only explanations grounded in nature are necessary (Giere, 2006; Laudan, 1990). Naturalism also holds that no a priori claims are needed; that is, when accounting for the natural world all prior knowledge claims (even those made with great certainty) are fallible (Giere, 2006; Laudan, 1990). Giere (2006) also accepts realism as his second fundamental assumption, acknowledging that there is a world "out there." However, this world does not exist independently of time and space, and one's knowledge of this world is always bounded by one's individual perspective (Brante, 2010; Giere, 2006, 2009). Giere calls this position *perspectival realism*.

Given these assumptions, Giere (2006) uses several detailed examples, such as color vision and scientific observation, to illustrate how perspectival realism bridges the gap between *objectivist realism* and *social constructivism*. In one example, he argues that, despite unique backgrounds and experiences, most people see the world as containing objects that have color. Human color vision is determined by different electromagnetic wavelengths within a very narrow band of the electromagnetic spectrum. Even though each person has a subjective experience of color, most people can reasonably agree on the colors of objects that they see in common. Thus, colors have both objective and subjective qualities that are rooted in the natural world but also experienced uniquely by each individual. When individuals report the same color to a given wavelength on the spectrum, they share what Giere (2006) calls *inter-subjective objectivity*. This concept is emblematic of perspectival realism and provides a "genuine alternative to both objectivist realism and social constructivism" (Giere, 2006, p. 14).

Giere (2006) argues that the output of scientific observation is also perspectival because the instruments used to make observations are uniquely tailored to measurements that have meaning in a human context. For example, astronomical observations use various instruments to provide unique, but incomplete, perspectives on the nature of the cosmos, and brain imaging equipment captures unique slices of the functioning brain. Each of these scientific perspectives on the world represents an imperfect and distinctly human experience of that world that suits scientists' purposes in a specific context (Lipton, 2007). Through the development of consensus standards for instrumentation and measurement, scientists establish a basis for intersubjective objectivity for their observations. Their ongoing interactions in a community of scientists and researchers do not eliminate the fact that their knowledge of the world is fundamentally perspectival.

Another important concept in Giere's (2006) perspectivism is the presence of what he called *contingencies* in the process of science. He draws on Pickering's (1995) description of the *mangle* of scientific practice to show how science is situated within specific historical, disciplinary, social, and conceptual contexts. These various contextual influences, Giere (2006) asserts, function as contingencies that impact scientific knowledge claims by influencing how science is practiced. Pickering's (1995) account, like those of others (Cushing, 1994; McGuire, 1986; Tebes, 2005), illustrates how contingencies operate during the research process because science is embedded in various contexts. Giere's (2006) *contingency thesis* stipulates that knowledge produced through science cannot be disentangled from these contingencies, and in fact, "that some contingency is always present in any science" (p. 93). As a result, there can be no "universal laws of nature" but only "highly generalized models that characterize a theoretical perspective" (Giere, 2006, p. 14).[1] Such

---

[1]Giere's discussion of models raises the question about the relationship of a *model* to a *paradigm*. Like others (Biesta, 2010; Gorard, 2010; Greene & Hall, 2010), I prefer to avoid use of the term *paradigm* in this context because its definition has become so broad as to not be particularly useful here.

models form the basis for scientific practice, communication across disciplines, and interdisciplinary integration (Brante, 2010).

Giere's (2006) scientific perspectivism thus entails several interlocking arguments: (a) All knowledge is human and, thus, perspectival; (b) because observation, instrumentation, and measurement are all dependent on human activity and designed for human purposes, they also are perspectival; (c) shared perspectival knowledge is possible through intersubjectivity despite the limits of human cognitive capacities and other constraints; (d) contingencies are an inevitable component of all knowledge claims; and (e) generalizable models derived from theory and supported by observation can only offer "a good but never perfect fit to aspects of the world" (p. 93).

Scientific perspectivism holds important implications for research, particularly mixed methods research. If knowledge claims are perspectival, then a broader portfolio of research methods—both quantitative and qualitative—is essential so that they match the perspectives on the world under investigation. If observation, instrumentation, and measurement are perspectival, then no one method is more valuable than any other in all circumstances. If intersubjectivity provides the basis for shared perspectival knowledge, then mixed methods may offer the best opportunity to advance communication among researchers because quantitative and qualitative approaches together are likely to yield multiple shared perspectives on the world. If contingencies (e.g., social, historical, cultural) are inherent to the research process, then methods that capture such contingencies, particularly qualitative approaches (e.g., ethnography, narrative), should be incorporated into standard research practice. And if generalizable models can never offer a perfect fit for making sense of the world, then the search for objective truth through research may be unrealistic.

IMPLICATIONS OF PRAGMATISM AND PERSPECTIVISM FOR RESEARCH PRACTICE

Dewey's pragmatism and Giere's scientific perspectivism, although separated by almost 100 years, have much in common, and their commonalities provide a philosophical foundation not only for mixed methods research but also for science and current research practice. In the next section, I discuss these implications with a particular emphasis on community-based research.

Intersubjectivity and the Research Process

Intersubjectivity is central to pragmatism and scientific perspectivism because it offers a legitimate way of addressing the subjectivism–objectivism dichotomy that continues to shape research. The concept of intersubjectivity offers a practical and realistic objective for research—to create an "intersubjectively objective" perspective on human behavior that can guide effective action. Some scholars have argued that qualitative approaches (e.g., ethnography, case study, participant observation) lend themselves better to understanding human behavior, whereas quantitative approaches (e.g., survey research, social indicator analysis, randomized controlled trials) are more useful for explaining behavior because the former seeks to identify meanings and the latter mechanisms (Biesta, 2010). Mixed methods, by definition, involve the systematic integration of these approaches in the same study or research program, thus creating opportunities that can foster intersubjectivity among scholars. Researchers who follow a single methodological tradition will have a narrower perspective on the human condition, thus making intersubjectivity across meanings and mechanisms more difficult.

It may be instructive in this context for researchers to consider the words of the late Donald Campbell in his Kurt Lewin address at the 1974 meeting of the Society for the Psychological Study of Social Issues (Campbell, 1974). Campbell was one of the most prominent social scientists associated with the quantitative, experimental tradition who had conducted numerous large-scale social experiments. Yet, on this occasion he titled his talk "Qualitative Knowing in Action Research" and focused on how qualitative knowledge ultimately provides the foundation for quantitative knowledge. Campbell's explicit recognition of the centrality of qualitative knowing challenges researchers who rigidly adhere to a single tradition to consider the benefits of mixed methods inquiry, particularly for community-based research (Tebes & Kraemer, 1991). More recently, O'Donnell and Tharp (2011) argued that intersubjectivity provides the basis for the integration of psychological concepts relevant to understanding culture and community. They urged community researchers to embrace an eclectic array of quantitative and qualitative methods that will enable them to capture the intersubjectivity that is characteristic of shared cultural meanings derived from common experiences in activity settings.

Theoretical and Methodological Pluralism

Pragmatism and perspectivism provide justification for not only mixed methods research but also theoretical and methodological pluralism. Since the decline of logical empiricism as a justification for scientific practice, scholars have increasingly moved toward *critical multiplism* to guide research (Tebes, 2005). Critical multiplism assumes that there is inherent bias in any method and that the use of multiple methods, including mixed methods, will minimize any single source of methodological bias (Cook, 1985; Cook & Campbell, 1979; Shadish, Cook, & Campbell, 2002). Critical multiplism, standing squarely within the realist tradition in philosophy, thus implicitly advocates for methodological pluralism and legitimizes the use of methods from both the quantitative and qualitative traditions (Maxwell & Mittapalli, 2010). Methodological pluralism is especially relevant to community-based research because multiple methods and mixed methods may be necessary to measure behavior in multiple community contexts (see Chapter 3, this volume). Tebes (2005) noted this in relation to community science in which quantitative population-level data on psychological and social indicators are collected along with qualitative data about stakeholder relationships and program leadership.

A perspectival realist view of the world, as advanced by Giere (2006), also acknowledges the value to knowledge of generating multiple theories about that world (McGuire, 1986). If there is no one objective truth but only an infinite number of perspectival realities, then generating plausible empirically supported theories about the world becomes an integral part of the research process (Jaeger & Rosnow, 1988; McGuire, 1997). What this implies for scientific inquiry is that researchers benefit when they are able to examine simultaneously multiple theories in the same study or program of research (McGuire, 2004). This is especially welcome in community-based research because human behavior is embedded in both social ecological (e.g., individual, family, group, organization, neighborhood, community, and society) and biological (e.g., organs, cells, molecules, and genes) contexts—that is, it represents an embodied social ecology (Tebes, in press)—in what has been referred to as the "society–behavior–biology nexus" (Glass & McAtee, 2006, p. 1661). Multiple theories are necessary to examine the reciprocating influences in these multiple contexts (Glass & McAtee, 2006; Shinn, 1990).

Culturally Situated Inquiry

Both pragmatism and perspectivism make clear the importance of culture, history, and other social contexts in shaping perspectival reality. As a result, knowledge claims are also situated within multiple "cultural" contexts, such as gender, race, ethnicity, age, sexual orientation, religion, disability status, or any number of individual contexts emblematic of human diversity (Cohen, 2009; Tebes, 2010). Research on human behavior must be oriented toward identifying and understanding these critical perspectival realities, and mixed methods approaches provide a variety of means for doing so.

Cohen (2009) has argued for further study of individual cultural identities, whereas Trickett (1996; Trickett & Schensul, 2009) and Tebes (2000, 2010) have also emphasized the need to examine cultural identities in community contexts. Further study of individual cultural identities is a focus of researchers who study *intersectionality* (Warner, 2008), a term derived from feminist theory that describes the multiple cultural identities (e.g., Black, female, adolescent) that must be considered to fully understand human experience (Shields, 2008). Multiple cultural identities are a challenge for research of all kinds but especially for community-based research because intersectional realities represent another layer of complexity within the embodied social ecologies described earlier. Tebes (2000, 2005) has argued that better specification of cultural identities within community contexts will not only promote the generalizability of research findings to community settings but also improve population-based interventions and research with specific cultural groups.

A related challenge for culturally situated inquiry is how to develop community-based preventive interventions for specific cultural groups. Barrera, Castro, and Steiker (2011) describe four different types of approaches for developing such interventions: (a) the prevention intervention research cycle, (b) cultural adaptations of evidence-based interventions, (c) culturally grounded approaches that are investigator initiated, and (d) indigenous approaches that are community initiated. They summarize considerations by which one or another approach may be appropriate in various cultural contexts and note how the use of mixed methods offers distinct advantages for cultural adaptations of interventions to specific groups. In contrast, Trickett (2011) challenges the premise underlying the framework offered by Barrera et al. He recommends that community-based researchers first seek to understand a particular cultural group before implementing or adapting a community-based intervention. Such understanding would require a variety of methods, including the integration of knowledge derived from both qualitative and quantitative approaches.

Interdisciplinarity and Heterarchy in Research

Research characterized by theoretical and methodological pluralism that attempts to address multiple levels of reciprocating influences on human behavior requires increasing collaboration across disciplines. Over the past 50 years, research from many fields, including the physical sciences, engineering, and the social sciences, has found that publications and innovations are most commonly produced in research teams, many of which consist of researchers from different disciplines (Jones, Wuchty, & Uzzi, 2008; Wuchty, Jones, & Uzzi, 2007). Interdisciplinary team science has also enabled researchers to address complex public health challenges that could not be addressed by a single discipline (Börner et al., 2010; Kessel, Rosenfield, & Anderson, 2008).

The emergence of interdisciplinary team science has also changed how research is practiced, with interdisciplinary research teams often organized

24   JACOB KRAEMER TEBES

heter

heterarchically rather than hierarchically (Rosenfield & Kessel, 2008; Tebes, 2009). A heterarchy is a biological or social organizational system that consists of an interconnected and overlapping network of components that operate dynamically to both emerge from and govern the interactions of constituent components (Gunji & Kamiura, 2004). Tebes (2009) provides the following examples of heterarchies: (a) individuals acting as dynamic members of interrelated groups (e.g., families, organizations, political economies), (b) biological signaling processes (e.g., regulatory processes within living cells), (c) evolutionary systems, (d) participatory democracies, and (e) Wikipedia. Interdisciplinary team science initiatives can operate heterarchically because different investigators can provide leadership for various parts or phases of the research. Similar interdisciplinary and intersectoral collaborative models have had a long tradition in community-based research (Kelly, 1988; Tolan, Keys, Chertok, & Jason, 1990). In this connection, Stokols (2006) describes opportunities for community-based researchers willing to collaborate with colleagues from other disciplines, community members, policymakers, and relevant stakeholders to solve large-scale community problems using a participatory action research framework.

Truth as a Research Objective

Although the search for truth is generally accepted as the central objective of scientific research, the history of science has shown that scientific theories are all eventually found to be false to some degree (Oddie, 2007; Popper, 1963; Zamora Bonilla, 2000). Scientific researchers are thus left searching for approximations of the truth so as to determine the *truthlikeness* (or verisimilitude) of their proposed theories about reality (Popper, 1963). They do this with the understanding that a given theory is destined to be replaced by another, slightly less flawed theory (Oddie, 2007; Zamora Bonilla, 2000). Although Kuhn's (1962/1970) revolutionary view of science (as influenced by social and cultural contexts) came to replace Popper's more rational view of scientific progress, Popper's concept of truth as a research objective remains a cornerstone among scientific researchers.

The late Richard Rorty (1991), a contemporary pragmatist, argued that objective truth is not possible and, therefore, not a realistic goal for science. He contends that because truth cannot be recognized as such because of people's fallibility, it should not be the focus of scientific inquiry. Adopting this view, a cynic might even argue that the scientific search for truth is doomed to yield only *truthiness*—the satirical term adopted by the comedian Stephen Colbert to capture the misinformation, or ersatz truth, often found in political discourse (Zimmer, 2010). But in the absence of a search for truth, what are scientific researchers to do?

McGuire (1989) and Tebes (2005) maintain that even though objective truth is unattainable, there is much to be gained when scientific researchers seek successive approximations of it, despite knowing that their inquiry will be flawed and perspectival. Proposing and examining imperfect models can advance knowledge incrementally, particularly if one uses multiple and mixed methods and critically assesses perspectival realities constrained by (as shown previously) intersubjectivity, theory, methodology, culture, and discipline. In practical terms, scientific researchers ultimately search for *trueness*—a term commonly used at the turn of the 19th century to signify "the characteristic of being true" (Whitney & Smith, 1897). Although trueness may conjure up in the contemporary mind the more cynical truthiness, it represents a realistic objective for research and thus serves as both a noble aspiration and a humbling reminder that discoveries are perspectival and ultimately emblematic of human fallibility.

REFERENCES

Anderson, E. (2010). Feminist epistemology and philosophy of science. In E. N. Zalta (Ed.), *The Stanford encyclopedia of philosophy*. Retrieved from http://plato.stanford.edu/entries/feminism-epistemology/

Barrera, M., Castro, F. G., & Steiker, L. K. H. (2011). A critical analysis of approaches to the development of preventive interventions for subcultural groups. *American Journal of Community Psychology*. Retrieved from http://www.springerlink.com/content/np65243575k08577/ doi:10.1007/s10464-010-9422-x

Beilin, H. (1992). Piaget's enduring contribution to developmental psychology. *Developmental Psychology, 28,* 191–204. doi:10.1037/0012-1649.28.2.191

Berger, P. L., & Luckmann, T. (1966). *The social construction of reality: A treatise in the sociology of knowledge*. Garden City, NY: Anchor Books.

Biesta, G. (2010). Pragmatism and the philosophical foundations of mixed methods research. In A. Tashakkori & C. Teddlie (Eds.), *SAGE handbook of mixed methods in social & behavioral research* (2nd ed., pp. 95–117). Thousand Oaks, CA: Sage.

Bhaskar, B. R. (1975). *A realist theory of science*. London, England: Verso Books.

Börner, K., Contractor, N., Falk-Krzesinski, H. J., Fiore, S. M., Hall, K. L., Keyton, J., . . . Uzzi, B. (2010). A multi-level systems perspective for the science of team science. *Science Translational Medicine, 2*(49), cm24. doi:10.1126/scitranslmed.3001399

Brante, T. (2010). Perspectival realism, representational models, and the social sciences. *Philosophy of the Social Sciences, 40,* 107–117. doi:10.1177/0048393109352771

Campbell, D. T. (1974, August). *Qualitative knowing in action research*. Kurt Lewin address at the meeting of the American Psychological Association, New Orleans, LA.

Capaldi, E. J., & Proctor, R. W. (1994). Contextualism: Is the act in context the adequate metaphor for scientific psychology. *Psychonomic Bulletin & Review, 1,* 239–249. doi:10.3758/BF03200775

Cohen, A. B. (2009). Many forms of culture. *American Psychologist, 64,* 194–204. doi:10.1037/a0015308

Cook, T. D. (1985). Postpositivist critical multiplism. In L. Shotland & M. M. Mark (Eds.), *Social science and social policy* (pp. 21–62). Newbury Park, CA: Sage.

Cook, T. D., & Campbell, D. T. (1979). *Quasi-experimentation: Design and analysis issues for field settings*. Boston, MA: Houghton Mifflin.

Creswell, J. W., & Plano Clark, V. L. (2007). *Designing and conducting mixed methods research*. Thousand Oaks, CA: Sage.

Cushing, J. T. (1994). *Quantum mechanics: Historical contingency and the Copenhagen hegemony*. Chicago, IL: University of Chicago Press.

Dewey, J. (1896). The reflex arc concept in psychology. In J. A. Boydston (Vol. Ed.) & L. Hickman (Electronic Ed.), *The collected works of John Dewey, 1882–1953*. Retrieved from http://pm.nlx.com/xtf/view?docId=dewey/dewey.05.xml;chunk.id=div.ew.5.20;toc.depth=1;toc.id=div.ew.5.7;brand=default

Dewey, J. (1903). Logical conditions of a scientific treatment of morality. In J. A. Boydston (Vol. Ed.) & L. Hickman (Electronic Ed.), *The collected works of John Dewey, 1882–1953*. Retrieved from http://pm.nlx.com/xtf/view?docId=dewey/dewey.08.xml;chunk.id=div.mw.3.6;toc.depth=1;toc.id=div.mw.3.6;brand=default

Dewey, J. (1905). The postulate of immediate empiricism. In J. A. Boydston (Vol. Ed.) & L. Hickman (Electronic Ed.), *The collected works of John Dewey, 1882–1953*. Retrieved from http://pm.nlx.com/xtf/view?docId=dewey/dewey.08.xml;chunk.id=div.mw.3.42;toc.depth=1;toc.id=div.mw.3.6;brand=default

Dewey, J. (1925). Experience and nature. In J. A. Boydston (Vol. Ed.) & L. Hickman (Electronic Ed.), *The collected works of John Dewey, 1882–1953*. Retrieved from http://pm.nlx.com/xtf/view?docId=dewey/dewey.21.xml;chunk.id=div.lw.1.6;toc.depth=1;toc.id=div.lw.1.6;brand=default

Feyerabend, P. (1965). Reply to criticism. In R. S. Cohen & M. W. Wartofsky (Eds.), *Boston studies in the philosophy of science* (Vol. 2, pp. 223–261). New York, NY: Humanities Press.

Feyerabend, P. (1975). *Against method: Outline of an anarchistic theory of knowledge*. London, England: New Left Books.

Gergen, K. J. (1985). The social constructionist movement in modern psychology. *American Psychologist, 40,* 266–275. doi:10.1037/0003-066X.40.3.266

Giere, R. N. (2006). *Scientific perspectivism*. Chicago, IL: University of Chicago Press.

Giere, R. N. (2009). Scientific perspectivism: Behind the stage door. *Studies in History and Philosophy of Science, 40,* 221–227. doi:10.1016/j.shpsa.2009.03.004

Giere, R. N. (2010). An agent-based conception of models and scientific representation. *Synthese, 172,* 269–281. doi:10.1007/s11229-009-9506-z

Glass, T. A., & McAtee, M. J. (2006). Behavioral science at the crossroads in public health: Extending horizons and envisioning the future. *Social Science & Medicine, 62,* 1650–1671. doi:10.1016/j.socscimed.2005.08.044

Gorard, S. (2010). Research design, as independent of methods. In A. Tashakkori & C. Teddlie (Eds.), *SAGE handbook of mixed methods in social & behavioral research* (2nd ed., pp. 237–251). Thousand Oaks, CA: Sage.

Greene, J. C. (2007). *Mixed methods in social inquiry.* San Francisco, CA: Jossey-Bass.

Greene, J. C., & Hall, J. N. (2010). Dialectics and pragmatism: Being of consequence. In A. Tashakkori & C. Teddlie (Eds.), *SAGE handbook of mixed methods in social & behavioral research* (2nd ed., pp. 119–143). Thousand Oaks, CA: Sage.

Gunji, Y.-P., & Kamiura, M. (2004). Observational heterarchy enhancing active coupling. *Physica D: Nonlinear Phenomena, 198,* 74–105. doi:10.1016/j.physd.2004.08.021

Hickman, L. A. (2009). Dewey: His life and work. In L. A. Hickman, S. Neubert, & K. Reich (Eds.), *John Dewey: Between pragmatism and constructivism* (pp. 3–19). New York, NY: Fordham University Press. doi:10.5422/fso/9780823230181.003.0001

Hookway, C. J. (2008). Pragmatism. In E. N. Zalta (Ed.), *The Stanford encyclopedia of philosophy.* Retrieved from http://plato.stanford.edu/archives/fall2008/entries/pragmatism/

Jaeger, M. E., & Rosnow, R. L. (1988). Contextualism and its implications for psychological inquiry. *British Journal of Psychology, 79,* 63–75. doi:10.1111/j.2044-8295.1988.tb02273.x

Jones, B. F., Wuchty, S., & Uzzi, B. (2008, November 21). Multi-university research teams: Shifting impact, geography, and stratification in science. *Science, 322,* 1259–1262. doi:10.1126/science.1158357

Kelly, J. G. (1988). *A guide to conducting prevention research in the community: First steps.* New York, NY: Haworth Press.

Kessel, F., Rosenfield, P. L., & Anderson, N. B. (Eds.). (2008). *Interdisciplinary research: Case studies from health and social science.* New York, NY: Oxford Press.

Kuhn, T. S. (1970). *The structure of scientific revolutions* (2nd ed.). Chicago, IL: University of Chicago Press. (Original work published in 1962)

Knorr-Cetina, K. D. (1981). *The manufacture of knowledge: An essay on the constructivist and contextual nature of science.* Oxford, England: Pergamon Press.

Lakatos, I. (1970). Falsification and the methodology of scientific research programs. In I. Lakatos & A. Musgrave (Eds.), *Criticism and the growth of knowledge* (pp. 91–196). Cambridge, England: Cambridge University Press.

Lakatos, I. (1978). *The methodology of scientific research programs.* Cambridge, England: Cambridge University Press.

Lather, P. (1991). *Getting smart: Feminist research and pedagogy with/in the postmodern.* New York, NY: Routledge, Chapman & Hall.

Laudan, L. (1990). Normative naturalism. *Philosophy of Science, 57,* 44–59. doi:10.1086/289530

Laudan, L. (1996). *Beyond positivism and relativism: Theory, method, and evidence.* Boulder, CO: Westview Press.

Longino, H. (2002). The social dimensions of scientific knowledge. In E. N. Zalta (Ed.), *The Stanford encyclopedia of philosophy.* Retrieved from http://plato.stanford.edu/archives/sum2002/entries/scientific-knowledge-social/

Lipton, P. (2007, May 11). Philosophy of science: The world of science. *Science, 316,* 834. doi:10.1126/science.1141366

Maxwell, J. A., & Mittapalli, K. (2010). Realism as a stance for mixed methods research. In A. Tashakkori & C. Teddlie (Eds.), *SAGE handbook of mixed methods in social & behavioral research* (2nd ed., pp. 95–117). Thousand Oaks, CA: Sage.

McGuire, W. J. (1986). A perspectivist looks at contextualism and the future of behavioral science. In R. L. Rosnow & M. Georgundi (Eds.), *Contextualism and understanding in behavioral science* (pp. 271–303). New York, NY: Pergamon Press.

McGuire, W. J. (1989). A perspectivist approach to the strategic planning of programmatic scientific research. In B. Gholson, W. R. Shadish, Jr., R. A. Neimeyer, & A. C. Houts (Eds.), *Psychology of science: Contributions to metascience* (pp. 214–245). Cambridge, England: Cambridge University Press.

McGuire, W. J. (1997). Creative hypothesis generating in psychology: Some useful heuristics. *Annual Review of Psychology, 48,* 1–30. doi:10.1146/annurev.psych.48.1.1

McGuire, W. J. (1999). *Constructing social psychology: Creative and critical processes.* Cambridge, England: Cambridge University Press.

McGuire, W. J. (2004). Appendix: Perspectivist worksheets for generating a program of research. In J. T. Jost, M. R. Banaji, & D. A. Prentice (Eds.), *Perspectivism in social psychology: The yin and yang of scientific progress* (pp. 319–332). Washington, DC: American Psychological Association.

Morgan, D. L. (2007). Paradigms lost and pragmatism regained: Methodological implications of combining qualitative and quantitative methods. *Journal of Mixed Methods Research, 1,* 48–76. doi:10.1177/2345678906292462

Morse, J. M., & Niehaus, L. (2009). *Principles and procedures of mixed methods design.* Walnut Creek, CA: Left Coast Press.

Oddie, G. (2007). Truthlikeness. In E. N. Zalta (Ed.), *The Stanford encyclopedia of philosophy.* Retrieved from http://plato.stanford.edu/archives/fall2007/entries/truthlikeness/

O'Donnell, C. R., & Tharp, R. G. (2011). Integrating cultural community psychology: Activity settings and the shared meanings of intersubjectivity. *American Journal of Community Psychology.* Retrieved from http://www.springerlink.com/content/q1141310825471m1/ doi:10.1007/s10464-011-9434-1

Pickering, A. (1995). *The mangle of practice: Time, agency, and science.* Chicago, IL: University of Chicago Press.

Popper, K. (1959). *The logic of scientific discovery*. New York, NY: Basic Books. Retrieved from http://www.questia.com/PM.qst?a5o&d59219121 (Original work published in 1935)

Popper, K. (1963). *Conjectures and refutations*. London, England: Routledge.

Rorty, R. (1991). *Objectivity, relativism, and truth: Philosophical papers* (Vol. 1). Cambridge, England: Cambridge University Press.

Rosenfield, P. L., & Kessel, F. (2008). Closing commentary: Fostering interdisciplinary research: The way forward. In F. Kessel, P. L. Rosenfield, & N. B. Anderson (Eds.), *Interdisciplinary research: Case studies from health and social science* (pp. 429–464). New York, NY: Oxford Press.

Rosnow, R. L., & Georgoudi, M. (Eds.). (1986). *Contextualism and understanding in behavioral science: Implications for research and theory*. New York, NY: Praeger.

Shadish, W. R., Cook, T. D., & Campbell, D. T. (2002). *Experimental and quasi-experimental designs for generalized causal inference*. Boston, MA: Houghton Mifflin.

Shields, S. A. (2008). Gender: An intersectionality perspective. *Sex Roles, 59,* 301–311. doi:10.1007/s11199-008-9501-8

Shinn, M. (1990). Mixing and matching: Levels of conceptualization, measurement, and statistical analysis in community research. In P. Tolan, C. Keys, F. Chertok, & L. Jason (Eds.), *Researching community psychology: Issues of theory and methods* (pp. 111–126). Washington, DC: American Psychological Association. doi:10.1037/10073-010

Siegfried, C. H. (2002). John Dewey's pragmatist feminism. In C. H. Siegfried (Ed.), *Feminist interpretations of John Dewey* (pp. 47–77). University Park, PA: Pennsylvania State University Press.

Stokols, D. (2006). Toward a science of transdisciplinary action research. *American Journal of Community Psychology, 38,* 63–77.

Tebes, J. K. (2000). External validity and scientific psychology. *American Psychologist, 55,* 1508–1509. doi:10.1037/0003-066X.55.12.1508

Tebes, J. K. (2005). Community science, philosophy of science, and the practice of research. *American Journal of Community Psychology, 35,* 213–230. doi:10.1007/s10464-005-3399-x

Tebes, J. K. (2009, November). *Evaluating interdisciplinary team science: Theory and methods for an emerging field of inquiry*. Expert lecture at the meeting of the American Evaluation Association, Orlando, FL.

Tebes, J. K. (2010). Community psychology, diversity, and the many forms of culture. *American Psychologist, 65,* 58–59. doi:10.1037/a0017456

Tebes, J. K. (in press). Community psychology, community research and action, and 21st century scholarship. *American Journal of Community Psychology*.

Tebes, J. K., Kaufman, J. S., & Connell, C. M. (2003). The evaluation of prevention and health promotion programs. In T. P. Gullotta & M. Bloom (Eds.), *Encyclopedia of primary prevention and health promotion* (pp. 42–61). New York, NY: Kluwer Academic.

Tebes, J. K., & Kraemer, D. T. (1991). Quantitative and qualitative knowing in mutual support research: Some lessons from the recent history of scientific psychology. *American Journal of Community Psychology, 19*, 739–756. doi:10.1007/BF00938042

Teddlie, C., & Tashakkori, A. (2009). *Foundations of mixed methods research.* Thousand Oaks, CA: Sage.

Teddlie, C., & Tashakkori, A. (2010). Overview of contemporary issues in mixed methods research. In A. Tashakkori & C. Teddlie (Eds.), *SAGE handbook of mixed methods in social & behavioral research* (2nd ed., pp. 1–41). Thousand Oaks, CA: Sage.

Tolan, P., Keys, C., Chertok, F., & Jason, L. (Eds.). (1990). *Researching community psychology: Issues of theory and methods.* Washington, DC: American Psychological Association. doi:10.1037/10073-000

Trickett, E. J. (1996). A future for community psychology: The contexts of diversity and the diversity of contexts. *American Journal of Community Psychology, 24*, 209–234. doi:10.1007/BF02510399

Trickett, E. J. (2011). From "water boiling in a Peruvian town" to "letting them die": Culture, community intervention, and the metabolic balance between patience and zeal. *American Journal of Community Psychology, 47*, 58–68. doi:10.1007/s10464-010-9369-y

Trickett, E. J., & Schensul, J. (2009). Summary comments: Multi-level community based culturally situated community interventions. *American Journal of Community Psychology, 43*, 377–381. doi:10.1007/s10464-009-9237-9

Vanderstraeten, R. (2002). Dewey's transactional constructivism. *Journal of Philosophy of Education, 36*, 233–246. doi:10.1111/1467-9752.00272

Warner, L. R. (2008). A best practices guide to intersectional approaches in psychological research. *Sex Roles, 59*, 454–463. doi:10.1007/s11199-008-9504-5

Webb, C. (1993). Feminist research: Definitions, methodology, methods and evaluation. *Journal of Advanced Nursing, 18*, 416–423. doi:10.1046/j.1365-2648.1993.18030416.x

Whitney, W. D., & Smith, B. E. (1897). *The century dictionary and cyclopedia.* Retrieved from http://www.global-language.com/CENTURY/

Wuchty, S., Jones, B. F., & Uzzi, B. (2007, May 18). The increasing dominance of teams in production of knowledge. *Science, 316*, 1036–1038. doi:10.1126/science.1136099

Zamora Bonilla, J. P. (2000). Truthlikeness, rationality, and scientific method. *Synthese, 122*, 321–335. doi:10.1023/A:1005269826141

Zimmer, B. (2010, October 17). Truthiness. *The New York Times Magazine*, p. 22.

3

METHODOLOGICAL PLURALISM: IMPLICATIONS FOR CONSUMERS AND PRODUCERS OF RESEARCH

CHRIS BARKER AND NANCY PISTRANG

Within the field of community psychology, methodological pluralism in research has achieved a motherhood and apple pie status. Most community psychologists, such as Tolan, Keys, Chertok, and Jason (1990), agree that it is something to which researchers ought to aspire. However, possibly precisely because of its feel-good quality, the concept of pluralism is widely venerated but rarely analyzed. Few authors have attempted to elucidate how the pluralist position actually would play out in practice in terms of how research ideally should be conducted and evaluated.

Therefore, building on our previous treatment (Barker & Pistrang, 2005), in this chapter, we aim to clarify what is meant by the concept of methodological pluralism and to explore its implications for community psychology research. We examine how a pluralistic ethos guides both consuming research, that is, evaluating research quality, and producing research, that is, carrying out individual studies or whole research programs.

Methodological pluralism is enshrined in the third of the four guiding principles of the Society for Community Research and Action (2010), which has stated that "community research . . . uses multiple methodologies" (para. 3). The basic sentiment behind this statement is certainly one with which we would agree; yet on closer examination this apparently simple and incontrovertible idea starts to become more complicated. Should all community psychology researchers use multiple methodologies? In every study? What exactly is meant by a methodology? How can research using multiple methods be evaluated? What is the difference between pluralism and mixed methods research?

In this chapter, we attempt to address these and other questions from the standpoint both of research consumers (by which we mean general readers, journal reviewers and editors, grant reviewers, and funding bodies) and research producers (the researchers themselves, either individuals or research teams or groupings). We start by examining what is meant by *methodological pluralism* and its related terms. Then we examine the question of standards in research: If there is a pluralistic ethos, does this then mean that there is no unitary way to evaluate the quality of a piece of research? If there is no such unitary way, is this necessarily a bad thing? Finally, we address how pluralism can be put into practice both by individual researchers and by the field as a whole.

WHAT IS PLURALISM?

In general, the term *pluralism* refers to the appreciation and encouragement of variety. It has several subtypes. For instance, political pluralism describes societies in which a wide spectrum of different political viewpoints can coexist and be openly expressed (e.g., Connolly, 2005) in contrast to rigidly controlled one-party states. Cultural pluralism, or multiculturalism (Lott, 2010), refers to societies in which different cultural or ethnic groups amicably rub shoulders with each other, and each of their various cultural traditions contributes to the cultural life of the whole society. Such a state of affairs more or less exists in many North American and European cities (this is not to deny the existence of racism or ethnic tensions but merely to assert that they are not highly prevalent). Other important subtypes of pluralism are religious (e.g., Beneke, 2006) and legal (e.g., Berman, 2006) pluralism.

However, the pluralist position is not without its inherent difficulties. One is the issue of whether any general principles exist that transcend the rights of particular subgroups within society to live as they see fit. The problem is that there must be some limits on what constitutes acceptable variety. For instance, the attitude and behavior of the Afghanistan Taliban toward women currently violates basic human rights such as freedom of choice, freedom of expression, and the right to receive an education. Therefore, for pluralism to be viable, all subgroups must subscribe to some higher principles that place constraints on what is acceptable.

A second intrinsic difficulty with pluralism is that of divided loyalties. In a multicultural society is the individual's primary loyalty to the larger, superordinate society (e.g., the nation-state) or to the subgroup to which he or she belongs? If it is to the subgroup, then is the superordinate society as a whole in danger of becoming fatally subdivided? This may occur when individuals' identification with a particular religious, ethnic, or political group is stronger than that toward the country in which they reside.

Both of these issues—higher order principles and potential social fragmentation—are relevant to our subsequent discussion of methodological pluralism in research.

Methodological Pluralism

Pluralism in research is referred to as methodological pluralism. It is characterized by the valuing, within a field of science or scholarship, of a variety of different research approaches. As we have previously defined it, methodological pluralism is the belief that

> no single approach to research is best overall; rather, what is important is that the methods be appropriate for the questions under investigation. No single research method is inherently superior to any other: all methods have their relative advantages and disadvantages. (Barker, Pistrang, & Elliott, 2002, p. 245)

It is the converse of the belief that certain research methods are inherently more scientifically valid or respectable than others. For instance, randomized controlled trials often are regarded as a gold standard research design, a status that methodological pluralists would question. This is not to deny that randomized controlled trials are excellent designs for tackling certain questions, particularly those concerning causality, but it is also important to acknowledge their limitations and the strengths of alternative approaches.

Within methodological pluralism, a similar problem arises to that within cultural pluralism, namely, where does one draw the boundary lines? Are there some approaches to research that simply fail to follow basic maxims about how research should be carried out and therefore cannot be defined as research at all? This is an age-old issue with which philosophers of science have grappled. How can (or should) science be demarcated from pseudoscience? What is the essential difference, if any, between astronomy and astrology? Why do we trust chemotherapy for cancer more than crystal healing therapy?

The seminal text on methodological pluralism in the social sciences is Fiske and Shweder's (1986) edited volume *Metatheory in Social Science: Pluralisms and Subjectivities* in which a number of eminent contributors set out the case for a pluralistic approach. However, during the same time period in which that text was published, the picture was more troubled on other fronts. The 1980s and especially the 1990s were characterized by fierce "paradigm wars" (Oakley, 1999), particularly between proponents of quantitative and qualitative research methods, in which the debates became increasingly vociferous and unproductive. Happily, these paradigm wars seem to have abated, and this chapter is intended as a small attempt to further soothe whatever passions may remain.

Methodological Pluralism in Community Psychology

Historically, community psychology has been dominated by quantitative approaches, although somewhat less so in recent years. Luke (2005) compared the contents of the *American Journal of Community Psychology* over a 20-year time span in the two 3-year periods 1981–1983 and 2001–2003. In the earlier period the proportion of articles using qualitative methods was very small (4%); in the later period it had grown markedly to 17%.

Within this historical context, several community psychologists (e.g., Kelly, 2003; Tebes & Kraemer, 1991; Trickett, 1996) have set out the methodological pluralist agenda, largely advocating a greater use of qualitative methods. For example, Tebes and Kraemer (1991) explicated the pluses and minuses of quantitative and qualitative ways of knowing within the context of mutual support group research.

Several authors (e.g., Banyard & Miller, 1998; Orford, 2008; Stewart, 2000) have argued that qualitative methods have a natural resonance with community psychology's ethos in that they are more attuned to contexts, are good for giving voice to underrepresented populations, and may reduce the power differential between researcher and participant (see Pistrang & Barker, 2012). In traditional quantitative research, particularly randomized trials, it is hard to avoid a power differential in which the "subject" is subordinated to the researcher.

Our own underlying philosophical approach is a pragmatic one. We hold that particular research methods are suitable for answering particular research questions. In other words, research should be question driven, rather than method driven. Although qualitative methods do have their characteristic advantages for community psychology research, we believe that it is entirely possible to do quantitative research in a way that is perfectly consistent with community psychology's underlying value system.

CRITERIA FOR EVALUATING RESEARCH

Having laid out some of the background to pluralism, we next examine how it can be applied to specifying criteria by which research can be evaluated, both by those producing it and those consuming it. As discussed previously, one of the main problems posed by adopting a pluralist stance in general is that there is no longer a unitary set of standards by which to make judgments. Within methodological pluralism in research, the issue is how to appraise the quality of different pieces of work that were conducted within different genres of research, each genre having its own philosophy and procedures. As in our previous treatment (Barker & Pistrang, 2005), we draw on the work of Elliott, Fischer, and Rennie (1999), who attempted to resolve this problem by proposing two sets of quality standards. The first is a set of criteria applicable to all research; the second is a set of genre-specific criteria, one subset applicable to qualitative research and one to quantitative. Elliott et al.'s analysis was situated within the clinical and counseling psychology context; here we expand and adapt it to the community psychology context.

Following Elliott et al. (1999), we propose first some general principles to which all community psychological research should aspire and then some particular genre-specific ones. We take as our main focus the qualitative–quantitative distinction, but in principle the analysis can be extended to other distinctions between research genres that may be part of the pluralistic debate. For example, the distinction between experimental and correlational research, or that between randomized and nonrandomized (naturalistic) experiments, tends to define different research genres or methodologies.

Our quality criteria for research thus fall under four headings: (a) criteria applicable to all research, (b) research-relevant community psychology values and principles, (c) criteria specifically applicable to quantitative research, and (d) criteria specifically applicable to qualitative research.

Criteria Applicable to All Research

This first set of criteria is intended to apply to all types of research and is not specifically tied to community psychology research. These criteria represent some global principles to which all research is expected to adhere.

Explication of Context and Purpose

The first criterion concerns clearly articulating what the research is attempting to do and what conceptual and empirical background it is drawing on. This provides the theoretical context in which to situate the methods and findings and also helps the reader to judge the advances in knowledge (if any) made by the research. For example, Ahrens (2006) studied how rape victims disclose (or do not disclose) the rape to potential sources of support. The study was conducted from a feminist standpoint, which situated it within the general literature on the silencing of women and the denial of voice to oppressed people. Not only does the purpose of the research become clearer by being thus situated but also the findings can be fed back into the larger theoretical contexts.

Use of Appropriate Methods

The appropriate methods criterion specifies that the study should use research methods that are explicitly linked to the research question being addressed. If the study is aiming to address the efficacy of a community intervention, methods that are capable of ruling out alternative explanations for change and attributing it to the intervention in question are needed. These usually will involve an experimental or quasi-experimental design with some kind of comparison group. On the other hand, if the researchers are interested in personal experiences of a community program, then an attitude survey or a qualitative approach would be a better alternative.

The phrase *appropriate methods* intentionally echoes the phrase *appropriate technology* from Schumacher's (1973) *Small Is Beautiful: A Study of Economics as if People Mattered*. In the technological context the idea is that one uses the simplest mechanism that will get the job done. For instance, a simple water extraction method may be all that is needed to transform lives in a Ugandan village. Similarly, researchers should seek to use the simplest design and methods that put the least burden on participants but still provide an answer to the research questions (Peterson, 2009).

Transparency of Procedures

It is a fundamental scientific criterion that exactly how the researchers carried out the study needs to be made manifest in order that other investigators may replicate it. If a result cannot be replicated by other investigators, this undermines its trustworthiness. Furthermore, a full description of the methods enables readers to know exactly what was done so that they can understand and evaluate the meaning of the results.

Ethical Treatment of Participants

Clearly, all research must treat participants ethically. Research ethics principles and codes of conduct, such as those of the American Psychological Association (2010), detail the specific considerations that researchers need to take into account.

Importance of Findings

The final general criterion is the hardest to judge. It is that the research findings be important, a consideration that complements the need for the research to be methodologically sound. As Rozin (2009) argued, psychologists are often so preoccupied with methodological rigor that they lose sight of the larger picture. Some deficiencies in methodology may be forgivable if the research has something important to say.

Research-Relevant Community Psychology Values and Principles

The set of criteria discussed in the previous section is intended to be applicable to all psychological research. This second set is specific to community psychology, which is a unique subfield of psychology in that it has not only a content focus but also a strong set of values. Here we attempt to distill those values that are relevant to conducting research into a set of criteria that can be used to guide and evaluate studies. They are drawn from the Society for Community Research and Action's (2010) guiding principles and other sources (Banyard & Miller, 1998; Langhout, 2003; Nelson & Prilleltensky, 2010; Orford, 2008; Ryerson Espino & Trickett, 2008; Stewart, 2000).

Sensitivity to People's Contexts

It is almost a definition of community psychology that it takes context into account. Lewin's (1951) formulation that behavior is a joint function of the person and the environment and Bronfenbrenner's (1979) analysis of social ecology provide the conceptual foundation. The norm in other branches of psychology, including, oddly, in much of social psychology, is to focus on purely intrapsychic variables. Community psychology researchers, on the other hand, strive to avoid individualistic approaches and to embrace contextual effects (Ryerson Espino & Trickett, 2008; Trickett, 1996). For example, Ahren's (2006) study of the silencing of rape victims, mentioned previously, potentially could have been conducted from an individualistic standpoint, examining which individual factors were associated with speaking out and which with remaining silent. Instead, Ahrens used a more contextual method, examining how victims' social environment supported or inhibited disclosure.

Respect for Diversity Among People and Settings

Researchers live in a diverse world, and it desirable that their research reflects that diversity, in terms of both populations and settings. At a basic level, this can be considered as a sampling issue, namely, that researchers ensure that their studies are demographically representative with respect to such variables as gender, social class, ethnicity, or sexual orientation. However, at a more profound level, this entails conducting research in settings and cultures that may be radically different from the researcher's home territory. This is often easier said than done. The narratives assembled by Bond and Harrell (2006) in an *American Journal of Community Psychology* special issue on diversity challenges strikingly illustrate the difficulties faced by researchers working in areas well outside of their comfort zones.

Giving Voice to Traditionally Underrepresented Populations

A related criterion is that the research "gives voice" to underrepresented populations. For example, historically the voices of people with intellectual disability or serious mental illness were rarely heard in psychological research. A classic example of how things might be done differently is an article by two sociologists, Bogdan and Taylor (1976), who carried out a life history study of Ed Murphy, a man with intellectual disability (then labeled "mental retardation") who had been cared for in state institutions. The article is remarkable in that it consists almost entirely of the participant's own words and demonstrates his articulate awareness and insight.

Addressing Competencies

The approach of community psychology is to view people in a rounded way, as possessing both strengths and weaknesses, in contrast, for example, to clinical psychology's predominant focus on deficit and psychopathology. In research terms this translates into measurement of competencies as well as deficits and to a focus on well-being as well as problems. These ideas are closely allied to humanistic psychology's notions of human potential and personal growth and to positive psychology's focus on well-being and its rather more limited notion of happiness (Seligman & Csikszentmihalyi, 2000).

Promoting Empowerment

Empowerment is a key concept in community psychology. Indeed, Rappaport (1990) proposed that it be considered as its central organizing principle from which the other criteria that we are discussing can be derived. For instance, focusing on competencies can be seen as empowering because it accentuates strengths rather than weaknesses. Rappaport outlined how an empowerment focus translates into research terms, such as using collaborative research methods and conducting action-oriented research.

Promoting Social Justice

Several authors have urged community psychologists to transcend the individual level of analysis in favor of examining the structure of society as a whole. The central organizing concept is that of social justice, in other words, documenting inequalities and promoting greater movement toward equality. An exemplar of such research is the epidemiologist Michael Marmot's work on social gradients in health. His recent official report for the British government on health inequalities (Marmot, 2010, p. 2) has an epigraph from the poet Pablo Neruda that easily could stand as a strapline for emancipatory community psychology generally, "Rise up with me against the organization of misery."

Research Using Multiple Methodologies

The last principle, that the research use multiple methodologies, is explicated in the final section of this chapter in which we examine how this maxim translates into practice at the level of the individual study, the research program, and the field as a whole.

Criteria Specifically Applicable to Quantitative Research

The criteria for evaluating quantitative research have been analyzed thoroughly elsewhere (e.g., Shadish, Cook, & Campbell, 2001), and we do not belabor them here. It is, however, perhaps worth reiterating that we do not regard quantitative research as inherently antithetical to community psychology's research-related values that are outlined in the previous sections. Granted it may be easier to translate these values into research using, for example, participatory action research methods, but we contend that it is perfectly possible to carry out quantitative research in a way that is also compatible with these values.

Criteria specific to evaluating quantitative research derive from the seminal work of the late Donald Campbell and his colleagues on the validity of research (Campbell & Stanley, 1966; Cook & Campbell, 1979; Shadish et al., 2001). The authors of these books describe the fundamental criteria for judging the validity of research, particularly research that seeks to make claims about causality: statistical conclusion validity, internal validity, construct validity, and external validity. For present purposes, they are best thought about in the context of research examining the effects of a community intervention in which the researcher is attempting to demonstrate causality, that is, that the intervention results in a positive outcome.

Statistical Conclusion Validity

The first criterion, statistical conclusion validity, is whether the study has demonstrated that there is any effect worth bothering about. The criterion revolves around the word significance, both in its statistical sense (at a minimum, chance variations must be ruled out as likely explanations) and then in its deeper meaning of important (statistically significant effects can still be trivial in terms of any meaningful impact on people's lives). Thus, the question is not only whether an effect has been shown statistically (by using the appropriate statistical tests) but also what its magnitude is (in terms of p values, effect sizes, and importance to real individuals).

Internal Validity

After it has been established that a significant relationship exists between variables, the internal validity question is whether the relationship can plausibly be considered causal, rather than, for example, due to variables extraneous to the research (e.g., the tendency for changes to occur over time independently of the intervention being tested). Mostly this involves the researcher using experimental or quasi-experimental designs, with appropriate control or comparison groups designed to eliminate alternative explanations. However, some plausible causal inferences can also be made from uncontrolled longitudinal correlational designs.

Construct Validity

Once it has been established that a causal relationship exists, the next question to ask is, What does it mean? Construct validity issues involve examining both the nature of the intervention (What exactly does it consists of? What are its active ingredients?) and the nature of the outcome variables (What exactly has changed in the participants or the community?).

External Validity

Following the determination that within the confines of the study meaningful change has occurred that can be attributed to the presence of a causal relationship, the external validity question is, To what extent does the relationship generalize? In other words, does it hold up under different times, places, settings, and cultures? One key way to establish external validity is by replication, particularly by researchers independent of the original research group.

Criteria Specifically Applicable to Qualitative Research

The criteria for judging qualitative research are less straightforward than those for judging quantitative research, partly because qualitative research procedures are more flexible. The main research instrument in qualitative research is often said to be the person of the researcher, with regard to both the collection of the data and the interpretation of the data. For example, in a semistructured interview, different questions may be asked of each interviewee, so the notion of standardization and replicability of methods applies in a weaker sense than in quantitative research. In addition, qualitative researchers acknowledge that the researchers themselves actively construct meaning from their data; there is no single correct reading of the data but rather multiple possible readings.

Furthermore, for many qualitative researchers the whole notion of validity is contentious because it implies a realist epistemology, that is, that there is a real world out there that can be described more or less accurately. Instead, many qualitative researchers hold a constructionist position. That is, they view the social world as constructed by each individual, and it is the task of research to understand how these constructions are achieved (Willig, 2008). Therefore, instead of the validity of findings, qualitative researchers tend to speak of the trustworthiness of the methods and findings.

There are several possible criteria for judging trustworthiness. We have attempted to synthesize some of the more prominent ones (e.g., Creswell, 1998; Elliott et al., 1999; Mays & Pope, 2000; Stiles, 1999; Yardley, 2000). They are intended to apply to all the various subgenres of qualitative research, although we recognize that qualitative research is not a unitary entity and that some of the criteria are more contentious when applied to the more radical relativist approaches (Willig, 2008).

Disclosure of Perspective

Given that the person of the researcher influences both the collection and interpretation of the data, it is important for readers to know what the researchers' preconceptions were about the topics under investigation to judge the extent to which these may have influenced the conclusions drawn. (No malpractice is implied here, simply a recognition that researchers' prior perspectives inevitably influence how they interpret their material.) It is, therefore, good practice in qualitative research for the researchers to briefly describe their background (e.g., in terms of status, gender, and ethnicity) and what their preconceptions (if any) were about the phenomena being researched. This is an extension of the criterion discussed previously of *explication of context and purpose* applicable to all research. It is, however, typically taken further by qualitative researchers, who will reflect on what they as individuals have brought to the research process.

Grounding Interpretations in the Data

Qualitative research is a process of inductive inference, going from the raw data to the researchers' conceptualizations of the data. One way to ensure that these conceptualizations are trustworthy is to anchor them in the original data, a process known as *grounding*. In this way, the reader is able to verify the inductive steps that have been taken and to tally the more abstract conclusions against the concrete original material. Furthermore, readers can use the data presented to test their own alternative conceptualizations of the phenomena. Grounding was the distinguishing feature of one of the first systematic approaches to qualitative research, namely, grounded theory (Glaser & Strauss, 1967), but it has come to be regarded as a common feature of all qualitative approaches.

Coherence of Interpretive Framework

Qualitative research findings normally are presented within a conceptual structure, often consisting of a set of themes or categories. In a good qualitative study, these categories hang together to form a logically coherent framework of ideas, as opposed to a list of categories with no underlying order or meaning. The set of categories as a whole should throw new light on the phenomenon under investigation.

Credibility Checks

The final criterion, credibility checks, is a set of procedures that involve checking the researchers' conceptualizations against other sources (e.g., Elliott et al., 1999; Stiles, 1999). Ways to achieve this include *consensus*, in which members of a research team discuss and agree on the best ways of understanding the data (see Hill, Thompson, & Williams, 1997); *auditing*, in which a researcher outside the research team reviews the findings, examining the "audit trail" that leads from the raw data to the final conclusions; *respondent validation* (also known as *testimonial validity* and *member validation*), in which the researchers obtain participants' comments on the accuracy of the interpretations drawn from the data; and *triangulation*, in which the findings of the study are compared with the findings of other studies or with other sources of information from within the same study. For example, in mixed methods studies, the quantitative and qualitative results can be compared with each other.

These credibility checks should be applied flexibly; we are not proposing that all of them be applied to every study. For example, some studies may be carried out by a single researcher, so consensus is not possible, or there may be a single source of data, which limits the possibilities of triangulation. However, we would expect that all qualitative researchers take some steps to uphold the credibility of their findings.

PUTTING PLURALISM INTO PRACTICE

Having addressed how judgments about research quality might be made under pluralism, we now attempt to set out the implications of a pluralistic stance for how community psychology researchers might plan and conduct their studies. It is useful to distinguish three levels of application at which pluralism might occur: the individual study, the research program, and community psychology as a discipline. We address each of these in turn. Again, following the literature, we focus on the qualitative–quantitative methodological distinction, but the issues are general ones that can be applied to any set of research genres.

Pluralistic Studies

The first level of pluralism is the combination of different research approaches within the same study. This is known as *mixed methods research* and is the subject of a large and growing methodological literature with its own handbook (Tashakkori & Teddlie, 2002) and a recently established journal, the *Journal of Mixed Methods Research*, which began publication in 2007.

Methods can be combined within a study in various ways. Each methodological component (qualitative or quantitative) may have different relative prominence and be sequenced differently over time (Morgan, 1998). For example, the qualitative component may be carried out first and be of lesser importance, as in the case of qualitative interviews being used to develop a quantitative measure with which an extensive reliability and validity study is subsequently performed. Or vice versa, the quantitative component may be carried out first and be of lesser importance, as when a small quantitative survey is followed up by in-depth qualitative interviews. Or yet another possibility is that qualitative and quantitative methods be interwoven and be of equal importance, as in a face-to-face interview study that has both open-ended questions analyzed qualitatively and fixed-response questions analyzed quantitatively.

Pluralistic Research Programs

The second level at which pluralism can occur is across a program of studies conducted by the same investigator or research team on the same general topic. Thus, an initial survey study, an experimental trial, and a discourse analysis could be used to investigate the same topic. The use of complementary methodologies allows a rich and multifaceted picture of the phenomenon to be constructed. One example of how this can be achieved is the work by Humphreys and Moos on self-help groups for addictions. They have carried out quasi-experimental studies showing the health, economic, and clinical benefits of users engaging in 12-step support groups (Humphreys & Moos, 2001). At the same time, Humphreys (2000) wrote a narrative analysis of the stories told by Alcoholics Anonymous members in their self-help groups. This program of research thus addresses both the outcome of self-help groups (To what extent do they assist recovery and meet other goals for their members?) and also their process (What goes on in them, and what are the mechanisms by which they might work?).

A Pluralistic Research Discipline

The third level at which pluralism can occur is that of the field as a whole. Various definitions of the term *field* are possible, from the narrower one of a broad research topic area (e.g., research into domestic violence) to the broader one of an entire discipline (e.g., community psychology or even psychology in general). Indicators that the field is a pluralistic one are the balance of publications in journals, the types of methods used in funded research grants, the spread of presentations in conferences, the types of methodologies drawn on in review articles, and methodological recommendations in standard textbooks and in more specialized methods texts such as the present volume.

These judgments are made at a level beyond that of the individual investigator. Thus, it is perfectly possible for individual researchers to be monomethod in their approach; nothing in what we are saying should be taken to imply that all individual studies or even individual investigators need to be pluralistic. Investigators have their own individual methodological strengths and predilections, and it seems silly for them not to play to those strengths. What is important, however, is that the field as a whole show a healthy mix of different approaches and that this diversity occur within a framework of mutual tolerance and respect.

Are We There Yet?

The community psychology field has moved a long way since its early post-Swampscott Conference days in the 1960s and 1970s. Then, despite its rebellion against many of the assumptions of traditional psychology, its research methods remained fairly mainstream quantitative (Luke, 2005). As Luke's (2005) survey of the *American Journal of Community Psychology* showed, the proportion of qualitative papers increased in the 20-year period from the early 1980s. It would be interesting to examine other indices of pluralism (e.g., other community psychology journals, funded grants, conferences). Within psychology more generally there has been a greater acceptance of a wide variety of approaches to qualitative research (Pistrang & Barker, 2012).

In parallel to these developments in qualitative methods, methodological advances are also being made in quantitative approaches. It is heartening that several of the chapters in the present volume explore the utility of quite complex statistical modeling procedures. This means that the community psychology field is developing in both directions, simultaneously taking on board new qualitative approaches and new quantitative ones.

However, one could question how open the field is to a plurality of theoretical perspectives. Some theoretical orientations and their associated methodological approaches have been noticeable by their absence in community journals. Learning-theory methods, for instance, have been underrepresented (Bogat & Jason, 2000). Biological approaches, such as behavioral ecology, evolutionary psychology, and genetics, have been almost totally ignored, surprisingly so because there is considerable work in these areas on mutual aid and cooperative behavior (e.g., Axelrod, 2006), which are core community psychology constructs. The fact that community psychology has not yet embraced these approaches suggests that community psychology still has some distance to go before it can claim to be a fully pluralistic field. ✓

CONCLUSION

In this chapter, we have attempted to elucidate the methodological pluralist approach, analyzing the meaning and implications of the term, how standards hold up if there are diverse pluralistic approaches, and what a pluralistic agenda would mean in practice. The issues that we have examined are relevant both to research consumers, who are principally interested in how to appraise completed studies, and to research producers, who are principally interested in how to design individual studies and plan out research programs. Of course, this distinction is less than watertight because all producers of research are necessarily also consumers. However, the dichotomy does highlight the different demands on each side. For research consumers, the main task is to develop "research literacy" in each of the different genres of research; for individual researchers, the primary task is to hone their expertise in the genres in which they are conducting their own studies.

Finally, in the spirit of pluralism, we want to reiterate that we are not attempting to lay down rigid rules or to tell researchers how they ought to be going about their business. Our message is really addressed at a higher level, to the community psychology discipline as a whole; it is our hope that those of us in the field are able to give ourselves periodic methodological health checks and to foster a spirit of pluralistic diversity.

REFERENCES

Ahrens, C. E. (2006). Being silenced: The impact of negative social reactions on the disclosure of rape. *American Journal of Community Psychology, 38,* 263–274. doi:10.1007/s10464-006-9069-9

American Psychological Association. (2010). *Ethical principles of psychologists and code of conduct (2002, Amended June 1, 2010)*. Retrieved from http://www.apa.org/ethics/code/index.aspx

Axelrod, R. (2006). *The evolution of cooperation* (Rev. ed.). New York, NY: Basic Books.

Banyard, V. L., & Miller, K. E. (1998). The powerful potential of qualitative research for community psychology. *American Journal of Community Psychology, 26,* 485–505.

Barker, C., & Pistrang, N. (2005). Quality criteria under methodological pluralism: Implications for doing and evaluating research. *American Journal of Community Psychology, 35,* 201–212. doi:10.1007/s10464-005-3398-y

Barker, C., Pistrang, N., & Elliott, R. (2002). *Research methods in clinical psychology: An introduction for students and practitioners* (2nd ed.). Chichester, England: Wiley. doi:10.1002/0470013435

Beneke, C. (2006). *Beyond toleration: The religious origins of American pluralism.* New York, NY: Oxford University Press.

Berman, P. S. (2006). Global legal pluralism. *Southern California Law Review, 80,* 1155–1237.

Bogat, G. A., & Jason, L. A. (2000). Toward an integration of behaviorism and community psychology. In J. Rappaport & E. Seidman (Eds.), *Handbook of community psychology* (pp. 101–114). New York, NY: Kluwer Academic. doi:10.1007/978-1-4615-4193-6_5

Bogdan, R., & Taylor, S. (1976). The judged, not the judges: An insider's view of mental retardation. *American Psychologist, 31,* 47–52. doi:10.1037/0003-066X.31.1.47

Bond, M. A., & Harrell, S. P. (2006). Diversity challenges in community research and action: The story of a special issue of AJCP. *American Journal of Community Psychology, 37,* 157–165. doi:10.1007/s10464-006-9013-z

Bronfenbrenner, U. (1979). *The ecology of human development: Experiments by nature and design.* Cambridge, MA: Harvard University Press.

Campbell, D. T., & Stanley, J. C. (1966). *Experimental and quasi-experimental designs for research.* Chicago, IL: Rand McNally.

Connolly, W. E. (2005). *Pluralism.* Durham, NC: Duke University Press.

Cook, T. D., & Campbell, D. T. (1979). *Quasi-experimentation: Design and analysis issues for field settings.* Chicago, IL: Rand McNally.

Creswell, J. W. (1998). *Qualitative inquiry and research design: Choosing among five traditions.* Thousand Oaks, CA: Sage.

Elliott, R., Fischer, C. T., & Rennie, D. L. (1999). Evolving guidelines for publication of qualitative research studies in psychology and related fields. *British Journal of Clinical Psychology, 38,* 215–229. doi:10.1348/014466599162782

Fiske, D. W., & Shweder, R. A. (Eds.). (1986). *Metatheory in social science: Pluralisms and subjectivities.* Chicago, IL: University of Chicago Press.

Glaser, B. G., & Strauss, A. L. (1967). *The discovery of grounded theory: Strategies for qualitative research.* Chicago, IL: Aldine.

Hill, C. E., Thompson, B. J., & Williams, E. N. (1997). A guide to conducting consensual qualitative research. *The Counseling Psychologist, 25,* 517–572. doi:10.1177/0011000097254001

Humphreys, K. (2000). Community narratives and personal stories in Alcoholics Anonymous. *Journal of Community Psychology, 28,* 495–506. doi:10.1002/1520-6629(200009)28:5<495::AID-JCOP3>3.0.CO;2-W

Humphreys, K., & Moos, R. H. (2001). Can encouraging substance abuse patients to participate in self-help groups reduce demand for health care? A quasi-experimental study. *Alcoholism: Clinical and Experimental Research, 25,* 711–716. doi:10.1111/j.1530-0277.2001.tb02271.x

Kelly, J. G. (2003). Science and community psychology: Social norms for pluralistic enquiry. *American Journal of Community Psychology, 31,* 213–217. doi:10.1023/A:1023998318268

Langhout, R. D. (2003). Reconceptualizing quantitative and qualitative methods: A case study dealing with place as an exemplar. *American Journal of Community Psychology, 32,* 229–244. doi:10.1023/B:AJCP.0000004744.09295.9b

Lewin, K. (1951). *Field theory in social science.* New York, NY: Harper.

Lott, B. (2010). *Multiculturalism and diversity: A social psychological perspective.* Chichester, England: Wiley.

Luke, D. A. (2005). Getting the big picture in community science: Methods that capture context. *American Journal of Community Psychology, 35,* 185–200. doi:10.1007/s10464-005-3397-z

Marmot, M. (2010). *Fair society, healthy lives.* Retrieved from http://www.marmotreview.org

Mays, N., & Pope, C. (2000). Qualitative research in health care: Assessing quality in qualitative research. *BMJ, 320,* 50–52.

Morgan, D. L. (1998). Practical strategies for combining qualitative and quantitative methods: Applications to health research. *Qualitative Health Research, 8,* 362–376. doi:10.1177/104973239800800307

Nelson, G., & Prilleltensky, I. (Eds.). (2010). *Community psychology: In pursuit of liberation and well-being* (2nd ed.). New York, NY: Palgrave MacMillan.

Oakley, A. (1999). Paradigm wars: Some thoughts on a personal and public trajectory. *International Journal of Social Research Methodology, 2,* 247–254. doi:10.1080/136455799295041

Orford, J. (2008). *Community psychology: Challenges, controversies and emerging consensus.* Chichester, England: Wiley.

Peterson, C. (2009). Minimally sufficient research. *Perspectives on Psychological Science, 4,* 7–9. doi:10.1111/j.1745-6924.2009.01089.x

Pistrang, N., & Barker, C. (2012). Varieties of qualitative research: A pragmatic approach to selecting methods. In H. Cooper (Ed.), *APA handbook of research methods in psychology* (pp. 5–18). Washington, DC: American Psychological Association.

Rappaport, J. (1990). Research methods and the empowerment social agenda. In P. Tolan, C. Keys, F. Chertok, & L. Jason (Eds.), *Researching community psychology: Issues of theory and methods* (pp. 51–63). Washington, DC: American Psychological Association. doi:10.1037/10073-005

Rozin, P. (2009). What kind of empirical research should we publish, fund, and reward? A different perspective. *Perspectives on Psychological Science, 4,* 435–439. doi:10.1111/j.1745-6924.2009.01151.x

Ryerson Espino, S. L., & Trickett, E. J. (2008). The spirit of ecological inquiry and intervention research reports: A heuristic elaboration. *American Journal of Community Psychology, 42*, 60–78. doi:10.1007/s10464-008-9179-7

Schumacher, E. F. (1973). *Small is beautiful: A study of economics as if people mattered.* London, England: Blond & Briggs.

Seligman, M. E. P., & Csikszentmihalyi, M. (2000). Positive psychology: An introduction. *American Psychologist, 55*, 5–14. doi:10.1037/0003-066X.55.1.5

Shadish, W. R., Cook, T. D., & Campbell, D. T. (2001). *Experimental and quasi-experimental designs for generalized causal inference.* Boston, MA: Houghton Mifflin.

Society for Community Research and Action. (2010). *Principles.* Retrieved from http://www.scra27.org/about

Stewart, E. (2000). Thinking through others: Qualitative research and community psychology. In J. Rappaport & E. Seidman (Eds.), *Handbook of community psychology* (pp. 725–736). New York, NY: Kluwer Academic. doi:10.1007/978-1-4615-4193-6_30

Stiles, W. B. (1999). Evaluating qualitative research. *Evidence-Based Mental Health, 2*, 99–101. doi:10.1136/ebmh.2.4.99

Tashakkori, C., & Teddlie, C. (Eds.). (2002). *Handbook of mixed methods in social and behavioral research.* Thousand Oaks, CA: Sage.

Tebes, J. K., & Kraemer, D. T. (1991). Qualitative and quantitative knowing in mutual support research: Some lessons from the recent history of scientific psychology. *American Journal of Community Psychology, 19*, 739–756. doi:10.1007/BF00938042

Tolan, P., Keys, C., Chertok, F., & Jason, L. (Eds.). (1990). *Researching community psychology: Issues of theory and methods.* Washington, DC: American Psychological Association. doi:10.1037/10073-000

Trickett, E. J. (1996). A future for community psychology: The context of diversity and the diversity of contexts. *American Journal of Community Psychology, 24*, 209–234. doi:10.1007/BF02510399

Willig, C. (2008). *Introducing qualitative research in psychology: Adventures in theory and method* (2nd ed.). Buckingham, England: Open University Press.

Yardley, L. (2000). Dilemmas in qualitative health research. *Psychology & Health, 15*, 215–228. doi:10.1080/08870440008400302

4

INTEGRATING QUALITATIVE AND QUANTITATIVE APPROACHES: AN EXAMPLE OF MIXED METHODS RESEARCH

REBECCA CAMPBELL, KATIE A. GREGORY,
DEBRA PATTERSON, AND DEBORAH BYBEE

In his call for pluralistic inquiry in community psychology, Kelly (2003) *champion* noted that "complexity is the given reference point for the community psychologist" (p. 215). If community psychologist researchers want to capture complexity and context, then their methodologies must be similarly diverse. Innovative qualitative, quantitative, and mixed methods designs, from their own discipline and most likely beyond, must become part of their methodological nomenclature. Indeed, the field's interest and use of qualitative methods has grown rapidly since Banyard and Miller's (1998) special issue of the *American Journal of Community Psychology* highlighted how these approaches are particularly well suited for the study of such core values as diversity, culture and context, and empowerment.

On the quantitative front, Luke (2005) noted that although the field of community psychology has historically overrelied on quantitative techniques too simplistic for its theoretical propositions, this too is changing with the expanding use of complex modeling techniques, as further evidenced

Research for this chapter was supported by a grant (2005-WG-BX-0003) to Rebecca Campbell from the National Institute of Justice. The opinions expressed in this document are those of the authors and do not reflect the official position of the U.S. Department of Justice.

throughout this edited volume. In the pursuit of methodological pluralism, community psychologists must also consider mixed methods as a distinct approach to social inquiry (Langhout, 2003; see also Chapter 3, this volume). Mixed methods research combines quantitative and qualitative methods to leverage the unique points of view afforded by each tradition. Such designs are particularly well suited for studying complex phenomena in real-world settings, whereas the use of one single method would be unlikely to reveal a complete picture.

As a methodological paradigm, mixed methods research is not simply an A + B operation of adding qualitative methods to a quantitative study (or vice versa). It is often referred to as a "third paradigm" (Denscombe, 2008) and a holistic enterprise (Langhout, 2003) with its own multidisciplinary history and unique epistemological, methodological, and practical challenges and solutions. In this chapter, we first review briefly the history and current epistemological and design debates in the mixed methods literature. We then present a case study of one specific mixed methods design, the sequential explanatory mixed methods design, in an evaluation of a community-based intervention to improve postassault care for sexual assault survivors (for other mixed methods case examples, see Chapter 11, this volume).

WHAT ARE MIXED METHODS, AND WHY ARE THEY USEFUL?

What does the term *mixed methods* mean? Many answers have been proposed over the past 50 years. Johnson, Onwuegbuzie, and Turner (2007) reviewed the most influential conceptualizations in the field to derive a common, synthesized definition:

> Mixed methods research is the type of research in which a researcher or team of researchers combined elements of qualitative and quantitative research approaches (e.g., use of qualitative and quantitative viewpoints, data collection, analysis, inference techniques) for the broad purposes of breadth and depth of *understanding and corroboration* [emphasis added]. (p. 123)

Historically, there has been more emphasis on the corroboration element, tracing back to D. T. Campbell and Fiske's (1959) classic work on convergent and discriminant validity by the multitrait–multimethod matrix. Even Denzin's (1978) classic text on sociological methods framed the use of mixed methods as a strategy for triangulation, that is, using different methods to collect data on the same subject to compare and contrast the findings obtained through each to see if the findings converge. Denzin argued that triangulation can strengthen confidence in the accuracy and validity of one's findings, particularly because between-methods triangulations cancel out the biases inherent in each method. Yet, the concept of corroboration implies that there is an objective, known world of "truths" to be discovered and verified, and the rise of constructivist theories of social science in the 1980s and 1990s challenged that fundamental assumption (Guba & Lincoln, 1989). As such, from a constructivist point of view, the utility of mixed methods was questionable (at best).

However, for scholars who were not completely smitten with the essentialist positions of the "paradigm wars" (Gage, 1989), the utility of mixed methods was still worth exploring, particularly for their potential to bring about more nuanced understanding of social phenomena. If one sidesteps the issue of triangulation, mixed methods provide diverse perspectives on a phenomenon of interest, whereas the use of any single method, however complicated, is unlikely to yield as much detail. Indeed, Greene, Caracelli, and Graham's (1989) influential review of the literature demonstrated that the mixed methods field had grown beyond its original scope of triangulation. Greene et al.'s conceptual framework outlined five major purposes of mixed methods: (a) triangulation; (b) complementarity—to elaborate, illustrate, and/or clarify findings generated by one method with the other; (c) development—to use results from one method to inform the other method; (d) initiation—to discover contradictions and paradoxes and to develop new perspectives and frameworks; and (e) expansion—to push the boundaries on the breadth and depth of inquiry by using different methods for different components of a project. *collaboratn.*

To that list, Collins, Onwuegbuzie, and Sutton (2006) highlighted four additional reasons for using mixed methods designs that are particularly relevant in community-based research and intervention studies. First, mixed methods can foster participant enrichment, by which Collins et al. meant participant recruitment and selection into a study. In studies of social problems, the population of interest is almost always presumed to be diverse and heterogeneous, and formative mixed methods studies can be instrumental in learning how to access and develop trusting relationships with different sectors of a community. Second, these designs can improve instrument fidelity. Mixed methods projects can be useful for determining whether existing measures are culturally meaningful and contextually grounded for the target population. Third, the use of qualitative methods within quantitative randomized control intervention trials can be extraordinarily helpful in assessing treatment fidelity and treatment integrity. Qualitative methods can readily capture drift from a planned intervention as well as identify how an intervention could be modified for subsequent phases of a project. Finally, mixed methods can foster significance enhancement, meaning that the significance of an intervention ought to be construed more broadly than its statistical significance and that integrated analyses and interpretations can provide richer data on a social program's potential effectiveness.

THEORETICAL AND DESIGN ISSUES
IN MIXED METHODS RESEARCH

Mixed methods offer the promise of the best of both methodological traditions, but not without substantial challenges. The paradigm wars painted quantitative and qualitative methodologies as so distinct and, more to the point, oppositional that mixing methods seemed impossible. From an ontological and epistemological point of view, how it is possible to bring together radically different paradigms about the nature of what can be known and how it can be known within the same study, series of studies, or program of research? To some extent, paradigms are linked to a researcher's identity because they reflect a researcher's fundamental beliefs and values (R. Campbell, 2002). Can a researcher "be" one paradigm in one context, one study, or one part of a study and then be another paradigm in another? Such questions led to the incompatibility thesis: The "mixing" in mixed methods cannot occur at theoretical levels because of the fundamental conflict between positivist and constructivist models, "just as surely as the belief in a round world precludes belief in a flat one" (Guba, 1987, p. 31). Mixed methods studies were considered theoretically tangled at best and theoretically adrift at worst.

In an effort to dismantle the incompatibility thesis, mixed methods scholars have outlined multiple alternatives for addressing these epistemological tensions (see Greene, 2007; Tashakkori & Teddlie, 2003, 2010). First, the aparadigmatic stance promulgated the idea that methods and paradigms are independent. As Patton (1990) argued, "in real world practice, methods can be separated from the epistemology out of which they emerged" (p. 90). In essence, theoretical "navel gazing" was seen as distracting and unhelpful to the actual practice of social science research, and therefore the so-called requirement that theory and methods line up was best left ignored. Such arguments, though, were unsatisfying to many and led to a second approach for resolving theoretical tensions in mixed methods research, namely, the adoption of a single paradigm that could theoretically accommodate multiple methods.

For instance, postrealist pragmatism was heralded as a theoretical solution because of its emphasis on practice and method over theoretical cogitation (Greene & Hall, 2010; Howe, 1988; Patton, 2002; Rallis & Rossman, 2003). In this approach, the research question is paramount and must drive the selection of methods, which would be expected to vary within and across studies. More recently, other uniting theories, such as critical realism (Maxwell & Mittapalli, 2010) and transformative paradigms (Mertens, Bledsoe, Sullivan, & Wilson, 2010), have been proposed as single-paradigm solutions. Third, rather than ignoring theoretical sticking points or trying to bring them together under one umbrella, other mixed methods theorists called for embracing the tensions between paradigms and advocated for dialectical, multiparadigmatic

look-up

approaches. In this view, all paradigms are presumed to have merit. Therefore, allowing multiple theoretical models to guide a study is beneficial so long as researchers engage those tensions through explicit reflection and engagement (Greene & Caracelli, 1997; 2003; Greene & Hall, 2010). Finally, a fourth strain promoted theoretical plurality—different components of a study can in fact be guided by different paradigms (Creswell, Plano Clark, Gutmann, & Hanson, 2003). Design comes first, and researchers can "walk backwards" to its corresponding paradigms, allowing for multiple frameworks within a study.

At the same time that mixed methods scholars were working through these epistemological issues, a comprehensive taxonomy of mixed methods designs was evolving (for reviews, see Creswell & Plano Clark, 2007; Tashakkori & Teddlie, 2003, 2010). A multitude of designs can be created by varying the timing or sequence of different methods, the relative priority of the approaches, the intended function or purpose of using multiple methods, and the stage of the research process at which qualitative and quantitative methods are to be integrated. First, with respect to timing, mixing can occur within the same study (usually termed *parallel* or *simultaneous*) or across studies within a series (usually termed *sequential*). Second, mixing methods does not necessarily mean that qualitative and quantitative approaches have the same relative priority in a project. Sometimes the work is predominately quantitative, with qualitative methods used in a supplemental fashion; at other times, the reverse is true. However, in yet other designs, the priority is balanced, with both methods used with equal importance.

Third, with respect to function, researchers must sort out why they need both methods and what they hope to gain from their integration. In some circumstances, exploration is the purpose; this is particularly common in new areas of inquiry in which there are no guiding frameworks, theories, measures, or instruments. By contrast, both methods may be needed for explanation, with the findings generated through one method needing to be unpacked further using a different method for a more complete understanding of the results. Methods could be combined for examining triangulation (i.e., seeking convergence and corroboration of findings across different methods studying the same phenomenon). For example, sequential designs (e.g., first qualitative and then quantitative or vice versa) could be used for different purposes. In a sequential explanation-focused design, the findings of one method would be used to shape what happens in the next method; by contrast, in a sequential triangulation design, there may be more independence of method until the final comparing and contrasting of findings.

Finally, the stage of integration can vary across designs. To date, most mixed methods studies have typically integrated data at the interpretation stage. Data from each method are analyzed in their own tradition and then the results from each are brought together during interpretation of the overall findings. However, one of the most rapidly developing sectors within the mixed methods literature is the creation of techniques for jointly analyzed data (Onwuegbuzie & Combs, 2010). Because qualitative data can be numerically coded, integrated analyses are often quantitative. McConney, Rudd, and Ayers (2002) noted that because qualitative data often contain unique information otherwise not captured in quantitative study components, conversion methods must be sensitive to that issue so that the distinctive perspectives captured through qualitative means are not lost. Alternatively, Bazeley (2010) noted that retaining information in its original form—be it visual, numerical, or textual—will likely become more common with continued advancement in software for computer-assisted joint analysis.

The ever-evolving taxonomy of mixed methods designs presents researchers with a bevy of creative options, depending on the nature of the research questions and goals of the project. Recently, Creswell (2010) noted that more and more unusual blends of methods and techniques that do not necessarily fit existing design typologies are emerging. As such, this literature must rely (as it has historically) on the presentation of case examples that highlight various epistemological, design, and analytic strategies for integrating qualitative and quantitative methods. In other words, true to form, this field develops both inductively and deductively. In that tradition, in the rest of this chapter, we discuss a mixed methods case example from community psychology that used a sequential explanatory design to evaluate the effectiveness of a community intervention for victims of sexual assault.

CASE EXAMPLE OF MIXED METHODS IN COMMUNITY PSYCHOLOGY

The case example we are presenting here is part of our ongoing research examining what happens when rape survivors turn to their communities for assistance after a sexual assault. Traditionally, victims are directed to hospital emergency departments for forensic evidence collection (Martin, 2005). Unfortunately, emergency department personnel rarely know how to collect such evidence correctly and frequently treat survivors in ways that are experienced as retraumatizing (for reviews, see R. Campbell, 2008; Martin, 2005). If victims try to pursue legal prosecution, their experiences with the criminal justice system are not markedly better. Only 14% to 18% of all reported sexual assaults are successfully prosecuted (R. Campbell, 2008). Medical forensic evidence is important in prosecution because injury and DNA evidence can carry substantial weight with judges and juries (Spohn, Beichner, & Davis-Frenzel, 2001). However, due to a lack of communication and coordination between the legal and medical systems, police and prosecutors rarely receive medical exam findings in time to affect the outcome of a case (Human Rights Watch, 2009). As a result, it is not uncommon for rape survivors to have to endure an invasive, traumatizing medical exam that has no bearing on their legal case.

In light of these problems with the medical and legal systems, the nursing profession created Sexual Assault Nurse Examiner (SANE) programs (Ledray, 1999) as an alternative model of postassault care. Specially trained nurses provide 24-hour care to sexual assault victims in either hospital or nonhospital clinic settings (R. Campbell, Patterson, & Lichty, 2005). To address survivors' psychological needs, SANEs strive to preserve victims' dignity and ensure that they are not retraumatized by the exam. Many SANE programs work with their local rape crisis centers so that rape victim advocates can also be present for the exam to provide crisis intervention and emotional support. For victims' physical health needs, SANE programs offer emergency contraception and prophylactic antibiotics for sexually transmitted infections. For forensic evidence collection, SANEs conduct a comprehensive head-to-toe examination of the survivor's body to document and treat injuries. The forensic evidence collected by the SANEs is sent to the state crime lab for analysis, and the results are forwarded to the police and prosecutors. If a case is prosecuted, the SANE may provide expert witness testimony in the trial.

SANE programs have spread quite quickly throughout the United States, growing from a handful of programs in the 1970s and 1980s to nearly 500 programs currently in existence (International Association of Forensic Nurses, 2010). However, this diffusion occurred despite minimal evaluative data on the effectiveness of SANE programs. Although SANE programs address the legal, medical, and mental health needs of rape survivors, the few evaluation studies that have been conducted on these interventions have focused on legal outcomes because of the pressing need to identify successful programs that can systemically change prosecution rates (for exceptions, see R. Campbell, Patterson, Adams, Diegel, & Coats, 2008). Several case studies have suggested that SANE programs increase prosecution rates because the forensic evidence provided by the nurses is so compelling to judges and juries (Littel, 2001). In a quasi-experimental pre–post design, Crandall and Helitzer (2003) found that rates of successful prosecutions significantly increased. Such findings are promising but merit replication to determine whether such successes can be duplicated in other community contexts.

Developing a Mixed Methods Design

Our goal in this project was to determine if and how a community-based SANE program could contribute to increased prosecution rates in the community, which is not to say that legal change is the only appropriate outcome to examine, but it was readily identified by multiple stakeholders as a critical issue of interest. To plan this project, we began by considering our epistemological stance and decided to adopt the single-paradigm approach. Consistent with a postrealist pragmatist approach, we allowed our research questions to dictate the methods needed for our evaluation. We wanted to capture both outcome and process—whether SANE programs could contribute to increased prosecution rates and, if so, how. Capturing the processes of this intervention were particularly important because, as Kazdin (2008) noted, intervention research has not paid nearly enough attention to understanding the mediating mechanisms by which programs work. Understanding how, why, and under what circumstances interventions produce desired effects helps identify critical ingredients of change. Such information may be even more impactful because it promotes the adoption of "evidence-based *mechanisms*" (Kazdin, 2008, p. 152; emphasis added) rather than specific programs. Such flexibility is critical because it gives communities the option of varying intervention structure and function in ways that suit local contexts while retaining an emphasis on the key processes that create change. Mixed methods were a natural choice because outcomes are traditionally assessed quantitatively, and qualitative methods are particularly well suited for capturing process.

For this project, we used a sequential explanatory mixed methods design (Creswell et al., 2003). This design is characterized by the collection and analysis of quantitative data followed by qualitative data. The purpose of this design is to "use qualitative results to assist in *explaining* [emphasis added] and interpreting the findings of a primarily quantitative study" (Creswell et al., 2003, p. 227). In such designs, primacy is typically given to the quantitative data, although Creswell et al. (2003) noted that both methods can be treated as equal components, which is how we implemented this design in our project. The two methods are usually integrated during the final interpretation phase of the study, but the design can be modified to work reflexively with both methods throughout the project. Creswell et al.'s original description of the design characterized it as one cycle of mixed methods, that is, quantitative followed by qualitative data collection. Given the complexity of our project and its twin goals of identifying outcomes and processes, our design included two full cycles of sequential quantitative and qualitative methods. In addition, because multiple stakeholders were involved in this intervention (i.e., nurses, police, prosecutors, survivors, advocates), we decided to collect data from different perspectives throughout the cycles because we suspected that the explanation for the success or failure of the intervention could be understood only by capturing the varied points of view of all of it major constituents.

The final design of our project is depicted in Figure 4.1. We started with quantitative methods. Study 1 used a quasi-experimental, nonequivalent

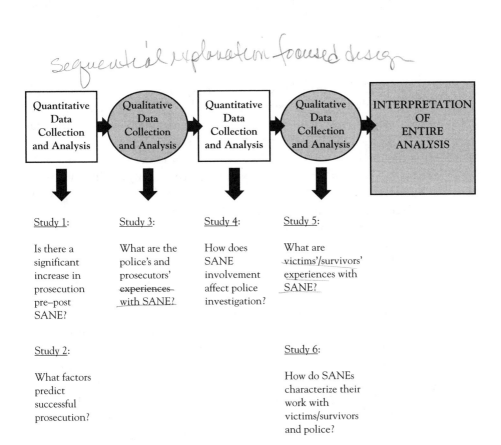

sequential explanation focused design

Study 1:

Is there a significant increase in prosecution pre–post SANE?

Study 3:

What are the police's and prosecutors' ~~experiences~~ with SANE?

Study 4:

How does SANE involvement affect police investigation?

Study 5:

What are victims'/survivors' experiences with SANE?

Study 2:

What factors predict successful prosecution?

Study 6:

How do SANEs characterize their work with victims/survivors and police?

Figure 4.1. Multistudy project design. SANE = Sexual Encounter Nurse Examiner program.

comparison group cohort design (Shadish, Cook, & Campbell, 2002) to compare criminal justice system outcomes for adult sexual assault cases treated in county hospitals 5 years prior to the implementation of the SANE program to cases treated in the focal SANE program during its first 7 years of operation. Study 2 also used quantitative methods to examine what characteristics of the victim, the assault, and the medical forensic evidence were associated with successful prosecution. These data were analyzed as quickly as possible to inform data collection in the next sequence in the design.

For Study 3, we conducted qualitative interviews with police and prosecutors regarding their experiences working with the SANE program in an effort to explain what we had learned about the intervention's effectiveness. In Study 4, we returned to quantitative methods for a detailed content analysis of sexual assault police reports to determine whether the nature of police investigations differed as a function of SANE involvement in a case. These data enabled us to cross-check findings that emerged in Study 3 regarding possible pathways through which the SANE program was affecting prosecution outcomes. In Study 5, we cycled back to qualitative interviews with victims/survivors about their experiences with the SANE program and criminal justice system. These data were essential for exploring possible mechanisms of effectiveness through a completely different point of view. Prior to conducting the final study in the project, Study 6, we completed all other data analyses to identify any unanswered questions. In these final qualitative interviews, we asked the forensic nurses to reflect on their work with their patients and with their legal community. After these open-ended discussions, we shared the findings from the other studies and asked the nurses for their interpretations and comments.

Although the purpose of this chapter is to examine the methods of this project, it may be useful to highlight key findings prior to discussing the challenges and lessons learned during implementation. Using multilevel modeling, we found that prosecution rates significantly increased pre- to post-SANE (from 24% to 29%) and that these effects could be reasonably attributed to the program's efforts (for full methodological details, see R. Campbell, Bybee, Ford, Patterson, & Ferrell, 2009; for another example of multilevel modeling, see Chapter 10, this volume). The nurses provided police and prosecutors with valuable evidence and also helped streamline their investigational efforts, which allowed them to invest more time and effort into these cases. With the survivors/patients, the nurses emphasized health and recovery and did not pressure them to report to the police. This focus on well-being indirectly contributed to survivors' becoming more willing and able to participate in the lengthy prosecution process.

Issues in Implementation

Practical Problems

The story behind the design and our results is not nearly as tidy as Figure 4.1 would suggest. Practically, we were in a serious time crunch because we had bundled all six studies together into a single 2-year grant. We had limited time to collect and make sense of vast, diverse data. Beginning with the quantitative analyses to ascertain program outcomes certainly made sense, but we gained a deeper appreciation as to why many intervention evaluations stop at that question. In experimental randomized control trials, if an effect is significant, then it can quite reasonably (and quickly) be attributed to the intervention. By contrast, community-based quasi-experimental designs typically involve more complicated analyses and often have to be supplemented with additional archival information to rule out threats to internal validity. We were in trouble early on because we needed to start the qualitative data collection to explain findings that were still not entirely known.

Epistemological Headaches and Design Drift

The transition from Studies 1 and 2 (quantitative outcome findings) to Study 3 (qualitative process findings) was bumpy because of epistemological confusion and difficult decisions in data collection. How exactly were we supposed to use our quantitative findings (the increased prosecution rates pre–post SANE) to inform the next method in the sequence, the qualitative interviews with the police and prosecutors? Although guided by a pragmatist epistemological position, we could not quite escape our prior teachings in positivism and constructivism. From a positivist point of view (or even a kinder postpositivist perspective) how credible would our findings be if we let our research participants know our prior results? We planned for an explanatory design, but we felt tangled up in the need for triangulation. Would it not be better if the qualitative interviews would independently verify the results of the quantitative outcome evaluation? From a constructivist perspective, how appropriate would it be to approach qualitative data collection with preconceived notions about the nature of the story to be told?

From either point of view, it seemed that we needed to withhold the quantitative findings in the qualitative interviews with police and prosecutors. So we struggled to forget the findings we had rushed to produce and tried to approach data collection with police and prosecutors from an open perspective. Over time, we began to discover how we were using our prior findings in the interviews. When the police and prosecutor interviews naturally flowed into topics that could speak to the mechanisms of the intervention's effectiveness, our interviewing style shifted. We became more targeted, using extensive probing to ferret out all information we could obtain regarding possible pathways from the SANE program to prosecution success. There was an intensity to this line of questioning that otherwise would have been quite unlikely.

Analyses, Interpretation, and Integration

We were then in a quandary as to which qualitative data analysis methods would be appropriate for these interview data, and unfortunately the mixed methods literature does not yet provide much guidance on that issue. In traditional qualitative research, epistemological, methodological, and analytic options are often bundled together into different subtypes (e.g., phenomenological, grounded theory), but we did not have "pure" qualitative data. Traditional grounded theory analysis seemed inappropriate given how the data were collected. After extensive review, we reasoned that modified analytic induction (AI) could work within our mixed methods paradigm (for more discussion on our use of AI, see R. Campbell, Patterson, & Cabral, 2010). AI is similar to grounded theory in that both approaches work inductively from the data to develop explanatory models. Rather than trying to develop a constructivist theory, AI techniques emphasize identifying and empirically testing qualitative assertions (i.e., mechanistic building blocks of a theory; Erickson, 1986; Robinson, 1951). Moreover, the AI literature encourages researchers to make use of all data when formulating and testing their assertions (Erickson, 1986), which we interpreted to mean that our quantitative findings need not be forgotten at this stage of the analysis.

The Cycle of Challenges Repeats

We ended this first cycle of quantitative–qualitative data collection and analysis with findings suggesting that the intervention did contribute to increased prosecution, and we had identified clear mechanisms through which SANEs had an influential early impact on the police investigation itself. Then, we sought to repeat the cycle by returning to quantitative analyses to unpack further the influence of SANEs on police work specifically. We conducted a detailed quantitative content coding of sexual assault police reports to capture how SANE involvement in a case had a demonstrable impact on the investigation and affected the critical decision to move a case forward to prosecutors. At this transition back to quantitative methods, our intentions for using mixed methods became muddled. Although explanation had been our goal, we were drifting to triangulation; we were wondering if the findings from the qualitative police interviews would be replicated in the new quantitative police report analyses. We were still pursuing an explanation for the intervention's effectiveness, but we saw an opportunity for a rigorous test of triangulation if we forced some separation between these components of the project. No doubt such ideas were rooted in unresolved epistemological confusions, and in our crunch for time, we duly noted this theoretical mess and moved forward.

We decided the team members coding the police files should not be the same people who did the police qualitative interviews and analyses. We began functioning in subgroups and deliberately held off on any integrative discussions until the next phase of quantitative data was further along. When the quantitative data were ready for analysis, we met as a collective to identify variables of interest and brainstorm ideas for possible mediational models to explore. In that sense, we were again using prior findings to inform the next phase of work. At the same time, though, the qualitative team held back and did not put forward all of its details. When the quantitative analyses nicely triangulated the qualitative findings, which together advanced our explanation of how and why this intervention was effective, we wondered if we had made things more complicated than they needed to be.

Meanwhile, the next piece of the project was to interview rape survivors about their experiences with the SANE program and the criminal justice system. We knew from prior projects that recruiting survivors for interview research can be time consuming, so these data were collected concurrently with all other aspects of the project. Because we were so weighed down with the logistics and theoretical confusions of the prior phases, we found it easier to approach this study from a purer qualitative perspective. These interviews were structured such that survivors were asked to describe what happened in the assault itself and then, in whatever order they saw fit, to trace the steps of their postassault help seeking. Interestingly, the survivors never framed their experiences solely around legal prosecution, which was a refreshing change from the rest of our data and indeed proved to be a substantively critical piece in the puzzle. The survivors discussed how the SANE program helped them feel safe and how it helped them heal from the assault.

We then wondered why it was that the rest of our data were so clearly showing that the SANE program was contributing to increased prosecution rates. We had to consider the possibility that the survivors' data were not going fit with the rest of the picture; for them, the SANE program did not seem to have anything to do with prosecution. But again, when the survivors' interviews came around to a discussion of their experiences with police and prosecutors, our interviewing probed around this seeming missing link, and we discovered that it was not missing, just indirect. The SANE program's focus on health care and recovery did in fact eventually lead to survivors' increased engagement and participation in the criminal justice system because they were more ready, willing, and able to deal with the challenges of the investigation because the initial trauma of the assault had been responded to so effectively by the SANE program staff. From these data, the explanation of the intervention's effectiveness became far more complete and nuanced.

As we approached the final stages of data collection, we were running low on time and patience, so we put all of our findings on the table, figured out what we knew, and made a list of unanswered questions, potential contradictory findings, and odd things that did not line up. That list of unknowns became the guiding force in the last wave of data collection, the qualitative interviews with the SANE nurses themselves. This was our last chance to put the pieces together, and vestigial concerns and pretenses about postpositivist and constructivist notions of right and wrong fell by the wayside. It was only at the end that we functioned as mixed methodologists in that all data were allowed and all team members knew everything and shared everything. Such openness was instrumental for identifying the ultimate explanation of the intervention's effectiveness: The SANEs work in parallel processes with their patients and with the police, and these separate pathways are mutually reinforcing, thereby contributing to increased prosecution. Ironically, our own parallel methods came together in the end as well.

CONCLUSION

We began this project well versed in the mixed methods literature; we had a methodologically diverse research team with staff trained in both quantitative and qualitative methods; and yet our experiences were still quite challenging. The epistemological issues were surprisingly sticky, and our original plan for a single-paradigm pragmatist approach did not sustain us through the entire project. Precisely because we had histories with post-positivist and constructivist approaches, we had no choice but to try to reconcile these conflicts, and in the end our approach would be better characterized as the dialectical, multiparadigmatic approach. We had to divide into subgroups, and we then rejoined in the end for the kind of dialectical debates advocated by Greene and her colleagues (Greene & Caracelli, 1997, 2003; Greene & Hall, 2010). Greene and Hall (2010) recently noted that there are multiple conceptual and practical similarities between the dialectic and pragmatic stances, but in projects with recursive designs (and in instances in which the findings are surprising or dissonant), the dialectic approach may be particularly well suited.

In this project, we used both stances. At times, the findings across studies appeared completely contradictory, and the dialectical approach helped normalize that occurrence and pushed us to make the most of our final stages of data collection and the interpretive phases to figure out whether the findings were in fact at odds or were sufficiently complex that the big picture was just taking a little longer to see. The press for time did not always foster in-depth reflection when we were in the middle of everything, but our interpretive phases were necessarily conversational and reflective.

Our goal was to explain how and why a SANE program contributed to increased prosecution rates, and to that end we believe we succeeded. The resulting model could not have been produced with only one type of data or one stakeholder perspective. For instance, without the qualitative data from the survivors themselves, we might have erroneously concluded from the quantitative data that SANE programs should directly encourage victims to report and prosecute their assaults. Our findings seriously question the utility of such recommendations. The SANE program's deemphasis on legal matters and its focus on patient health were paramount, and in the end, this practice philosophy did contribute to increased victim participation in the criminal justice system. We did not fully understand that fact until we interviewed the SANE nurses; this was the only component of the study in which we were working more fluidly with multiple data sources. Our study did not compare SANE programs with different practice models, so we cannot conclude that proprosecution messages would be detrimental. Our point here is that even within our own project, we would have come to different conclusions without the use of multiple methods.

Our case example illustrates how methodological pluralism can be invaluable for evaluating complex community interventions (Kelly, 2003).We were successful in explaining the mediating mechanisms of this intervention's effectiveness precisely because we used multiple methods from multiple stakeholders. These differing data sources and points of view at times appeared to be contradictory, but with dialectical engagement we began to understand how the pieces came together into one, albeit complex, picture. The mixed methods literature offers community scholars a variety of design options of varying complexity for integrating multiple methods. As we have attempted to demonstrate, the benefits of such plurality are innumerable.

REFERENCES

Banyard, V. L., & Miller, K. E. (1998). The powerful potential of qualitative research for community psychology. *American Journal of Community Psychology, 26,* 485–505. doi:10.1023/A:1022136821013

Bazeley, P. (2010). Computer-assisted integration of mixed methods data sources and analyses. In A. Tashakkori & C. Teddlie (Eds.), *SAGE handbook of mixed methods in social & behavioral research* (2nd ed., pp. 431–468). Thousand Oaks, CA: Sage.

Campbell, D. T., & Fiske, D. W. (1959). Convergent and discriminant validation by the multitrait-multimethod matrix. *Psychological Bulletin, 56,* 81–105. doi:10.1037/h0046016

Campbell, R. (2002). *Emotionally involved: The impact of researching rape.* New York, NY: Routledge.

Campbell, R. (2008). The psychological impact of rape victims' experiences with the legal, medical, and mental health systems. *American Psychologist, 63,* 702–717. doi:10.1037/0003-066X.63.8.702

Campbell, R., Bybee, D., Ford, J. K., Patterson, D., & Ferrell, J. (2009). *A systems change analysis of SANE programs: Identifying mediating mechanisms of criminal justice system impact.* Washington, DC: National Institute of Justice.

Campbell, R., Patterson, D., Adams, A., Diegel, R., & Coats, S. (2008). A participatory evaluation project to measure SANE nursing practice and adult sexual assault patients' psychological well-being. *Journal of Forensic Nursing, 4,* 19–28. doi:10.1111/j.1939-3938.2008.00003.x

Campbell, R., Patterson, D., & Cabral, G. E. (2010). Using ecological theory to evaluate the effectiveness of an indigenous community intervention: A study of Sexual Assault Nurse Examiner (SANE) programs. *American Journal of Community Psychology, 46,* 263–276. doi:10.1007/s10464-010-9339-4

Campbell, R., Patterson, D., & Lichty, L. F. (2005). The effectiveness of Sexual Assault Nurse Examiner (SANE) programs: A review of psychological, medical, legal, and community outcomes. *Trauma, Violence, & Abuse, 6*, 313–329. doi:10.1177/1524838005280328

Collins, K. M. T., Onwuegbuzie, A. J., & Sutton, I. L. (2006). A model incorporating the rationale and purpose for conducting mixed-methods research in special education and beyond. *Learning Disabilities: A Contemporary Journal, 4*, 67–100.

Crandall, C., & Helitzer, D. (2003). *Impact evaluation of a Sexual Assault Nurse Examiner (SANE) program* (U.S. Department of Justice Document No. 203276; NIJ Award No. 98-WT-VX-0027). Retrieved from https://www.ncjrs.gov/pdffiles1/nij/grants/203276.pdf

Creswell, J. W. (2010). Mapping the developing landscape of mixed methods research. In A. Tashakkori & C. Teddlie (Eds.), *SAGE handbook of mixed methods in social & behavioral research* (2nd ed., pp. 45–68). Thousand Oaks, CA: Sage.

Creswell, J. W., & Plano Clark, V. L. (2007). *Designing and conducting mixed methods research*. Thousand Oaks, CA: Sage.

Creswell, J. W., Plano Clark, V. L., Gutmann, M. L., & Hanson, W. E. (2003). Advanced mixed methods research designs. In A. Tashakkori & C. Teddlie (Eds.), *Handbook of mixed methods in social & behavioral research* (pp. 209–240). Thousand Oaks, CA: Sage.

Denscombe, M. (2008). Communities of practice: A research paradigm for the mixed methods approach. *Journal of Mixed Methods Research, 2*, 270–283. doi:10.1177/1558689808316807

Denzin, N. K. (1978). *The research act: A theoretical introduction to sociological methods*. New York, NY: Praeger.

Erickson, F. (1986). Qualitative methods in research on teaching. In M. C. Wittrock (Ed.), *Handbook of research on teaching* (3rd ed., pp. 119–161). New York, NY: Macmillan.

Gage, N. (1989). The paradigm wars and their aftermath: A "historical" sketch of research and teaching since 1989. *Educational Researcher, 18*, 4–10.

Greene, J. C. (2007). *Mixed methods in social inquiry*. San Francisco, CA: Jossey-Bass.

Greene, J. C., & Caracelli, V. J. (Eds.). (1997). *Advances in mixed-method evaluation: The challenges and benefits of integrating diverse paradigms: New directions for evaluation*. San Francisco, CA: Jossey-Bass.

Greene, J. C., & Caracelli, V. J. (2003). Making paradigmatic sense of mixed methods practice. In A. Tashakkori & C. Teddlie (Eds.), *Handbook of mixed methods in social & behavioral research* (pp. 91–110). Thousand Oaks, CA: Sage.

Greene, J. C., Caracelli, V. J., & Graham, W. F. (1989). Toward a conceptual framework for mixed-method evaluation designs. *Educational Evaluation and Policy Analysis, 11*, 255–274.

Greene, J. C., & Hall, J. N. (2010). Dialectics and pragmatism: Being of consequence. In A. Tashakkori & C. Teddlie (Eds.), *SAGE handbook of mixed methods in social & behavioral research* (2nd ed., pp. 119–144). Thousand Oaks, CA: Sage.

Guba, E. G. (1987). What have we learned about naturalistic evaluation? *Evaluation Practice, 8*, 23–43. doi:10.1016/S0886-1633(87)80037-5

Guba, E. G., & Lincoln, Y. S. (1989). *Fourth generation evaluation.* Newbury Park, CA: Sage.

Howe, K. R. (1988). Against the quantitative–qualitative incompatability thesis or dogmas die hard. *Educational Researcher, 17*, 10–16.

Human Rights Watch. (2009). *Testing justice: The rape kit backlog in Los Angeles City and County.* New York, NY: Author.

International Association of Forensic Nurses. (2010). *Database of the International Association of Forensic Nurses.* Retrieved from http://www.forensicnurse.org

Johnson, R. B., Onwuegbuzie, A. J., & Turner, L. S. (2007). Toward a definition of mixed methods research. *Journal of Mixed Methods Research, 1*, 112–133. doi:10.1177/1558689806298224

Kazdin, A. E. (2008). Evidence-based treatment and practice: New opportunities to bridge clinical research and practice, enhance the knowledge base, and improve patient care. *American Psychologist, 63*, 146–159. doi:10.1037/0003-066X.63.3.146

Kelly, J. G. (2003). Science and community psychology: Social norms for pluralistic inquiry. *American Journal of Community Psychology, 31*, 213–217. doi:10.1023/A:1023998318268

Langhout, R. D. (2003). Reconceptualizing quantitative and qualitative methods: A case study dealing with place as an exemplar. *American Journal of Community Psychology, 32*, 229–244. doi:10.1023/B:AJCP.0000004744.09295.9b

Ledray, L. (1999). *Sexual Assault Nurse Examiner (SANE) development & operations guide.* Washington, DC: U.S. Department of Justice, Office for Victims of Crime.

Littel, K. (2001). Sexual Assault Nurse Examiner programs: Improving the community response to sexual assault victims. *Office for Victims of Crime Bulletin, 4*, 1–19.

Luke, D. A. (2005). Getting the big picture in community science: Methods that capture context. *American Journal of Community Psychology, 35*, 185–200. doi:10.1007/s10464-005-3397-z

Martin, P. Y. (2005). *Rape work: Organizations and rape victims.* New York, NY: Routledge.

Maxwell, J. A., & Mittapalli, K. (2010). Realism as a stance for mixed methods research. In A. Tashakkori & C. Teddlie (Eds.), *SAGE handbook of mixed methods in social & behavioral research* (2nd ed., pp. 145–168). Thousand Oaks, CA: Sage.

McConney, A., Rudd, A., & Ayers, R. (2002). Getting to the bottom line: A method for synthesizing findings within mixed-method program evaluations. *The American Journal of Evaluation, 23*, 121–140.

Mertens, D. M., Bledsoe, K. L., Sullivan, M., & Wilson, A. (2010). Utilization of mixed methods for transformative purposes. In A. Tashakkori & C. Teddlie (Eds.), *SAGE handbook of mixed methods in social & behavioral research* (2nd ed., pp. 193–214). Thousand Oaks, CA: Sage.

Onwuegbuzie, A. J., & Combs, J. P. (2010). Emergent data analysis techniques in mixed methods research: A synthesis. In A. Tashakkori & C. Teddlie (Eds.), *SAGE handbook of mixed methods in social & behavioral research* (2nd ed., pp. 397–430). Thousand Oaks, CA: Sage.

Patton, M. Q. (1990). *Qualitative research and evaluation methods* (2nd ed.). Thousand Oaks, CA: Sage.

Patton, M. Q. (2002). *Qualitative research and evaluation methods* (3rd ed.). Thousand Oaks, CA: Sage.

Rallis, S. F., & Rossman, G. B. (2003). Mixed methods in evaluation contexts: A pragmatic approach. In A. Tashakkori & C. Teddlie (Eds.), *Handbook of mixed methods in social and behavioral research* (pp. 491–512). Thousand Oaks, CA: Sage.

Robinson, W. S. (1951). The logical structure of analytic induction. *American Sociological Review, 16*, 812–818. doi:10.2307/2087508

Shadish, W. R., Cook, T. D., & Campbell, D. T. (2002). *Experimental and quasi-experimental designs for generalized causal inference*. Boston, MA: Houghton Mifflin.

Spohn, C., Beichner, D., & Davis-Frenzel, E. (2001). Prosecutorial justifications for sexual assault case rejection: Guarding the "gateway to justice." *Social Problems, 48*, 206–235. doi:10.1525/sp.2001.48.2.206

Tashakkori, A., & Teddlie, C. (Eds.). (2003). *Handbook of mixed methods in social and behavioral research*. Thousand Oaks, CA: Sage.

Tashakkori, A., & Teddlie, C. (Eds.). (2010). *SAGE handbook of mixed methods in social and behavioral research* (2nd ed.). Thousand Oaks, CA: Sage.

II

METHODS INVOLVING GROUPING OF DATA

5

CLUSTERING AND ITS APPLICATIONS IN COMMUNITY RESEARCH

ALLISON B. DYMNICKI AND DAVID B. HENRY

Seventy years ago, Tryon (1939) proposed what he believed was a simplified method of factor analysis that could be used to form groups of variables or individuals. This method, which he called *cluster analysis*, could be used, for example, to form groups of individual children on the basis of their levels of anxiety, aggression, delinquency, and cognitive difficulties. Doing this might result in useful typologies that could increase understanding of co-occurring mental disorders and lead to more appropriate treatments for specific individuals (e.g., Tolan & Henry, 1996). In time, cluster analysis was expanded by others (Johnson, 1967; Wolfe, 1970), and it found its way into areas as diverse as child development (Macfarlane, 1943), sociology (Backman, 1956), and personality research (Button, 1956).

Cluster analysis has evolved into a vast array of methods, many of which are tailored to the needs of diverse fields (Arabie & Hubert, 1992). In Table 5.1, we present a brief overview of different clustering methods and the type of data each method uses. Readers interested in more advanced

Research for this chapter was supported in part by grants from the Centers for Disease Control and Prevention and the National Institute on Drug Abuse.

TABLE 5.1

Choosing the Appropriate Clustering Method

Method	Aim of study	Type of variable
Hierarchical	Determine optimal number of clusters Detect outliers	Continuous or binary
K-means	Determine how cases are classified based on preassigned number of clusters	Continuous or binary
Model-based clustering[a]	Identify groupings of cases, particularly when clusters are not spherical in shape	Binary, ordinal, or continuous
Latent profile analysis[b, c] and latent class clustering[b, c]	Classify and compare solutions using fit statistics	Continuous
Growth mixture modeling[d]	Identify clusters of individual growth patterns	Continuous
Latent class analysis[e]	Identify groupings of cases	Categorical or continuous
Latent transition analysis[e]	Identify people who transition from one group to another over time	Continuous

Note. [a]For additional information, see Fraley and Raftery (1998, 2006). [b]For additional information, see Vermunt and Magidson (2000). [c]For additional information, see Muthén and Muthén (2007). [d]For additional information, see Jones, Nagin, and Roeder (2001). [e]For additional information, see Lanza, Lemmon, Schafer, and Collins (2008).

discussions of clustering approaches are referred to additional resources, such as Aldenderfer and Blashfield (1984); Everitt, Landau, and Leese (2004); and Fraley and Raftery (1998).

Data from community studies often require methods that account for clustering, either because of overtly clustered structure, such as the type of data that occur with communities, schools, or organizations, or because the data have a more covertly clustered structure in which the definition of clusters is unknown. In this chapter, we focus on methods applicable to the second type of problem. Specifically, we focus on the methods of cluster analysis that are relevant and useful when addressing questions that arise in community-based research. We review the uses of these methods with data that are frequently encountered in community research, and we detail one application of cluster analysis to a community data set (Sheidow, Gorman-Smith, Tolan, & Henry, 2001).

INTRODUCTION TO CLUSTER ANALYSIS

We use the term *cluster analysis* to refer to a general approach composed of several multivariate methods for delineating natural groups or clusters in data sets (Aldenderfer & Blashfield, 1984; Seber, 1984). Referred to by some as *person-oriented methods* (Bergman, 1998; Bergman & Magnusson, 1997; Cairns, Bergman, & Kagan, 1998), in contrast to *variable-oriented methods*, cluster analysis identifies and describes groups of cases (e.g., individuals, neighborhoods, classrooms) defined by similarities on multiple dimensions. Because community research regards cross-context variation in relations among variables to be an important focus for research, clustering methods, by creating groups from data, can help community researchers to better model variation in development; contextual risk, promotive, and protective factors; or differential intervention effects. Such modeling, however, uses different logic from that used when studying relations among variables, as with correlation or regression. Fundamentally, clustering involves sorting cases or variables according to their similarity on one or more dimensions. This creates groups that maximize within-group similarity and minimize between-groups similarity (Henry, Tolan, & Gorman-Smith, 2005).

More generally, we can define a cluster as an *approximation to uniqueness*. Just as the sample mean produces an unbiased approximation of a population mean, a cluster approximates the unique configurations of characteristics found in individuals, whether the "individual" is a person, a group, or a community. Estimates of population means become more accurate as sample sizes increase and we draw closer to sampling an entire population. Clusters become more accurate for identifying individuals as the number of identifying characteristics and the number of clusters increases.

In this chapter, we first discuss the uses of clustering in community research. We then review the steps in conducting a cluster analysis and describe the application of those steps to a community data set. We close the chapter with a discussion of the benefits and drawbacks of this approach.

USES OF CLUSTERING METHODS IN COMMUNITY RESEARCH

Recent years have seen multiple uses of clustering methods in community and prevention research. These may be summarized in the seven categories discussed in the sections that follow.

Classifying Differences Rather Than Controlling for Them

Almost 20 years ago, Rapkin and Luke (1993) suggested that cluster analysis should be of interest to community psychologists and community-based researchers because it could reveal diversity and unknown heterogeneity within data. They explained that cluster analysis "stands in contrast to traditional modeling where heterogeneity is handled by using covariates to control or adjust for these individual differences" (Rapkin & Luke, 1993, p. 196). As Rapkin and Luke pointed out, approaches that covary out individual variation imply that individual differences are not of scientific interest, although, in fact, they could be of great interest. For example, rather than treat self-esteem as a single variable, DuBois, Felner, Brand, and George (1999) used cluster analysis to derive five different profiles of individual self-esteem. Some of these were defined by high or low levels, but others were person-setting interactions according to which self-esteem varied depending on the context (e.g., school, peer relations). They found that these profiles during adolescence were related to outcomes such as depression, anxiety, and social functioning 2 years later. By using clustering, they were able to incorporate context into their analysis, producing a richer understanding of individual differences. Community researchers have traditionally tried to understand any single feature in the context of other features, especially when looking across domains of individual functioning (e.g., school, family) or across development (e.g., adolescence, early adulthood; Gest, Mahoney, & Cairns, 1999).

Cluster analysis can also reveal types of neighborhoods or other social structures. For example, McWayne, McDermott, Fantuzzo, and Culhane (2007) used a three-stage clustering procedure with administrative data on 1,801 block groups in low-socioeconomic-status neighborhoods of a large metropolitan area. The researchers identified six clusters of racial composition and property structure variables. They found that clusters of housing units predicted children's academic outcomes, even when the contributions of neighborhood racial composition, neighborhood structural danger (e.g., lead paint, residential fires), and neighborhood social stress were controlled for in the analysis.

Locating the Contextual Limits of Interventions

Using clustering in community research is consistent with contextualist epistemology, according to which the validity of a theory or the effectiveness of an intervention is a function of particular configurations of characteristics found in particular contexts (Maton, 1990). Illustratively, this speaks to the recent call for violence prevention researchers to move beyond assessing overall intervention effectiveness to address three more specific questions, namely, what works, for whom, and under what conditions (Guerra, Boxer, & Cook, 2006). Similarly, using data from the Metropolitan Area Child Study, Henry et al. (2000) clustered school classrooms according to whether children regarded aggressive children as unpopular and the extent to which teachers responded to student aggression. They found that classroom clusters moderated the effects of a universal social-cognitive curricular intervention (Henry & Schoeny, 2007). Specifically, the universal social-cognitive intervention was most effective in classrooms with preexisting student norms against aggression but little teacher enforcement.

Making Complex Interactions Interpretable

Researchers are frequently confronted with situations in which variables are associated with outcomes only in the presence of other variables. Interpretation of interactions becomes very difficult when multiple variables interact. Cluster analysis can make it possible to understand interactions of multiple variables. For example, Henry, Tolan, and Gorman-Smith (2001) used clustering to explore the longitudinal patterns among family and parenting characteristics, peer violence or nonviolence, and individual delinquency for male adolescents. They identified four clusters, or family types, that predicted violent and nonviolent delinquency above and beyond the three family relationships and two parenting practices measures that had been used to create the clusters. They interpreted this to suggest that the clusters were predicting variance due to the complex interactions among the five predictor variables.

Analyzing Data With Poor Distributions

Community data frequently violate key assumptions of models that assume normal distributions of data. Although recent statistical advances provide more flexibility in analyzing data through generalized linear models, the presence of subsamples and multimodality are intractable problems frequently encountered in community data. Clustering approaches can be used with such data and are particularly useful when it is possible that an underlying latent distribution is categorical, despite numeric measurement. For example, numeric data on the use of specific substances in representative samples are often characterized by low rates of use of any particular substance. Aiming to understand the patterns of substance use in a sample of American Indian youth, Mitchell and Plunkett (2000) used latent class analysis, a clustering approach appropriate for categorical data, to identify three different profiles of youth substance abusers in addition to the majority abstaining class, namely, (a) predominantly alcohol users, (b) alcohol and marijuana users, and (c) plural substance users. They found that the classes of substance users differed on such variables as substance use attitudes and peer values.

Targeting Interventions

Clustering can organize large quantities of multivariate data into groups that are more manageable and interpretable for practice (Clatworthy, Hankins, Buick, Weinman, & Horne, 2007). For example, Tolan and

Henry (1996) used latent class analysis to identify different profiles of psychopathology and comorbidity of symptoms in a sample of 4,000 urban and inner-city youth. Four groups were found on the basis of patterns of aggression, cognitive difficulties, and internalizing problems (e.g., two groups were marked by aggressive behavior and thought problems but differed in the presence or absence of internalizing problems). Hodges and Wotring (2000) used cluster analysis to describe groups of youth referred to community mental health service providers in terms of clinical diagnoses, overall functioning, and past and current use of services. These groupings formed the basis of a method of matching client needs to treatments (Hodges, Xue, & Wotring, 2004).

Detecting Multivariate Outliers

Clustering methods can be used to detect elusive and problematic multivariate outliers in a data matrix. This is particularly useful in small samples in which outliers can have strong and undue influence on the outcome of an analysis. For example, Allen, Mohatt, Fok, Henry, and the People Awakening Team (2009) used hierarchical cluster analysis to detect outlying observations in a study of suicide prevention in rural Alaska. Because of the small samples of youth available in rural native villages, these outliers could have caused erroneous conclusions in multivariate analyses.

Interfacing Between Qualitative and Quantitative Methods

Clustering also can be used to analyze data from qualitative studies, making it possible to organize complex ethnographic data and associate it with quantitative data (Maton, 1990). By coding interview data for the presence or absence of specific statements, it is possible to use cluster analysis on the resulting matrix of binary observations. Tandon, Azelton, Kelly, and Strickland (1998), in a study of African American community leaders, described applying a nonstatistical clustering approach that involved grouping coded interviews into "trees" representing different themes, such as reasons for involvement and activities, and facilitators or barriers to participation.

STEPS IN A CLUSTER ANALYSIS

Regardless of the clustering method being used, there are three main steps to completing a cluster analysis. The first step is data preparation. One needs to choose theoretically relevant and nonredundant measures and to prepare the data so that no single measure is given undue influence in the solution. The second step is to select a clustering method that is appropriate for the research question and the data. The third step is to find the optimal solution and display it in a manner that can be interpreted by researchers and community members.

Preparing the Data

Because the goal of cluster analysis is to determine if there is a clustered structure to the data and what that structure is, it is important to visually examine the data and to prepare the data appropriately for analysis. Results may be biased if redundant measures and constructs are included or if measures use different scales.

Goal of CA [handwritten annotation]

Use Theoretically Driven and Nonredundant Measures

Clustering algorithms will always find clusters, even in random data, so it is essential to select variables consistent with relevant theoretical perspectives. There is little benefit from including redundant or highly correlated measures of the same construct in a cluster analysis. If multiple measures are available that, although strongly correlated, provide some independent information about a construct, we recommend combining data into higher order measures on the basis of confirmatory factor analysis.

Visual Examination

Random data are often characterized by clumps or clusters of observations. Thus, an important issue in preparing data for cluster analysis is to estimate the extent to which the data are clustered beyond this random "clumpiness." Visual examination of the data, using plots in two or three dimensions, can provide an important source of evidence that may indicate the appropriateness of cluster analysis or assist in determining the appropriate number of clusters.

Scaling to Avoid Undue Influence

Clustering methods are fairly sensitive to differences in scaling. Although some recommend standardization to standard deviation units, converting to z scores sets all variances to 1.0, risking loss of information. A better procedure is to rescale to units of the range, which results in equivalent scaling of variables but leaves differences in variances intact (Henry et al., 2005). If the variable has a theoretical range (e.g., 1–4 on a Likert-type scale), we recommend subtracting the theoretical minimum from the score and dividing by the theoretical maximum less the theoretical minimum. Such a procedure facilitates comparisons across time in longitudinal analysis and makes scores easily interpretable. In the absence of a theoretical range, using the observed range is a reasonable alternative.

Choosing a Clustering Method

The choice of one out of the hundreds of different clustering methods should be determined primarily by the research question and the type of data being analyzed. In general, latent class methods (i.e., approaches that model categorical latent variables from categorical indicator variables) are recommended for binary and ordinal data with few categories because they provide fit indices that permit an all-or-nothing decision on whether a particular solution fits the data (McCutcheon, 1987). However, multiple methods are usually applicable to any problem, and method choices are limited only by the software available. Running the problem using a number of methods and comparing cluster assignments will provide an indication of how robust the solution is.

Determining the Correct Solution

One of the most difficult aspects of using cluster analysis is knowing how many clusters to retain. Visual representations, such as dendrograms (i.e., tree diagrams) showing the structure of a data set, can provide important evidence. Newer mixture methods or latent class methods provide Bayesian information criterion (BIC) values that can be plotted for multiple solutions, thereby allowing the researcher to see where increasing the number of clusters will improve the fit of the model to the data. Generally, the lower the value of the BIC, the better the model fit. Of primary importance in choosing a solution, however, is its interpretability according to theory.

In the next section, we illustrate the application of these steps to data from a research study aimed at understanding the developmental effects of community and family characteristics on youth delinquent behavior (Gorman-Smith, Tolan, & Henry, 2000). Data for this cluster analysis example are provided on the web appendix for this chapter (http://pubs.apa.org/books/supp/Jason-Glenwick).

APPLYING CLUSTER ANALYSIS:
PROFILES OF URBAN COMMUNITIES

Tolan, Gorman-Smith, and Henry (2003) factor analyzed census data (e.g., number of ethnic groups, percentage of female-headed households) and data from other archival sources to create three scales assessing structural characteristics of communities. The three scales, the variables they comprise, and their means and standard deviations were as follows: (a) Concentrated Poverty (indicator variables: unemployment rate, percentage of families living below the poverty level, percentage of female headed-households, and percentage of owner-occupied housing; M = 0.08, SD = 1.09), (b) Ethnic Heterogeneity (indicator variables: number of ethnic groups, proportion of people in most common ethnic group,[1] number of languages spoken; M = 20.27, SD = 0.86), and (c) Business Disinvestment (indicator variables: grocers per 1,000 residents, medical facilities per 1,000 residents, and nonmedical and nongrocery facilities per 1,000 residents; M = 0.02, SD = 0.68).

For the purpose of this example, we use these three factorially derived scales to suggest types of urban communities that share structural characteristics.

Visual Examination

Visual examination of the joint distributions of variables can help determine whether cluster analysis is appropriate and can sometimes aid in determining the optimal number of clusters. Many statistical programs, including SPSS, SYSTAT, and R, are capable of creating three-dimensional scatterplots. When there are more than three variables or it is difficult to interpret 3-D objects represented in 2-D, a scatterplot matrix may be preferable; an example of such a matrix is included in the web appendix for this chapter as Online Figure 5.1.

Finding the Appropriate Cluster Solution

A hierarchical cluster analysis can produce a tree diagram, or *dendrogram*. This provides another method of visually examining a data for clustered structure. Figure 5.1 was produced using hierarchical cluster analysis in SPSS on the three structural characteristics, selecting the between-groups option and squared Euclidian distance under Method and the dendrogram option under Plots. Hierarchical clustering requires the researcher to choose (a) a way of calculating the distances between different observations and clusters and (b) a way to define the distance between two clusters. The process of hierarchical clustering begins by grouping the closest observations together, which in this case are neighborhoods. Groups are then

---

[1]If a community had 46% African American residents as the largest ethnic group, the value for that community would be .46.

joined using the distance metric and linkage method selected by the researcher. Squared Euclidian distances work well with most continuous, ordinal, or binary data and are frequently used.

Different linkage methods represent different ways of conceptualizing the location of a cluster, and researchers should conduct analyses with different methods (e.g., farthest neighbor linkage or Ward's methods) to see how the results change. In Figure 5.1, we illustrate how we selected a three-cluster solution by dividing the sample at the longest joining distances. The two slash marks and the labels identify the three clusters we believe to be optimal. The numbers arranged vertically on the left side of the dendrogram represent the communities. Reading down the community numbers, the first cluster runs from Community 33 to Community 38, the second from Communities 15–21, and the third from Communities 2–13.

Because of the somewhat subjective nature of interpreting visual representations and other methods for selecting cluster solutions, newer approaches have attempted to incorporate indices of fit into the selection of a cluster solution, such as chi-square fit statistics and the BIC (Kass & Raftery, 1995). Two-step clustering in SPSS (SPSS Inc., 2006) and model-based clustering through R (Fraley & Raftery, 2006) provide automatic model selection based on BIC statistics. (SPSS does not report the BIC values for alternate solutions.) Model-based clustering also provides alternate solutions based on different models of cluster shapes (e.g., spherical, ellipsoidal) and degree of equality of variances. Programs for latent class analysis and mixture approaches to clustering (i.e., the e1073 module in R, PROC LCA, Latent GOLD, Mplus) and growth-mixture modeling (i.e., PROC TRAJ, Mplus, PROC LTA) also provide the BIC statistic as well as other indices of fit. We recommend the following articles for descriptions and examples using each approach: Fraley and Rafferty (1998) for model-based clustering; Vermunt and Magidson (2000) for latent profile and latent class clustering; Muthén et al. (2002) and Colder et al. (2001) for growth-mixture modeling; Mitchell and Plunkett (2000) for latent class analysis; and Spoth, Reyes, Redmond, and Shinn (1999) for latent transition analysis.

Interpreting the Solution

Once an optimal solution is found, it needs to be displayed in a manner that facilitates interpretation. The first step is to obtain the means on each variable for each cluster (e.g., means on Concentrated Poverty, Ethnic Heterogeneity, and Business Disinvestment for Cluster 1). It makes good sense to conduct a series of one-way analyses of variance for the variables used in the clustering, with cluster as the grouping variable, and to request post hoc tests of differences. The results of these tests allow one to determine which clusters

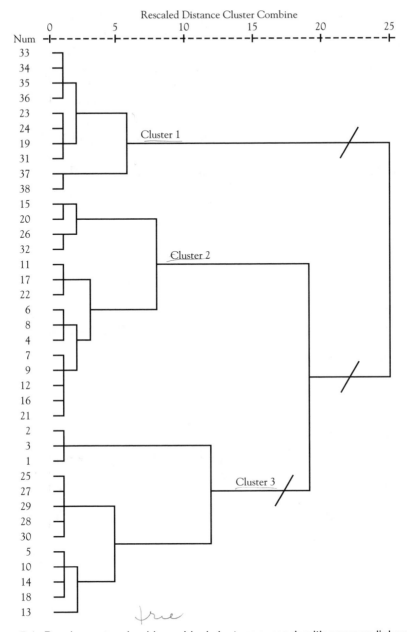

Figure 5.1. Dendrogram using hierarchical cluster approach with average linkage between groups. The *x*-axis is the joining distance, and the *y*-axis lists the communities by number.

differ significantly on which variables (e.g., Do Cluster 1 and Cluster 2 differ in the levels of Concentrated Poverty?). Clustering programs sometimes provide F ratios that indicate the extent to which the clusters differ on each variable used in their creation. These can be misleading and are not as useful as a simple one-way analysis of variance followed by post hoc tests of differences. Our recommended analysis allows one to determine not merely that the clusters differ but also where significant differences between the clusters lie.

Graphical methods are also very useful for communicating cluster results. Clustered bar charts work well when there are relatively few variables used in the clustering. Figure 5.2 is a clustered bar chart of the three-cluster solution for the community data. This figure describes each cluster using the means of Concentrated Poverty, Ethnic Heterogeneity, and Business

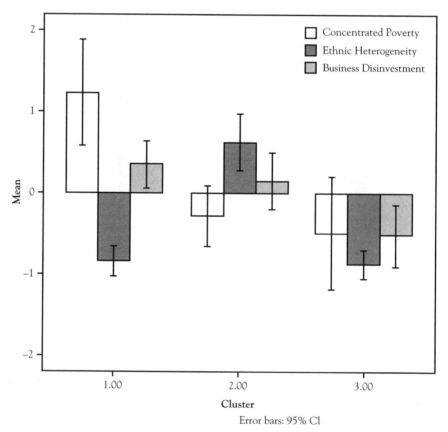

Error bars: 95% CI

Figure 5.2. Bar chart plotting three-cluster solution for the community data. CI = confidence interval.

Disinvestment and communicates which clusters differ on which variables. For example, Cluster 1 communities are ethnically homogeneous, have the highest levels of concentrated poverty, and lack business investment (because business investment is scaled so that higher scores represent less investment.). It seems that Cluster 1 communities are differentiated from Clusters 2 and 3 communities by their high concentrated poverty levels. Cluster 2 communities are differentiated from Cluster 3 communities by higher levels of Ethnic Heterogeneity and Business Disinvestment. Subsequent analyses were done to see how family characteristics predicted child delinquency in these three types of communities. In communities included in Cluster 3, only stress was related to child delinquency, whereas in communities included in Cluster 2, family cohesion, beliefs about family, and, to some extent, parental discipline mediated the impact of stress on child delinquency (Gorman-Smith et al., 2000). It seems that certain types of inner-city communities have social processes in place that moderate children's risk of delinquent behavior.

CAUTIONS AND LIMITS OF CLUSTERING METHODS

Like any analytic approach, cluster analysis has weaknesses. First, cluster analysis can find clusters even in random data. The possibility of detecting spurious clusters underscores the importance of researchers not being guided solely by quantitative results.

Second, many clustering programs do not function well if clusters are not circular or spherical in shape. To illustrate the importance of cluster shapes, we compared the performance of five clustering approaches (i.e., k-means, latent class analysis with continuous indicators in Mplus, two-stage clustering in SPSS, model-based clustering in R, and latent class clustering in Latent GOLD) for identifying true cluster membership for two data sets with known cluster membership. One data set had three spherical clusters (i.e., clusters are shaped like circles), created using three bivariate normal distributions. The second data set had two elongated clusters (i.e., shaped like footballs), created using two linear models. All five clustering approaches performed well in identifying membership of spherical clusters (accuracy ranged from 88% for two-stage clustering to 94% for latent class clustering). However, when trying to correctly identify cluster membership in data with two elongated clusters, only k-means (68%) and model-based clustering (95%) identified cases at better than chance levels. The other three approaches correctly identified between 52% and 56% of cases, barely better than guessing.

Third, even if clusters are spherical in shape, unless they are clearly separated, it is possible to find multiple and conflicting best-fitting solutions

(Arabie & Hubert, 1992). This has led some researchers to question the validity of clustering itself (Blashfield & Aldenderfer, 1988). However, we believe this should lead researchers to proceed with caution, particularly when interpreting solutions for clusters that are not clearly separate, and not to abandon the approach entirely.

CONCLUSION

In summary, we recommend that researchers choose indicators on the basis of theory and previous literature and construct hypotheses about the types or clusters that may be found in a particular data set. It is also important to use multiple sources of information when seeking an appropriate solution. Such sources include visual representations of the data, fit indices (if available), and the fit of the solution with theory. Once a solution is determined, it is important to report it in a manner that permits others, particularly community members, to understand how the clusters differ and on which characteristics they differ. If such care is taken, we believe that cluster analysis has much to contribute to community-based research and that the effects of its limitations and weaknesses can be minimized.

Clustering methods range from interpreting visual representations of data to sophisticated methods for clustering growth trajectories over time. There are multiple clustering methods for every field that uses them and several that are useful for community research. In this chapter, we have only touched on the vast array of methods that community researchers might find useful. We have provided examples of some potential uses of clustering in community research, steps in conducting a cluster analysis, and some benefits and drawbacks of the method. Clustering is particularly relevant for community-based research because of its ability to handle problem distributions; explore the influence of contexts, which is a key focus of community research; and make complex interactions interpretable. Other benefits of clustering include its ability to organize large amounts of multivariate data into more manageable groups; detect multivariate outliers, which are problematic, especially in small samples; and provide an interface between qualitative and quantitative data. Enthusiasm for the method is tempered somewhat by its limitations, including, perhaps most important, the possibility of finding clusters in random data and the occurrence of multiple and conflicting cluster solutions.

As we have seen, clustering has been used productively by community researchers for decades. In addition to past uses, there are multiple emerging areas of community research, as indicated in the volume by Jason et al. (2004), in which clustering methods may be relevant, such as identifying Gene ×

Environment interactions that predict risk behaviors (e.g., Caspi, et al., 2005; Moffitt, 2005) and assessing differential intervention effectiveness by clusters of individuals, interventionists, intervention components, and intervention settings that are associated with positive outcomes (Gregory, Henry, Schoeny, & Metropolitan Area Child Study Research Group, 2007; Metropolitan Area Child Study Research Group, 2002). Overall, the unique and difficult problems posed by the analysis of community data ensure an important role for cluster analysis in community-based research.

REFERENCES

Aldenderfer, M. S., & Blashfield, R. K. (1984). *Cluster analysis*. Beverly Hills, CA: Sage.

Allen, J., Mohatt, G. V., Fok, C. T., Henry, D. B., & the People Awakening Team. (2009). Suicide prevention as a community development process: Understanding circumpolar youth suicide prevention through community-level outcomes. *International Journal of Circumpolar Health, 68*, 274–291.

Arabie, P., & Hubert, L. J. (1992). Combinatorial data analysis. *Annual Review of Psychology, 43*, 169–203. doi:10.1146/annurev.ps.43.020192.001125

Backman, C. W. (1956). Sampling mass media content: The use of the cluster design. *American Sociological Review, 21*, 729–733. doi:10.2307/2088425

Bergman, L. R. (1998). A pattern-oriented approach to studying individual development: Snapshots and processes. In R. B. Cairns, L. R. Bergman, & J. Kagan (Eds.), *Methods and models for studying the individual* (pp. 83–122). Thousand Oaks, CA: Sage.

Bergman, L. R., & Magnusson, D. (1997). A person-oriented approach in research on developmental psychopathology. *Development and Psychopathology, 9*, 291–319. doi:10.1017/S095457949700206X

Blashfield, R. K., & Aldenderfer, M. S. (1988). The methods and problems of cluster analysis. In J. R. Nesselroade & R. B. Cattell (Eds.), *Handbook of multivariate experimental psychology* (2nd ed., pp. 447–473). New York, NY: Plenum Press.

Button, A. D. (1956). A study of alcoholics with the Minnesota Multiphasic Personality Inventory. *Quarterly Journal of Studies on Alcohol, 17*, 263–281.

Cairns, R. B., Bergman, L. R., & Kagan, J. (1998). *Methods and models for studying the individual: Essays in honor of Marion Radke-Yarrow*. Thousand Oaks, CA: Sage.

Caspi, A., Moffitt, T. E., Cannon, M., McClay, J., Murray, R., Harrington, H., & Craig, I. W. (2005). Moderation of the effect of adolescent-onset cannabis use on adult psychosis by a functional polymorphism in the catechol-O-methyltransferase gene: Longitudinal evidence of a Gene × Environment interaction. *Biological Psychiatry, 57*, 1117–1127. doi:10.1016/j.biopsych.2005.01.026

Clatworthy, J., Hankins, M., Buick, D., Weinman, J., & Horne, R. (2007). Cluster analysis in illness perception research: A Monte Carlo study to identify the most appropriate method. *Psychology & Health, 22,* 123–142. doi:10.1080/14768320600774496

Colder, C. R., Mehta, P., Balanda, K., Campbell, R. T., Mayhew, K. P., Stanton, W. R., & Flay, B. R. (2001). Identifying trajectories of adolescent smoking: An application of latent growth mixture model. *Health Psychology, 20,* 127–135. doi:10.1037/0278-6133.20.2.127

DuBois, D. L., Felner, R. D., Brand, S., & George, G. R. (1999). Profiles of self-esteem in early adolescence: Identification and investigation of adaptive correlates. *American Journal of Community Psychology, 27,* 899–932. doi:10.1023/A:1022218810963

Everitt, B. S., Landau, S., & Leese, M. (2004). *Cluster analysis* (4th ed.). New York, NY: Oxford University Press.

Fraley, C., & Raftery, A. E. (1998). How many clusters? Which clustering method? Answers via model-based cluster analysis. *The Computer Journal, 41,* 578–588. doi:10.1093/comjnl/41.8.578

Fraley, C., & Raftery, A. C. (2006). *MCLUST Version 3 for R: Normal mixture modeling and model-based clustering* (Tech. Rep. No. 504). Olympia, WA: University of Washington.

Gest, S. D., Mahoney, J. L., & Cairns, R. B. (1999). A developmental approach to prevention research: Configural antecedents of early parenthood. *American Journal of Community Psychology, 27,* 543–565. doi:10.1023/A:1022185312277

Gorman-Smith, D., Tolan, P. H., & Henry, D. (2000). A developmental-ecological model of the relation of family functioning to patterns of delinquency. *Journal of Quantitative Criminology, 16,* 169–198. doi:10.1023/A:1007564505850

Gregory, A., Henry, D., Schoeny, M., & Metropolitan Area Child Study Research Group. (2007). School climate and implementation of a preventive intervention. *American Journal of Community Psychology, 40,* 250–260. doi:10.1007/s10464-007-9142-z

Guerra, N., Boxer, P., & Cook, C. (2006). What works (and what does not) in youth violence prevention: Rethinking the questions and finding new answers. *New Directions for Evaluation, 110,* 59–71. doi:10.1002/ev.187

Henry, D. B., Guerra, N. G., Huesmann, L. R., Tolan, P. H., VanAcker, R., & Eron, L. D. (2000). Normative influences on aggression in urban elementary school classrooms. *American Journal of Community Psychology, 28,* 59–81. doi:10.1023/A:1005142429725

Henry, D. B., & Schoeny, M. E. (2007, June). *Moderation of universal intervention effects by norms and ethnicity.* Paper presented at the meeting of the Society for Community Research and Action, Pasadena, CA.

Henry, D. B., Tolan, P. H., & Gorman-Smith, D. (2001). Longitudinal family and peer group effects on violence and nonviolent delinquency. *Journal of Clinical Child Psychology, 30,* 172–186. doi:10.1207/S15374424JCCP3002_5

Henry, D. B., Tolan, P. H., & Gorman-Smith, D. (2005). Cluster analysis in family psychology research. *Journal of Family Psychology, 19*, 121–132. doi:10.1037/0893-3200.19.1.121

Hodges, K., & Wotring, J. (2000). Client typology based on functioning across domains using the CAFAS: Implications for service planning. *The Journal of Behavioral Health Services & Research, 27*, 257–270. doi:10.1007/BF02291738

Hodges, K., Xue, Y., & Wotring, J. (2004). Use of the CAFAS to evaluate outcome for youths with severe emotional disturbance served by public mental health. *Journal of Child and Family Studies, 13*, 325–339. doi:10.1023/B:JCFS.0000022038.62940.a3

Jason, L. A., Keys, C. B., Suarez-Balcazar, Y., Taylor, R. R., Davis, M., Durlak, J., & Isenberg, D. (2004). (Eds.). *Participatory community research: Theories and methods in action.* Washington, DC: American Psychological Association.

Johnson, S. C. (1967). Hierarchical clustering schemes. *Psychometrika, 32*, 241–254. doi:10.1007/BF02289588

Jones, B., Nagin, D., & Roeder, K. (2001). A SAS procedure based on mixture models for estimating developmental trajectories. *Sociological Methods & Research, 29*, 374–393. doi:10.1177/0049124101029003005

Kass, R. E., & Raftery, A. E. (1995). Bayes factors. *Journal of the American Statistical Association, 90*, 773–795. doi:10.2307/2291091

Lanza, S. T., Lemmon, D. R., Schafer, J. L., & Collins, L. M. (2008). *PROC LCA & PROC LTA user's guide.* State College, PA: Pennsylvania State University, The Methodology Center.

Macfarlane, J. W. (1943). Study of personality development. In R. G. Barker, J. S. Kounin, & H. F. Wright (Eds.), *Child behavior and development: A course of representative studies* (pp. 307–328). New York, NY: McGraw-Hill. doi:10.1037/10786-018

Maton, K. (1990). Toward the use of qualitative methodology in community psychology research. In P. H. Tolan, C. Keys, F. Chertok, & L. Jason (Eds.), *Researching community psychology: Issues of theory and methods* (pp. 153–156). Washington, DC: American Psychological Association.

McCutcheon, A. L. (1987). *Latent class analysis.* Newbury Park, CA: Sage.

McWayne, C. M., McDermott, P. A., Fantuzzo, J. W., & Culhane, D. P. (2007). Employing community data to investigate social and structural dimensions of urban neighborhoods: An early childhood education example. *American Journal of Community Psychology, 39*, 47–60. doi:10.1007/s10464-007-9098-z

Metropolitan Area Child Study Research Group. (2002). A cognitive–ecological approach to preventing aggression in urban settings: Initial outcomes for high risk children. *Journal of Consulting and Clinical Psychology, 70*, 179–194.

Mitchell, C. M., & Plunkett, M. (2000). The latent structure of substance use among American Indian adolescents: An example using categorical variables. *American Journal of Community Psychology, 28*, 105–125. doi:10.1023/A:1005146530634

Moffitt, T. E. (2005). Genetic and environmental influences on antisocial behaviors: Evidence from behavioral-genetic research. *Advances in Genetics, 55,* 41–104. doi:10.1016/S0065-2660(05)55003-X

Muthén, B., Brown, C. H., Masyn, K., Jo, B., Khoo, S. T., & Yang, C. C. (2002). General growth mixture modeling for randomized preventive interventions. *Biostatistics, 3,* 459–475. doi:10.1093/biostatistics/3.4.459

Muthén, L. K., & Muthén, B. O. (2007). *Mplus user's guide* (5th ed.). Los Angeles, CA: Muthén & Muthén.

Rapkin, B. D., & Luke, D. A. (1993). Cluster analysis in community research: Epistemology and practice. *American Journal of Community Psychology, 21,* 247–277. doi:10.1007/BF00941623

Seber, G. A. F. (1984). *Multivariate observations.* New York, NY: Wiley.

Sheidow, A. J., Gorman-Smith, D., Tolan, P. H., & Henry, D. (2001). Family and community characteristics: Risk factors for violence exposure in inner-city youth. *Journal of Community Psychology, 29,* 345–360. doi:10.1002/jcop.1021

Spoth, R., Reyes, M. L., Redmond, C., & Shinn, C. (1999). Assessing a public health approach to delay onset and progression of adolescent substance use: Latent transition and log-linear analyses of longitudinal family preventive intervention outcomes. *Journal of Consulting and Clinical Psychology, 67,* 619–630. doi:10.1037/0022-006X.67.5.619

SPSS Inc. (2006). *SPSS 15.0 for Windows.* Chicago, IL: Author.

Tandon, S. D., Azelton, L. S., Kelly, J. G., & Strickland, D. (1998). Constructing a tree for community leaders: Contexts and processes in collaborative inquiry. *American Journal of Community Psychology, 26,* 669–696. doi:10.1023/A:1022149123739

Tolan, P. H., Gorman-Smith, D., & Henry, D. B. (2003). The developmental ecology of urban males' youth violence. *Developmental Psychology, 39,* 274–291. doi:10.1037/0012-1649.39.2.274

Tolan, P. H., & Henry, D. B. (1996). Patterns of psychopathology among urban poor children: Comorbidity and aggression effects. *Journal of Consulting and Clinical Psychology, 64,* 1094–1099. doi:10.1037/0022-006X.64.5.1094

Tryon, R. C. (1939). *Cluster analysis.* Oxford, England: Edwards.

Vermunt, J. K., & Magidson, J. (2000). *Latent GOLD user's manual.* Boston, MA: Statistical Innovations.

Wolfe, J. H. (1970). Pattern clustering by multivariate mixture analysis. *Multivariate Behavioral Research, 5,* 329–350. doi:10.1207/s15327906mbr0503_6

6

THE PERSON-ORIENTED APPROACH AND COMMUNITY RESEARCH

G. ANNE BOGAT, NICOLE ZARRETT, STEPHEN C. PECK, AND ALEXANDER VON EYE

The data-analytic techniques that form the basis of most psychological research, including community-based research, are variable-oriented approaches, so named because they are concerned with the statistical relationship among variables. For example, suppose we want to study whether the length of time women stay in a domestic violence shelter is related to whether they leave the abusive relationship. We correlate these two variables and find a significant positive relationship. Thus, when we discuss our findings, we might say that more days spent in a domestic violence shelter is related to the probability of leaving a partner. In making this statement, we are saying that two variables (number of days spent in a shelter and leaving one's partner) are statistically related to each other; we are saying nothing about specific individuals. In fact, the relationship between the two variables assumes that, for all individuals, the more days one spends in a domestic violence shelter, the more likely it is that one will leave one's partner.

We also use variable-oriented approaches when we compare groups. A typical statistical technique would be to aggregate data across individuals and compare the mean scores of the two groups by, for example, analysis of variance (ANOVA). The significance tests for ANOVA are built on the assumption that these aggregate group scores generalize to populations. In other words, variable-oriented approaches assume that interindividual differences are minimal or random.

Recent research indicates that these assumptions may not be accurate. For example, von Eye and Bergman (2003) provided alcohol consumption data from four participants, each interviewed several hundred times. When the data were aggregated, there was a specific up-and-down pattern of drinking across the observational period; however, when the data from the four individuals were examined separately, not one person had a pattern of drinking that looked like the aggregate.

It is unfortunate for community-based researchers that the person-oriented approach has its moniker. Since its inception, community psychology has attempted to move its focus away from the individual and toward broader social systems, not always successfully. Thus, there is an inherent bias in the field to regard something that focuses on people to not be central to the field. This is unfortunate. As we explain and demonstrate, the goals of the person-oriented approach are to focus on individuals in context—a goal completely consonant with the focus of community psychology.

WHAT IS THE PERSON-ORIENTED APPROACH?

Person-oriented approaches assume that people act in unique ways and that those actions are influenced by the context in which individuals live. In other words, examining the aggregate may tell one nothing about a particular individual, and a fuller understanding of an individual's behavior occurs when the context within which the person lives is examined. Person-oriented approaches have been used predominantly in the fields of developmental psychology and developmental psychopathology in which research has focused mainly on individuals. However, as we demonstrate in the discussion that follows, person-oriented theory is well suited to understanding higher order systems, which are the purview of community-based research (Bogat, 2009; Bogat, Levendosky, & von Eye, 2005).

THEORY OF THE PERSON-ORIENTED APPROACH

First discussed by Jack Block (1971) in order to understand personality and its development, the person-oriented approach has garnered greater attention in recent years (e.g., Bergman & Magnusson, 1997; von Eye & Bergman, 2003). The person orientation has six tenets (Bergman & Magnusson, 1997): (a) an individual's behavior is based on the environment in which

Tenets

interindividual

he or she lives and is influenced by many different factors, ranging from biologically based factors to cultural influences; (b) because the etiology of behavior is so complex, an individual's behavior cannot be captured by any one piece of information; (c) there is discoverable organization to systems, individuals, and their interactions as well as to the change or constancy within these factors; (d) an individual's developmental process is systematic and involves multiple factors and their interactions, which can be described as profiles or patterns; (e) the meaning of the factors involved in describing an individual results from the interaction among the factors; and (f) in principle, the number of patterns that exist are infinite; however, the number of global patterns or profiles that exist is likely finite.

Since the original tenets were published, there have been meaningful reformulations and additions. First, regarding Tenet f, von Eye and Bogat (2006) proposed that *expectancies* can guide researchers' search for patterns. That is, theory, models, and/or population statistics allow researchers to propose expected patterns within the population in question, and researchers can then compare these to observed patterns (von Eye, 2010). This reformulation allows them to apply data-analytic tools to Tenet f (finding patterns or profiles) rather than to focus simply on descriptive statements (von Eye, 2010).

Second, von Eye and Bergman (2003) proposed the concept of *dimensional identity:* "A set of variables can be defined as displaying dimensional identity if the interrelations among the variables in this set remain unchanged across the levels or categories of other variables" (p. 554). This concept is similar to *measurement* or *factorial invariance* in which assessment instruments are ascertained to measure the same phenomenon (e.g., across time, across groups). Dimensional identity takes the idea of measurement invariance further. First, it suggests that until the search for subgroups occurs within a sample, the search for measurement invariance is pointless. If subgroups are present, then statements about the population or statements about differences between groups may not be valid because the assessment instruments used to detect these differences may not have dimensional identity across the subpopulations. Second, measurement invariance may be difficult to accomplish across subpopulations because "there may be members of this population for which a model or instrument does not apply" (von Eye, 2010, p. 280). It is likely that the researcher must develop alternative assessment instruments for different subpopulations, individuals, and developmental stages. Third, as noted previously, the person orientation states that human behavior is complex, and an individual cannot be described by one variable. Thus, dimensional identity suggests that the search for measurement invariance regarding a particular assessment instrument is not sufficient; it is vital to understand the relationship among the variables and how these relationships describe a subpopulation.

If variables have dimensional identity, then variable-oriented approaches are appropriate. However, if qualitatively different subgroups exist, person-oriented data techniques that allow for a focus on structural differences should be used (Bergman, Magnusson, & El-Khouri, 2003; von Eye & Bogat, 2007).

Third, Bogat (2009, p. 32) added three tenets to the person-oriented approach to increase its relevance for community psychology:

1. "The structure and dynamics of individual behavior are, at least in part, specific to the environment in which the individual lives and works."
2. "There is lawfulness and structure to (*i*) intra-systemic constancy and change and (*ii*) inter-systemic differences in constancy and change. These processes can be described as patterns of the involved factors."
3. "Validity is specific to individuals and environments."

These additional tenets address a problem inherent in the person-oriented approach; namely, the context is rarely well articulated or measured. Thus, the first additional tenet addresses a contradiction in current person-oriented approaches: Although the broad theory of the person-oriented approach emphasizes the importance of the environment, there has been an inadvertent oversimplification when measuring settings or contexts.

patterns

Regarding the second additional tenet, Bogat (2009) emphasized the importance of finding patterns that exist between individuals and their context. For example, most research on intimate partner violence focuses on individual factors (e.g., substance abuse) that affect its occurrence. However, social contagion theory suggests that environments may be crime promoting or crime limiting (Anderson, 1990; Fagan, Wilkinson, & Davies, 2000). Variable-oriented research has found that (a) higher rates of community violence are associated with higher rates of intimate partner violence (Richters & Martinez, 1993) and (b) intimate partner violence is related to women's mental health (e.g., Bogat, Levendosky, DeJonghe, Davidson, & von Eye, 2004; Bogat, Levendosky, Theran, von Eye, & Davidson, 2003).

Using a person-oriented approach, Bogat, Leahy, von Eye, Maxwell, and Levendosky (2005) examined whether there were individual or environment patterns among three variables: neighborhood crime, intimate partner violence, and women's mental health. The results did not support the associations among these variables found by variable-oriented research (noted previously). The discrepancy between the findings suggested that either (a) the variable-oriented results were true for some women but not others, including those in the Bogat, Leahy, et al. (2005) research sample or (b) the aggregated data did not reflect the pattern of variable relationships that existed for any woman in the population.

Bogat's (2009) third additional tenet related to community psychology is the importance of validity as it relates to settings. In Bogat, Leahy, et al.'s (2005) research, the setting variable may not have been valid for all women. The crime data were collected in the neighborhoods within which the women lived. Social contagion theory suggests that for those women and men who live together, the crime data in the woman's neighborhood might be a valid setting variable. However, when the women and men do not live together, the valid setting may be the rates of crime in the partner's neighborhood or some pattern of crime data from the woman's and the man's neighborhoods. As this simple example suggests, defining settings validly is an important challenge to discover regularities and irregularities within these settings. Validity is established by comparing setting patterns to variables not used to make the patterns.

HOW CAN THE PERSON-ORIENTED APPROACH BE APPLIED TO RESEARCH?

Three Assumptions

The most important methodological implication of the person-oriented approach involves the unit of data analysis—the person or setting. Given this, there are three assumptions underlying data analysis from a person-oriented approach (Bogat, Levendosky, & von Eye, 2005; von Eye & Bogat, 2006). The first assumption is that any sample is likely drawn from a population with more than one group. Discovering these groups and their differences is an important component of person-oriented research.

There are three broad types of groups: natural groups, created groups, and groups that form without the researchers' awareness (von Eye & Bogat, 2007). An example of a natural group is boys and girls. Both person- and variable-oriented researchers might examine differences between boys and girls on a specified variable. Person-oriented researchers would not make a priori assumptions that girls and boys are homogeneous groups; they would look for subgroups within these naturally occurring groups. Created groups are those that by virtue of an environmental manipulation, experiment, or accident have different experiences. For example, researchers might compare two types of schools—charter schools and public, noncharter schools. Or, as an experiment, researchers might create two groups by assigning mother–infant dyads to an early intervention group and a control group. Accidental groups might form as the result of individual experiences, such as those who develop cataracts and those who do not. Finally, the third type of group forms outside the researcher's awareness. Thus, the person-oriented researcher must be alert for possible heterogeneity within the sample that may not have occurred to him or her a priori.

The second assumption of data analysis is that the groups must be valid. In this case, the groups must differ from each other on variables that were not used to create the groups. For example, depressed people must differ from not-depressed people on the "happy-go-lucky" scale for the diagnosis to be meaningful.

The third assumption is that the groups must be meaningful. Groups can be generated theoretically and a priori, or they can be generated using statistical techniques that create groups. One distinction between the variable- and person-oriented approaches is that for the person-oriented approach, the size of the groups does not matter and cannot always be determined a priori. In fact, groups will probably differ in size, and some may be small. This can create problems for variable-oriented approaches (e.g., ANOVA significance tests are not valid if the group sizes differ significantly from each other), but the person-oriented approach is interested in the unusual (von Eye, Bogat, & Rhodes, 2006).

As an example, consider the technique of eliminating *outliers* before conducting variable-oriented data analysis. Outliers are extreme scores that are considered too large or likely to unduly influence the findings; that is, they are not valid. However, the person-oriented approach does not necessarily consider the outlier to be invalid. Unless the researcher knows for a fact (e.g., the malfunction of equipment) that the data are not valid, the assumption is made that the data are valid.

Statistical Techniques

Cluster analysis, latent class analysis, exploratory factor analysis, configural frequency analysis, and methods of data mining are techniques that fall under the purview of person-oriented research (for more on cluster analysis, see Chapter 5, this volume). These methods allow the researcher to identify groups within the sample, and they make no a priori assumptions about how many meaningful groups will be found. Single-subject methods, widely used by behavioral psychologists, are also person oriented such as Bogat and Jason (2000) and Glenwick and Jason (1980).

Another approach, Caramani's (2009) comparative method, reflects the postulate that all empirical research results are based on comparisons. The author proposed using the tools of predicate calculus and formal logic to perform such comparisons. Necessarily, the results of comparisons will include statements about the differences among individuals and groups of individuals. Therefore, the comparative method is very suitable for exploratory person-oriented research, despite the author's claim that the method is "ultimately variable-oriented" (Caramani, 2009, p. 90).

Symbolic data analysis is another person-oriented approach. Standard data analysis proceeds from the simplifying assumptions that to describe satisfactorily the unit of analysis (e.g., an individual, an object, or a setting) a well-designed set of random variables can be used and that a description involves just one value per unit (e.g., one value per unit per variable per observation point). However, often there is internal variation in the data. For example, individuals may differ in the list of pets they own. These lists, their ranges of scores, and the variation in these lists are called *symbolic data*, or *set-valued data* (Billard & Diday, 2006). A data table in symbolic data analysis is more complex than a standard rectangular data table because each data cell contains an entire qualitative or quantitative distribution instead of a single number. Because of this, descriptions of individuals can be richer and more diverse than standard descriptions, allowing researchers to do justice to intra- and interindividual differences.

In addition, techniques that are highly identified with the variable-oriented approach might be used in a person-oriented manner. For example, Sterba and Bauer (2010) discussed less restrictive variable-oriented longitudinal methods (e.g., latent growth curve modeling) that might be used by person-oriented researchers. Similarly, von Eye and Bogat (2007) suggested that some aspects of ANOVA might be of interest to person-oriented research.

One example is repeated measures ANOVA. In this method, individuals are assessed at more than one time period, allowing the researcher to determine (a) change or stability in the outcome and (b) group differences in that change or stability. Such a circumstance might involve three measurements of the outcome (e.g., scores on an educational achievement test) and two groups (children in charter vs. regular public schools). We focus on the polynomial decomposition of the results. Polynomials are contrasts among the levels of a factor. With three measurements of the outcome, there are two possible contrasts—linear and quadratic polynomials—in which, under the null hypothesis, both slopes are assumed to be the same for each participant. (The linear slope demonstrates whether the outcome increases, decreases, or stays constant over time. The quadratic slope examines whether the increases or decreases in the outcome occur at a constant rate.) These aspects of change or stability in the outcome are not of interest to the person-oriented researcher because of the assumption that the slope is the same for each individual. However, the person-oriented researcher is interested in whether the linear and quadratic slopes are the same for the two groups. In our example, we can determine whether children in charter versus regular public schools have the same change or stability in educational achievement over time (linear slope) and whether the increase or decrease in educational achievement occurs at a constant rate for both groups (quadratic slope). This is a person-oriented approach because, even though the groups are determined a priori, there is not an a priori assumption about the type or rate of change within these groups.

In the following section, we provide variable- and person-oriented approaches to the same data set. We also compare the results.

DATA EXAMPLE OF THE PERSON-ORIENTED APPROACH

A growing body of research indicates that how youths spend their time outside of school has important consequences for their development. Most of this research suggests that youths' participation in constructive out-of-schooltime activities (e.g., extracurricular activities, community-based youth organizations) has positive consequences for their academic, social, civic, and physical functioning (e.g., Durlak & Weissberg, 2007; Eccles, Barber, Stone, & Hunt, 2003; Mahoney, Larson, & Eccles, 2005; Zarrett, 2007). However, few studies have addressed alternative explanations for these relations. Perhaps youths who get involved in such activities have greater access to resources or are better adjusted and, thus, have a higher likelihood of continuing on positive developmental trajectories even without constructive out-of-schooltime activity participation. Thus, successfully translating out-of-school research findings into effective interventions requires careful attention to both (a) how selection factors are related to the impact of activity participation on development and (b) how these impacts vary for different kinds of youth developing in different kinds of contexts.

The data come from the Maryland Adolescent Development in Context Study, a longitudinal study that began in 1991. (The participants were originally in the Study of Adolescents in Multiple Contexts; see Cook, Herman, Phillips, & Setterson, 2002.) Data for the current analyses were collected in six waves: the beginning of seventh grade, the summer after seventh grade, the summer and early fall after eighth grade, at the end of 11th grade, and 1 and 3 years post high school. There were 784 participants (51% female) with sufficiently complete data across waves. The families were 66% African American, 30% European American, and 4% from other backgrounds. The median income was $40,000 to $45,000 for the two largest groups. The youths were on average 12.75 years old at Wave 1 and 21.34 years old at Wave 6. The measures had good reliability and validity. The researchers assessed six broad areas (problematic behaviors, positive activities, occupational plans, educational aspirations and expectations, mental health, and academic motivation and achievement) that described four developmental systems (youth motivation, parent socialization, community resources, and youth out-of-school activities).

Cluster solutions for each of the developmental systems were derived (Zarrett, Peck, von Eye, & Eccles, 2010). Clusters were validated by comparing them with theoretically relevant variables (cf. Zarrett, 2007). These clusters were then used to develop three predictor variables: (a) contextual support (1 = low, 2 = medium, 3 = high) was derived from a cross-categorization of community support and parent socialization patterns during the seventh grade; (b) youth motivation (1 = low, 2 = medium, 3 = high) was derived from patterns of youth motivation related to out-of-school activities (e.g., sports, socializing with friends) and academic achievement in the seventh grade; and (c) positive activity involvement (1 = no, 2 = yes) was based on out-of-school activity participation patterns in 11th grade that were predictive of positive educational attainment (cf. Peck, Roeser, Zarrett, & Eccles, 2008; Zarrett, 2007). The outcome variable, college attendance (1 = no, 2 = yes), indicated educational attainment up to 3 years after high school graduation.

We provide three ways of analyzing the data. The first is a variable-oriented approach examining relationships among the four variables. The second and third are person-oriented approaches that look for subgroups within the population. In addition, the third approach ascertains whether the relationship among the levels of the variables is similar or different for the various subgroups (i.e., dimensional identity).[1]

In the variable-oriented approach, we estimated a log–linear model using the statistical program Lem (Vermunt, 1997). A log–linear model that describes these data well is the hierarchical two-interaction model

$$\log \hat{m}^{A,B,C,D} = \lambda + \lambda_i^A + \lambda_j^B + \lambda_k^C + \lambda_l^D + \lambda_{il}^{A,D} + \lambda_{kl}^{C,D}, \tag{1}$$

for which we obtained the LR-X^2 = 10.89. For df = 10, this model can be retained (p = .366). This model suggests that Variable B (youth motivation) is independent of the remaining three variables and that Variable D (college attendance) is associated with both Variable A (contextual support) and Variable C (positive activity involvement).

The first person-oriented approach modeled pathways from the seventh to 11th grades that resulted in college attendance after high school (Zarrett et al., 2010). A multinomial general log–linear model was developed using a backward stepwise regression approach (cf. Marascuilo & Busk, 1987), beginning with the fully saturated model implied by the various pattern-specific relations between the four variables. In this approach, each higher order

---

[1]The chapter's web appendix (http://pubs.apa.org/books/supp/Jason-Glenwick) contains the data set as well as command code for running the latent class analysis for the second person-oriented approach. The first person-oriented approach is only described briefly because a fuller explanation is beyond the scope of this chapter.

component of the model (e.g., the four-way interaction) is separately removed from the equation, and the best-fitting model is selected from among the models in which the likelihood ratio is most similar to the degrees of freedom. Given this baseline model, contrast vectors were added (cf. Mair & von Eye, 2007) that represented alternative developmental pathways corresponding to hypotheses concerning positive activity involvement predicting later achievement. Such log–linear models are analogous to person-oriented models tested by configural frequency analysis.

Various subgroups (patterns and profiles of youths of different size ns) were identified from this approach (Zarrett et al., 2010). The most interesting conceptual findings were that adolescents with low contextual support and low youth motivation defied the normative prediction of not attending college if they had high levels of positive activity involvement.

In the second person-oriented approach, we estimated a latent class model, estimated as an unrestricted model with no particular constraints on the parameters, including the sizes of the latent classes (Goodman, 1974; Lazarsfeld & Henry, 1968). The reason for using an unrestricted model is first that, as was known from the results presented by Zarrett et al. (2010), individuals with particular profiles tend to come in groups that differ in size. Second, in the context of a person-oriented approach, we entertained no hypotheses concerning the number or the size of the groups to expect.

To find the optimal number of latent classes, several comparison runs were performed in which we varied the number of latent classes. We started with two latent classes and increased the number of classes by one until model fit became worse. We also made the decision to hypothesize only one latent variable. That is, we assumed that the associations among the four variables, A (contextual support), B (youth motivation), C (positive activity involvement), and D (college attendance), could be explained by just one categorical latent variable. In other words, we assumed that the manifest variables were independent of each other in each category of the sole latent variable (assumption of local independence). If this is the case, the latent variable explains the associations among the four variables in this study. The decision concerning the number of latent variables was mainly based on the fact that we analyzed only four manifest variables. Still, had the results suggested that acceptable fit required more than one latent variable, we would have increased the number of latent variables.

For the four manifest variables (A, B, C, and D) and the latent variable X, we estimated the latent class model (here given in log–linear form); subscripts indicate the parameters for the main effects and interactions, and superscripts indicate the variables involved in the terms. Note that this model

$$\log \hat{m}^{A,B,C,D} = \lambda + \lambda_i^X + \lambda_j^A + \lambda_k^B + \lambda_l^C + \lambda_m^D + \lambda_{ij}^{X,A} + \lambda_{i,k}^{X,B} + \lambda_{il}^{X,C} + \lambda_{i,m}^{X,D} \quad (2)$$

TABLE 6.1
Overall Goodness of Fit of Four Latent Class Models of the Four Variables: Contextual Support, Youth Motivation, Positive Activity Involvement, and College Attendance

Model (No. latent classes)	df	LR-X^2	p	AIC
2	22	43.8	<.01	5251.89
3	15	17.13	.31	5239.22
4	8	14.15	.08	5250.24
5	1	7.48	.01	5257.57

Note. LR-X^2 = likelihood-ratio chi-square test; AIC = Akaike information criterion.

formulation describes a hierarchical log–linear model for the incomplete frequency table $X \times A \times B \times C \times D$. In each of the following models, the number of classes was increased by one (see Table 6.1). Both the goodness-of-fit significance tests (which we did not want to suggest significant model–data discrepancies) and the Akaike information criterion (a goodness-of-fit statistic that we wanted to be relatively low) suggest that the model with three latent classes was the best among the four considered. Therefore, we interpreted this model.

Table 6.2 displays the observed and the expected cell frequencies for this model. It shows that the observed cell frequencies correspond very closely to the ones estimated for the three-class model. None of the standardized residuals is large enough to indicate significant model–data discrepancies. As expected, the sizes of the latent classes are discrepant. Specifically, we found the following class size proportions (conditional probabilities): $p(X = 1) = 0.5127; p(X = 2) = 0.1735;$ and $p(X = 3) = 0.3138$.

Table 6.3 displays the latent class output, that is, the probabilities with which individuals with a particular marginal response category in the four variables under study belong to the three latent classes. It shows that assignment to the latent classes is clearly possible for a selection of the individual categories of the four variables. As stated previously, Variable A (contextual support) and Variable B (youth motivation) each had three categories (1 = low, 2 = medium, 3 = high), and Variable C (positive activity involvement) and Variable D (college attendance) each had two categories (1 = no, 2 = yes). Looking across the rows, we can examine the conditional probability that each response reflects whether the adolescent who made that response is likely or unlikely to be a member of one of the three classes.[2] For example,

---

[2]Note that if we examine columns, rather than rows, we can determine the conditional probability of whether, overall, the people within that class are more likely to respond in a particular manner. For example, those adolescents in Class 1 are most likely to attend college (D = 2, 0.9857).

TABLE 6.2
Observed and Expected Cell Frequencies for a Model With Three Latent Classes

Pattern A B C D	Frequencies Observed	Estimated	Standardized residual	Pattern A B C D	Frequencies Observed	Estimated	Standardized residual
1 1 1 1	27.000	22.315	0.992	2 2 2 1	8.000	6.598	0.546
1 1 1 2	10.000	12.607	-.0734	2 2 2 2	35.000	35.484	-0.081
1 1 2 1	3.000	4.782	-0.815	2 3 1 1	43.000	37.287	0.936
1 1 2 2	13.000	9.325	1.203	2 3 1 2	48.000	44.838	0.472
1 2 1 1	16.000	15.567	0.110	2 3 2 1	6.000	9.808	-1.216
1 2 1 2	18.000	14.167	1.018	2 3 2 2	52.000	51.995	0.001
1 2 2 1	2.000	3.355	-0.740	3 1 1 1	17.000	15.952	0.262
1 2 2 2	8.000	10.092	-0.659	3 1 1 2	19.000	23.020	-0.838
1 3 1 1	14.000	19.338	-1.214	3 1 2 1	4.000	3.871	0.066
1 3 1 2	9.000	11.932	-0.849	3 1 2 2	21.000	20.797	0.045
1 3 2 1	8.000	4.429	1.697	3 2 1 1	11.000	11.126	-0.038
1 3 2 2	12.000	12.091	-0.026	3 2 1 2	29.000	24.207	0.974
2 1 1 1	37.000	42.639	-0.864	3 2 2 1	2.000	2.501	-0.317
2 1 1 2	47.000	44.601	0.359	3 2 2 2	16.000	17.244	-0.300
2 1 2 1	11.000	9.394	0.524	3 3 1 1	14.000	14.944	-0.244
2 1 2 2	34.000	33.697	0.052	3 3 1 2	36.000	35.800	0.033
2 2 1 1	30.000	29.848	0.028	3 3 2 1	8.000	7.247	0.280
2 2 1 2	45.000	49.812	-0.682	3 3 2 2	71.000	71.291	-0.034

TABLE 6.3
Conditional Probabilities of Univariate Marginals and Latent Classes

	X = 1 0.5127	X = 2 0.1735	X = 3 0.3138
A = 1	0.1607	0.0517	0.2780
A = 2	0.5648	0.2888	0.5270
A = 3	0.2745	0.6594	0.1950
B = 1	0.3355	0.0876	0.3911
B = 2	0.3811	0.0000	0.2716
B = 3	0.2834	0.9124	0.3373
C = 1	0.5840	0.2334	0.8272
C = 2	0.4160	0.7666	0.1728
D = 1	0.0143	0.0680	1.0000
D = 2	0.9857	0.9320	0.0000

adolescents who responded B = 3 are likely to be members of the second latent class. Adolescents who responded D = 1 are extremely likely to be members of the third latent class. Conversely, adolescents who responded A = 1 are rather unlikely to be members of the second latent class. Adolescents who responded B = 2 are extremely unlikely to be members of the second latent class. Finally, for D = 2 there is close to perfect separation between the third latent class and the first and second classes.

Online Figure 6.1 in the web appendix to this chapter (http://pubs. apa.org/books/supp/Jason-Glenwick) displays the profiles that the three latent classes have over the categories of the four manifest variables. Table 6.3 and Online Figure 6.1 show that the second, the smallest latent class, is the most extreme in the sense that it is described by four conditional probabilities close to 0 and two close to 1. The first and the third latent classes are similar to each other over the categories of Variables A and B but differ strongly over the categories of Variables C and D. We conclude that separation is very good. This result is reflected in the estimated expected proportion of classification errors, E, when model assignment is used; that is, assignment is made based on the largest row-wise probabilities in Table 6.3. Specifically, we calculated E = .12, indicating only 12% of the cases will be misclassified when modal assignment is used. Also, the proportionate reduction in the proportion of classification error is .75.[3]

The resulting three latent classes can be described as follows. Class 1 are the *bright underachievers*. These adolescents, with only average motivation and contextual support and no involvement in out-of-school activities, still attend

---

[3]This value of .75 can be compared in magnitude with a correlation of .75 or to a Cohen κ of .75.

college. Class 2 are the *superachievers*. These youths excel inside and outside the classroom in the context of strong community support and parental involvement. Class 3 are the *slackers*. These are youths whose average amount of community and parental support is not enough to overcome their own lack of motivation and activity level to create the impetus to enroll in college.

Taken together, the variable-oriented approach, in this case a log–linear analysis, allows us to understand how variables are related in the population represented by the sample. However, this analysis assumes that the population is homogeneous and that the variables have the same meaning for all individuals. The Zarrett et al. (2010) results show that the population is not homogeneous and is characterized by various profiles of individuals of different sizes. These results also tell us that particular patterns of the variables describe profiles of individuals who are more or less likely to attend college than expected by chance and relative to other patterns. The latent class analysis again lets us see that the population is not homogeneous. It examines whether specific levels of each of the four variables that are associated in the log–linear analysis and the first person-oriented analysis are associated differently in the classes that result from the latent class model (dimensional identity). In fact, we found that the variables are indeed associated differently in the three classes, and the latent variable is able to explain this. Thus, the results of the latent class model allow us to conclude that person-oriented results from these data are open to even more detailed and accurate descriptions of patterns and (group-specific) variable relationships.

BENEFITS AND DRAWBACKS OF THE PERSON-ORIENTED APPROACH

As community psychologists begin to conceptualize their research using a person-oriented approach, they should be cognizant of some of its benefits and drawbacks.

Benefits

There are a number of benefits of the person-oriented approach. We outline three: (a) a more objective view of the data, (b) a more nuanced view of the data, and (c) a more complex view of individuals and their environments.

Objective

The results obtained using person-oriented methods are often likely to be more objective than variable-oriented approaches. In large part, this results because person-oriented methods eliminate some sources of researcher bias at the point of data analysis. The person-oriented approach necessitates that the researcher explore the data for subpopulations or subsettings. Thus, a priori ideas about what specific groups or settings are important to examine or compare may not be validated by the data. In this way, the person-oriented approach shares a data discovery process with qualitative data collection techniques. For example, the grounded theory technique (Glaser & Strauss, 1967) involves an iterative discovery-based process; as the researcher learns more about the concepts through the process of interviewing, he or she may decide to ask additional questions or query additional participants. That is, the researcher's a priori ideas about theory or populations may or may not be present in the content of the interviews. Of course, the person-oriented approach is a quantitative approach, but like qualitative approaches, it encourages the researcher to learn something unexpected from the data.

Nuanced

Person-oriented analyses provide a more nuanced view of the data. If one does not mind brushing details under the carpet, then the variable-oriented approach is sufficient. Person-oriented analyses bring the details to the forefront. As discussed, one way is by discovering subpopulations or sub-settings within the sample. However, as a supplement to variable-oriented techniques, person-oriented approaches can provide a more fine-grained analysis of the original findings.

For example, Martinez-Torteya, Bogat, von Eye, and Levendosky (2009) examined risk and protective factors that led to adaptation among children who were exposed to intimate partner violence when they were 2, 3, and 4 years of age. Eight risk factors that affected adaptation were modeled (duration of intimate partner violence, race, income, positive parenting, easy temperament, cognitive ability, maternal depression, and stressful life events). Although, overall, a large proportion of variance was explained, only two predictors were significant: maternal depression and child temperament (less depression and easier temperament were associated with adaptation). This is a variable-oriented approach because it focuses on the relationship between a particular variable (one of the eight predictors) and another variable (adaptation). However, because only two of the predictors were significant, it was likely that profiles or patterns existed that would better explain the relationship between risk factors and adaptation.

Therefore, a person-oriented analysis was conducted to determine configurations of risk and protective factors. The four variables accounting for the most variance in the variable-oriented analysis were categorized: maternal depression (yes or no), easy temperament (high or low), intimate partner violence duration (one, two, or three time periods), and adaptation (positive or negative). Cross-classifying these variables yielded 24 patterns or configurations (e.g., yes/high/one/positive; yes/low/one/positive). For example, the pattern yes/high/one/positive describes a child whose mother was depressed, who had an easy temperament, who was exposed to violence during one time period, and who had positive adaptation.

Once variables are cross-classified, configural frequency analysis (von Eye, 2002; von Eye, Mair, & Mun, 2010) determines whether a particular pattern of variables occurs more or less often than expected by chance. Based on an a priori determined base model, which provides a reference for the expected frequency of each pattern, the observed cell frequency is compared with the expected cell frequency. If significant differences between the observed and expected frequencies are found, they can be one of two cases, either (a) a *type* in which a pattern contains more cases than expected or (b) an *antitype* in which a pattern contains fewer cases than expected. Most patterns are not types or antitypes because they contain the number of cases one would expect. Alpha is protected to reduce capitalizing on chance.

This analysis revealed three types. The first two were profiles of resilient children with easy temperaments and nondepressed mothers and either one or two time periods of exposure to intimate partner violence. The third was nonresilient children who had difficult temperaments, depressed mothers, and who were exposed to three periods of intimate partner violence.

The variable-oriented and person-oriented approaches to data analysis allowed for a more complete picture of the risk and resilience in children exposed to intimate partner violence. The variable-oriented analyses found that of the eight risk factors, only maternal depression and child easy temperament were significant predictors of adaptation. The other risk and protective variables, including duration of intimate partner violence exposure, were not. However, the person-oriented analyses found that duration of exposure to intimate partner violence does matter. Maternal depression and easy temperament were protective factors only when children were exposed to one or two time periods of intimate partner violence. Children who were chronically exposed (i.e., three time periods) were at heightened risk because they were unlikely to have the family and individual resources associated with maintaining resilience.

Complex

Tenets c, d, and e of the person-oriented approach delineate the importance and complexity of the ecological context. In community psychology, Kelly (e.g., Kelly, 1968; Kelly & Hess, 1987; Kelly, Ryan, Altman, & Stelzner, 2000; Kingry-Westergaard & Kelly, 1990) has argued that interdependence is the hallmark of the ecological perspective. Interdependence is about complexity. It affirms the importance of studying the relationships of people to each other, the relationships of people to the contexts in which they live and work, and the interaction of one social system with another. The system is dynamic such that effecting a change in one area of the system will influence another area (e.g., Bergman & Magnusson, 1997). Kelly et al. (2000) encouraged community psychologists to study these interdependencies. The person-oriented approach provides an important way to do so.

Drawbacks

There are also some drawbacks to the person-oriented approach. First, the approach often requires a large sample. Second, the profiles or subpopulations derived may not be theoretically meaningful. Third, reviewers are generally unfamiliar with these approaches.

Sample Size

Two of the data examples we described in this chapter (e.g., Bogat, Leahy, et al., 2005; Martinez-Torteya et al., 2009) used configural frequency analysis and involved relatively small sample sizes (e.g., about 200). However, fully implementing the tenets of the person-orientation may require large sample sizes. When variables are used to create profiles of individuals or settings, sometimes very small groups may result. As we noted previously, this has the benefit of identifying sectors of the sample that variable-oriented techniques cannot. However, dimensional identity may be impossible to verify if the number of individuals in the profile is extremely small (von Eye, 2010). Also, when researchers create variables, they often use aggregated data (e.g., a sum score of the climate of a setting). However, in creating aggregated variables and then using these variables to create profiles of groups, researchers assume that the components (e.g., items) of the "raw" variable hold dimensional identity across a subpopulation or subsetting. This may not be the case. If it is not, then aggregating the components of a variable may mean that for some subgroups the aggregated variable does not have dimensional identity. Large sample sizes allow the researcher to create cross-classification profiles involving, for example, individual items of scales. This is exemplified in the latent class analysis presented earlier in this chapter.

Theoretically Meaningful Profiles

Person-oriented researchers have often promoted data-analytic methods that create classifications using descriptive approaches such as cluster analysis (e.g., Bergman & Magnusson, 1997; von Eye & Bergman, 2003). Although, as we argued previously, such approaches allow researchers to examine the details in the data and encourage scientific objectivity, the downside is that such taxometric methods may create groups that are not meaningful (Sterba

& Bauer, 2010; von Eye & Bergman, 2003), for example, as a result of measurement problems. However, it is also the case that variable-oriented methods suffer from the same problem. And perhaps in the latter case it is even more of a problem because variable-oriented researchers do not recognize it as such. Thus, as we have emphasized many times in this chapter, variable-oriented methods examine groups in which data are aggregated, and "the average may be highly atypical" (Walls & Schafer, 2006, p. xiv). Thus, many groups examined or formed by variable-oriented approaches may not be theoretically meaningful. Variable-oriented approaches beg the question of what is typical. Person-oriented approaches attempt to answer that question by examining the heterogeneity of a population.

Unfamiliarity With the Approach

At present, the majority of researchers writing and reviewing grants and articles have been trained in variable-oriented but not person-oriented approaches. Thus, it is a definite drawback for the person-oriented researcher to submit a manuscript or grant with a focus on person-oriented data analyses. The variable-oriented researcher does not have to justify his or her approach, but the person-oriented researcher is often asked to do. Because the person-oriented approach represents a radically different paradigm for research, the reviewer may not understand the explanations, data analysis, or data interpretation of the author. As with all scientific paradigm shifts, the reception may be chilly, and adoption may be slow. What may be most difficult for variable-oriented researchers to realize is that the use of variable-oriented statistics, like any other long-held paradigm, represents a specific scientific bias (Kuhn, 1962).

CONCLUSION

In this chapter, we have provided an overview of the person-oriented approach to research, including discussion of some of the most recent advances in the field (e.g., dimensional identity) and its relevance to community-based research. The person-oriented approach is a theoretical and methodological perspective that is a dramatic paradigm shift for the social science researcher. It requires that researchers abandon widely held beliefs about data analysis, including the conviction that an average score represents reality for most individuals or adequately describes a group or setting. It encourages researchers to think about the interdependence of individuals and their environments and to measure them in complex ways. We believe that the person-oriented approach holds much promise and value for the community researcher.

REFERENCES

Anderson, E. (1990). *StreetWise: Race, class, and change in an urban community.* Chicago, IL: University of Chicago Press.

Bergman, L. R., & Magnusson, D. (1997). A person-oriented approach in research on developmental psychopathology. *Development and Psychopathology, 9,* 291–319. doi:10.1017/S095457949700206X

Bergman, L. R., Magnusson, D., & El-Khouri, B. (2003). *Studying individual development in an interindividual context: A person-oriented approach.* Mahwah, NJ: Erlbaum.

Billard, L., & Diday, E. (2006). *Symbolic data analysis. Conceptual statistics and data mining.* Chichester, England: Wiley. doi:10.1002/9780470090183

Block, J. (1971). *Lives through time.* Berkeley, CA: Bancroft Books.

Bogat, G. A. (2009). Is the person orientation necessary in community psychology? *American Journal of Community Psychology, 43,* 22–34. doi:10.1007/s10464-008-9215-7

Bogat, G. A., & Jason, L. A. (2000). Toward an integration of behaviorism and community psychology: Dogs bark at those they do not recognize. In J. Rappaport & E. Seidman (Eds.), *Handbook of community psychology* (pp. 101–114). New York, NY: Kluwer Academic/Plenum. doi:10.1007/978-1-4615-4193-6_5

Bogat, G. A., Leahy, K. L., von Eye, A., Maxwell, C., & Levendosky, A. A. (2005). The influence of community violence on the functioning of battered women. *American Journal of Community Psychology, 36,* 123–132. doi:10.1007/s10464-005-6237-2

Bogat, G. A., Levendosky, A. A., DeJonghe, E., Davidson, W. S., & von Eye, A. (2004). Pathways of suffering: The temporal effects of domestic violence on women's mental health. *Maltrattamento e abuso all'infanzia, 6,* 97–112.

Bogat, G. A., Levendosky, A. A., Theran, S., von Eye, A., & Davidson, W. S. (2003). Predicting the psychosocial effects of interpersonal partner violence (IPV): How much does a woman's history of IPV matter? *Journal of Interpersonal Violence, 18,* 1271–1291. doi:10.1177/0886260503256657

Bogat, G. A., Levendosky, A. A., & von Eye, A. (2005). The future of research on intimate partner violence (IPV): Person-oriented and variable-oriented perspectives. *American Journal of Community Psychology, 36,* 49–70. doi:10.1007/s10464-005-6232-7

Caramani, D. (2009). *Introduction to the comparative method with Boolean algebra.* Los Angeles, CA: Sage.

Cook, T. D., Herman, M. R., Phillips, M., & Setterson, R. A., Jr. (2002). Some ways in which neighborhoods, nuclear families, friendship groups, and schools jointly affect changes in early adolescent development. *Child Development, 73,* 1283–1309. doi:10.1111/1467-8624.00472

Durlak, J. A., & Weissberg, R. P. (2007). *The impact of after-school programs that promote personal and social skills.* Chicago, IL: Collaborative for Academic, Social, and Emotional Learning.

Eccles, J. S., Barber, B. L., Stone, M., & Hunt, J. (2003). Extracurricular activities and adolescent development. *Journal of Social Issues, 59*, 865–889. doi:10.1046/j.0022-4537.2003.00095.x

Fagan, J., Wilkinson, D. L., & Davies, G. (2000, May). *Social contagion of youth homicide in New York.* Paper presented at the Urban Seminar Series on Children's Health and Safety, John F. Kennedy School of Government, Harvard University, Boston, MA.

Glaser, B. G., & Strauss, A. L. (1967). *The discovery of grounded theory: Strategies for qualitative research.* New York, NY: Aldine de Gruyter.

Glenwick, D. S., & Jason, L. A. (Eds.). (1980). *Behavioral community psychology: Progress and prospects.* New York NY: Praeger.

Goodman, L. A. (1974). Exploratory latent structure analysis using both identifiable and unidentifiable models. *Biometrika, 61*, 215–231. doi:10.1093/biomet/61.2.215

Kelly, J. G. (1968). Toward an ecological conception of preventive interventions. In J. W. Carter, Jr. (Ed.), *Research contributions from psychology to community mental health* (pp. 75–99). New York, NY: Behavioral Publications.

Kelly, J. G., & Hess, R. E. (1987). *The ecology of prevention: Illustrating mental health consultation.* New York, NY: Haworth Press.

Kelly, J. G., Ryan, A. M., Altman, B. E., & Stelzner, S. P. (2000). Understanding and changing social systems: An ecological view. In J. Rappaport & E. Seidman (Eds.), *Handbook of community psychology* (pp. 133–159). New York, NY: Kluwer Academic/Plenum. doi:10.1007/978-1-4615-4193-6_7

Kingry-Westergaard, C., & Kelly, J. G. (1990). A contextualist epistemology for ecological research. In P. Tolan, C. Keys, F. Chertok, & L. Jason (Eds.), *Researching community psychology: Issues of theory and methods* (pp. 23–31). Washington, DC: American Psychological Association. doi:10.1037/10073-002

Kuhn, T. S. (1962). *The structure of scientific revolutions.* Chicago, IL: University of Chicago Press.

Lazarsfeld, P. F., & Henry, N. W. (1968). *Latent structure analysis.* Boston, MA: Houghton Mifflin.

Mahoney, J. L., Larson, R. W., & Eccles, J. S. (Eds.). (2005). *Organized activities as contexts of development: Extracurricular activities, after school and community programs.* Mahwah, NJ: Erlbaum.

Mair, P., & von Eye, A. (2007). Application scenarios for nonstandard log-linear models. *Psychological Methods, 12*, 139–156. doi:10.1037/1082-989X.12.2.139

Marascuilo, L. A., & Busk, P. L. (1987). Loglinear models: A way to study main effects and interactions for multidimensional contingency tables with categorical data. *Journal of Counseling Psychology, 34*, 443–455. doi:10.1037/0022-0167.34.4.443

Martinez-Torteya, C., Bogat, G. A., von Eye, A., & Levendosky, A. A. (2009). Resilience among children exposed to domestic violence: The role of protective and vulnerability factors. *Child Development, 80,* 562–577. doi:10.1111/j.1467-8624.2009.01279.x

Peck, S. C., Roeser, R. W., Zarrett, N., & Eccles, J. S. (2008). Exploring the roles of extracurricular activity quantity and quality in the educational resilience of vulnerable adolescents: Variable- and pattern-centered approaches. *Journal of Social Issues, 64,* 135–156. doi:10.1111/j.1540-4560.2008.00552.x

Richters, J. E., & Martinez, P. (1993). The NIMH Community Violence Project: I. Children as victims of and witnesses to violence. *Psychiatry: Interpersonal and Biological Processes, 56,* 7–21.

Sterba, S. K., & Bauer, D. J. (2010). Matching method with theory in person-oriented developmental psychopathology research. *Development and Psychopathology, 22,* 239–254. doi:10.1017/S0954579410000015

Vermunt, J. K. (1997). *Lem: A general program for the analysis of categorical data.* Tilburg, The Netherlands: Tilburg University. Unpublished program manual.

von Eye, A. (2002). *Configural frequency analysis: Methods, models, and applications.* Mahwah, NJ: Erlbaum.

von Eye, A. (2010). Developing the person-oriented approach: Theory and methods of analysis. *Development and Psychopathology, 22,* 277–285. doi:10.1017/S0954579410000052

von Eye, A., & Bergman, L. R. (2003). Research strategies in developmental psychopathology: Dimensional identity and the person-oriented approach. *Development and Psychopathology, 15,* 553–580. doi:10.1017/S0954579403000294

von Eye, A., & Bogat, G. A. (2006). Person-oriented and variable-oriented research: Concepts, results, and development. *Merrill-Palmer Quarterly: Journal of Developmental Psychology, 52,* 390–420. doi:10.1353/mpq.2006.0032

von Eye, A., & Bogat, G. A. (2007). Methods of data analysis in person-oriented research. The sample case of ANOVA. In A. Ittel, L. Stecher, H. Merkens, & J. Zinnecker (Eds.), *Jahrbuch Jugendforschung 6. Ausgabe 2006* (pp. 161–182). Weisbaden, Germany: Springer-Verlag.

von Eye, A., Bogat, G. A., & Rhodes, J. (2006). Variable-oriented and person-oriented perspectives of analysis: The example of alcohol consumption in adolescence. *Journal of Adolescence, 29,* 981–1004.

von Eye, A., Mair, P., & Mun, E. (2010). *Advances in configural frequency analysis.* New York, NY: Guilford Press.

Walls, T. A., & Schafer, J. L. (Eds.). (2006). *Models for intensive longitudinal data.* New York, NY: Oxford University Press.

Zarrett, N. (2007). The dynamic relation between out-of-school activities and adolescent development. *Dissertation Abstracts International: Section B. Sciences and Engineering, 67*(10), 6100.

Zarrett, N., Peck, S. C., von Eye, A., & Eccles, J. S. (2010). *Do extracurricular activities matter? Addressing the endogeneity problem.* Unpublished manuscript.

7

META-ANALYSIS IN COMMUNITY-ORIENTED RESEARCH

JOSEPH A. DURLAK AND MOLLY PACHAN

Meta-analyses began to gain acceptance within the social sciences after the publication of Smith and Glass's (1997) classic meta-analysis of the effects of psychotherapy. However, the lack of practical guidelines, software, and generally agreed-on principles of practice made it difficult for many people to understand this methodology and execute a well-done meta-analysis efficiently. Much has changed over the past decade, and there are now expert groups that have developed explicit procedures on how to conduct, analyze, and report meta-analyses. For example, for the first time, the *Publication Manual of the American Psychological Association* (American Psychological Association, 2010) offers guidelines to authors; there are several publications that offer detailed explanations and instructions about the various steps in a meta-analysis; there are additional sources that explain how to compute effect sizes for different situations; and software is available for conducting a complete meta-analysis efficiently (Cooper & Hedges, 2004; Durlak, 2009; Hunter & Schmidt, 2004; Lipsey & Wilson, 2001; Rosenthal, 2001).

The intent of this chapter is to demystify the aims and processes of a meta-analysis, provide helpful resources that can be consulted for additional information, and, finally, as an addendum to the chapter, supply an online

data set in which the interested reader can understand through a concrete example how to negotiate the several major steps that will result in a high-quality meta-analysis. Consistent with the general theme of this volume, the ultimate idea is to encourage more community-oriented researchers to take advantage of different research strategies that can help answer critical research questions. The specific procedures used in each meta-analysis can differ depending on the status of the literature being reviewed (e.g., the information that is available or missing in each report and how the original data were presented and analyzed). For ease of discussion, the focus here is on some typical situations that many meta-analysts encounter.

The five parts of this chapter consist of comments bearing on the definition and typical goals of meta-analysis, a brief explanation of the theory behind meta-analysis, a listing and extended discussion of the major steps involved in conducting a meta-analysis, some details about a meta-analysis we conducted on the impact of after-school programs, and concluding comments about the benefits and drawbacks of meta-analyses.

DEFINITION AND GOALS OF META-ANALYSIS

Any type of literature review, including a meta-analysis, usually has three basic goals: (a) to critically evaluate and summarize a body of research, (b) to reach some conclusions about the outcomes of this research, and (c) to offer suggestions or guidelines to improve future work. The unique feature of a meta-analysis compared with narrative or descriptive literature reviews is the way that a meta-analyst quantifies, combines, and then analyzes the data in a research area to evaluate the literature. In a meta-analysis, the data from each study are converted into a common quantitative metric, called an *index of effect*, that allows for a synthesis of the findings across the reviewed studies. There are several different indices of effect, and in this chapter, we discuss only standardized mean differences (SMDs), which are commonly used to evaluate the impact of interventions or treatments.

BASIC THEORY BEHIND META-ANALYSIS

An SMD is calculated by subtracting the mean of the control group at posttest from the mean of the intervention group at posttest on each outcome variable and dividing by the pooled standard deviation of the two groups. Several sources have offered suggestions for how to estimate effects when means and standard deviations are not available (Lipsey & Wilson, 2001; Rosenthal, 2001; Wolf, 1986). In other words, positive values reflect the intervention group's superiority over the control group at posttest. The higher the value of the SMD, the more effective the intervention, and this indicates a prime advantage of effect sizes over considering only the statistical signifi- *SmD* cance of outcome findings. SMDs inform about the magnitude of the effect, or, put another way, they tell researchers how much more the average person in the intervention group changed compared with his or her counterpart in the control condition. Traditional statistical tests do not provide this type of information. It is possible to achieve statistical significance with a large sample, but the actual difference between the intervention and control groups might be so slight as to be practically meaningless. For example, with samples of 250 in both the intervention and control groups, a between-groups t test might be significant at the .05 level, but the group means could differ by only a few points on a standardized intelligence test, and the SMD (depending on the size of the standard deviations in the two groups) could be of very low magnitude (e.g., .02). A mean effect of 0.00 indicates there is no difference *makes* at all between the groups. In a meta-analysis, the differences between groups *sense* are aggregated over the entire sample of studies to provide an estimate of how ✓ different the two groups are over repeated trials or experiments, thereby ✓ increasing the confidence in the findings. Thus, the ability to estimate the magnitude of effects across many studies in a systematic and quantifiable way is believed to lead to more reliable conclusions. This also depends, of course, on how well the review process has been conducted, which bring us to the *right* major steps involved in a meta-analysis.

✓CONDUCTING A META-ANALYSIS

A meta-analysis is a research methodology, and therefore its quality can be evaluated by using criteria to judge how well it has been conducted. Here, *quality* refers to the review's scientific rigor, or the extent to which the reader can have confidence in the review's major findings, conclusions, and implications. The more carefully a meta-analysis has been conducted, the more confidence can be placed in its findings and implications. Exhibit 7.1 summarizes six major steps in a meta-analysis and lists major aspects of each step that contribute to a high-quality review. All of these features cannot be discussed in this chapter, but the references in Exhibit 7.1 provide detailed discussions of the different steps.

Steps 1 Through 4

good writing

Good writing is a hallmark of good science, and good scientific writing is accurate, clear, simple, and direct (Bem, 1995). Although, technically

anticipating this chapter

EXHIBIT 7.1
Major Features of a Well-Done Meta-Analysis

1. The review is well written.
    a. The review contributes new knowledge to the field.
    b. The review offers a logical, coherent, and convincing story.
    c. The prose is concise and specific.
    d. The take-home message is clear and emphatic.
2. The review is guided by good research questions.
    a. The review's purpose is described clearly.
    b. The research topic is important empirically, theoretically, and/or practically.
    c. The research questions are reasonable and testable.
    d. A priori hypotheses are offered.
3. An unbiased sample of relevant studies is reviewed.
    a. The scope of the review is appropriate.
    b. The review is up-to-date.
    c. Explicit criteria clarify which type of studies are included and excluded.
    d. Multiple search strategies are used to identify relevant studies.
    e. Unpublished studies are included.
4. The most important information is derived from individual studies.
    a. The potential influence of methodological features is evaluated.
    b. The extent of missing information is acknowledged.
    c. A clear rationale is presented for the coding of the major variables.
    d. The coding of studies is reliable.
5. The statistical analyses are executed appropriately.
    a. The analyses competently address the major research question(s).
    b. Clear distinctions are made between primary and exploratory analyses.
    c. Discrepant or contradictory findings are handled appropriately.
    d. One effect size per study is used to assess each research question.
    e. Effects are weighted before analyses.
    f. The potential presence of statistical outliers is examined.
    g. Studies are grouped appropriately for analyses.
    h. The review considers and tries to rule out likely rival explanations.
6. The conclusions are appropriately presented and advance the field.
    a. The take-home message is emphatic and clear.
    b. The major conclusions are clearly supported by the evidence.
    c. Appropriate qualifications to the main conclusions are offered.
    d. The practical significance of the findings is assessed.
    e. The findings are placed in an appropriate context.
    f. Implications for theory, policy, and/or practice are discussed.
    g. Critical directions for future research are offered.

Note. For more details about specific features, see Bem (1995), Drotar (2000), Durlak (2000, 2003), Durlak et al. (2003), Galvan (2004), Oxman (1994), and Sternberg, Hojjat, Brigockas, & Grigorenko (1997).

speaking, writing the review is the last thing the meta-analyst does, writing is listed here as the first step because of its fundamental importance. The value and contribution of a meta-analysis can be undone by poor writing, regardless of how well the other steps of a meta-analysis are accomplished. Moreover, it is important that the review be organized and composed so that it tells a compelling story and culminates in a clear take-home message (Step 1 in Exhibit 7.1). Sternberg (1991) wrote:

> Literature reviews are often frustrating because they offer neither a point of view nor a take-home message. One is left with a somewhat undigested scattering of facts but little with which to put them together. I encourage authors to take a point of view based on theory and to offer readers a take-home message that integrates the review. . . . [Reviews that are lively and maintain reader interest] need to make a point, not simply to summarize all the points everyone else has made. (p. 3)

Ideally, individual experiments are planned to investigate specific and clear research questions, and a priori hypotheses guide the execution of the experiment and its analyses. The same is true for a meta-analysis (Step 2 in Exhibit 7.1). If the initial research questions are vague, so too will be the answers to these questions. Findings based on a priori hypotheses inspire more confidence in their trustworthiness. It is useful to consider the difference between these two types of research approaches: (a) We wanted to examine the preventive impact of stress management interventions on college students versus (b) we hypothesized that preventive stress management interventions would be effective in reducing internalizing symptoms and increasing academic performance in college students and that first-year students would benefit the most from such interventions.

In an individual experiment, one wants to avoid bias in the choice of participants. In a meta-analysis, the "participants" are the studies being reviewed, so it is important to avoid bias by conducting a careful, systematic search of the possible literature so as not to overlook relevant studies (Step 3 in Exhibit 7.1). Two important considerations here are (a) the extent to which multiple search strategies are used to identify and obtain relevant studies and (b) the existence of a clear rationale regarding inclusion and exclusion criteria. Multiple search strategies typically include computer searches of multiple data bases and inspection of prior research reviews as well as the reference lists of each reviewed study. Sometimes, authors in the area are contacted for copies of their most recent work or to obtain more information on the details of their prior studies. The aim of this step of the meta-analysis is to review a nonbiased representative sample of relevant studies. For example, reviewing only published reports can be problematic because of the possibility of publication bias, that is, the tendency for editors and reviewers to reject (and for authors not to submit for publication) studies with nonsignificant results. Because publication bias has not been found in all research areas, an empirical question that needs to be investigated in each review is whether the published and unpublished studies (e.g., conference papers, technical reports, dissertations) in that area differ in their results. There are now statistical procedures available so that the meta-analyst can estimate whether the sample of reviewed studies contains a search bias and if so, determine how to make adjustments for this possible bias (Duval & Tweedie, 2000).

It is important for the meta-analyst to develop a clear rationale for the information that is derived from each study (i.e., for coding studies, Step 4 in Exhibit 7.1). The meta-analyst develops a coding system to abstract what is presumed to be the most important information from each study, such as characteristics of the research design, participants, intervention procedures, and outcomes. The presence of good research questions and a priori hypotheses should guide study coding, and the reliability of coding procedures should always be calculated. Meta-analysts usually make their coding system, with its definitions and explanations of variables, available to interested readers.

In the coding process, it is important to keep in mind that the methodology contained in the original studies might be an important variable affecting the outcomes. Therefore, some methodological features of the studies should always be coded along with the theoretical or conceptual variables of interest. For example, effect sizes might differ between randomized and quasi-experimental designs or as a function of the type and psychometric adequacy of the outcome measures on which the effects were calculated. A good review will justify which methodological features were coded and why. The analyses might eventually indicate that, as a group, studies that were carefully designed did not produce statistically significant mean effects, whereas studies that contained several threats to their internal validity did yield significant mean effects. Such results should certainly temper any conclusions offered in the review.

Step 5

There are several technical aspects to the statistical analyses (Step 5 in Exhibit 7.1) that are conducted in a meta-analysis, and this section takes the reader through some basic conditions. In general, there are two stages to the analyses: (a) the effect sizes drawn from the reviewed studies are inspected and prepared for analysis, and then (b) the major analyses are conducted.

Preparing the Data

Meta-analysts use various strategies regarding how they assess outcomes with respect to (a) the types of outcomes that are evaluated (e.g., behaviors, attitudes, knowledge), (b) the number of different outcomes that are used in each study, (c) the source of data for each type of outcome (e.g., independent observers, parents, children, school records), and (d) the outcome measures' psychometric properties. As already noted, the reviewer should code for important methodological aspects, such as the psychometric properties of the outcome assessments and the source of the data, because these variables could be related to the magnitude of effect. For example, the less reliable the outcome measure, the lower the effect size will be, and if most of the outcomes in a review are based on measures whose validity is unknown, this is critical information for the meta-analyst to present and discuss.

It is now standard practice to weight each individual effect size that is drawn from a study by the inverse of its variance (Hedges & Olkin, 1985). This procedure gives more weight to studies with larger sample sizes, which makes sense in that effects based on 200 participants would be a better estimate of the true population effect than those based on only 20 participants. It is also essential that each individual analysis be based on one effect size per variable of interest per study, which means that when there are multiple effects for the same variable in a study (i.e., multiple effects related to a specific research question), they are averaged to produce one effect for the analysis. For example, if Study A contained two self-report measures assessing depression, the average effect size for these two measures would be used in the analysis. This would be done so that Study A did not carry more weight in the analysis than Study B, which only used one measure to assess depression.

Finally, prior to any analysis, the distribution of effects should be examined to detect possible outliers, that is, effects that are at the far tail of either end of the distribution (i.e., they are either very negative or very positive in value compared with the sample's mean value). Detecting outliers is important because their inclusion can skew the overall findings. For example, suppose that 10 studies yielded a mean effect of 0.30 with a standard deviation of 0.2 (and the individual effects from these studies ranged from 0.00 to 0.50) but that an 11th study produced an effect size of 1.40, which is seven standard deviations beyond the 10 studies' mean of 0.20. Including the 1.40 value as is would yield a mean effect for 11 studies of 0.40, which would be 25% higher than the mean of 0.30. Different tactics are available for dealing with outliers and may involve trimming their values down to a level that is no more than three standard deviations from the other studies' mean. In such a case, the outlier effect from the 11th study would be trimmed, that is, recalculated and entered into the analyses as 0.80, and the mean of the 11 studies would thus become 0.34. In other words, when outlier values are trimmed, then their corresponding studies can be retained in the analyses without distorting the overall findings.

Conducting the Major Analyses

Uninformed readers are often at a loss to critically evaluate the statistical analyses that are presented in a meta-analysis. Has the meta-analyst done the analyses appropriately? Can the reader trust the main findings? It is helpful to think of the task of a meta-analysis of interventions in the following way.

The main challenge confronting most meta-analysts is how to explain the variability in effects that appears in a research area. Why have different

Note: IV, moderate outcomes → interv.

MMR disc.

researchers obtained different results? Interventions rarely lead to similar results; if they did, this would be common knowledge, and it would be clear that everyone should be using the same intervention to achieve the same ends. The reality is that different studies have obtained different outcomes, although it is not clear why this has occurred. It is up to the meta-analyst, using a defensible, systematic, and quantitative approach, to explain (if possible) why effects vary across studies. In other words, the meta-analyst frequently wants to identify which variables moderate the outcomes of interventions.

One very common analytic strategy in meta-analysis is to subdivide the total groups of studies on the basis of one chosen's moderators and then to test whether this subdivision helps to explain variability in effects. If one has chosen the correct moderators, the new groups of studies should yield different mean effect sizes. Furthermore, one can conduct statistical tests on these study groupings to confirm if one's grouping of studies seems appropriate.

There are two statistical tests that aid in the identification of possible moderators. One is the Q statistic, which ascertains whether a group of studies contains a statistically significant amount of variability in effects (called *heterogeneity* in meta-analysis). Basically, the Q statistic assesses whether a group of studies yields effects that vary by more than sampling error. The Q statistic is distributed as a chi-square variable, and if it is statistically significant (e.g., at the .05 level), this is interpreted as indicating that the studies are *not* estimating the same effects and that the meta-analyst should use one or more variables to subdivide studies further. In other words, in contrast to traditional statistical testing in which one usually wants the finding to be significant, for the Q statistic, nonsignificance is desired in the search for potential moderators. A nonsignificant Q statistic suggests that the meta-analyst has found a variable that places studies with similar effects together.

A second test that is used in meta-analysis calculates I^2 values, which assess the magnitude of any variability that exists in the group of studies. I^2 values range along a 0% to 100% continuum. An I^2 value of 0% indicates no variability (i.e., heterogeneity) at all among the study effects, whereas values of 25%, 50%, and 75% are considered to reflect low, moderate, and high degrees of heterogeneity, respectively (Higgins, Thompson, Deeks, & Altman, 2003). I^2 values are a useful complement to the Q statistic because the latter's statistical power is positively related to the number of included studies. With larger numbers of studies (particularly ≥ 50) the Q statistic is often statistically significant, whereas analyses of fewer studies (e.g., < 20) can easily produce nonsignificant Q values.

In summary, by subdividing a total group of reviewed studies so that each smaller group yields nonsignificant Q statistics and low I^2 values, a meta-analyst tries to determine which coded study features moderate outcomes. If this occurs, then the mean effects for the different study groups will differ and can be interpreted; that is, one group should yield higher mean effects than another group. Meta-analysts usually begin by applying the Q statistic and I^2 values to the total group of reviewed studies. If these first analyses on the variability of effects for all reviewed studies yields a nonsignificant Q statistic and a low I^2 value, then there is no need to search for potential moderators. Such a finding would suggest that collectively the studies are producing similar effects regardless of the diversity of the studies' methodology and of the participant, intervention, and outcome characteristics represented among the studies.

Step 6 *great summary*

Reviews can be important not only because of the results they summarize but also because of what they suggest about future work. This is Step 6 (see Exhibit 7.1) in a meta-analysis. Therefore, in the discussion section of the review, the meta-analyst should carefully summarize the main findings, *Do* their practical and theoretical importance, and their possible limitations or qualifications. It is also critical that the reviewer provide others with a research agenda for the future. What important questions remain? What variables and constructs need more attention? How can researchers improve the methodology and thus the impact of future investigations? Good meta-analyses advance the field by summarizing what has been learned to date and what still needs to be learned in a particular area.

AN EXAMPLE OF A META-ANALYSIS

The online data set that accompanies this chapter (see web appendix *online dataset* for this chapter; http://pubs.apa.org/books/supp/Jason-Glenwick) is based on our meta-analysis of outcomes from after-school programs (ASPs) for school-age youths (Durlak, Weissberg & Pachan, 2010). ASPs now serve millions of school-age youths and are financed through both federal and local funds, but there is concern that programs may not be effective in their goal of fostering young people's social and personal development (Mahoney & Zigler, 2006). Therefore, we examined the impact of ASPs and tried to determine which types of programs were most effective in achieving different goals. We reviewed 66 programs that met our specific inclusion and exclusion criteria.

When we first examined the effects averaged across all 66 studies, the results of the Q and I^2 tests indicated that the heterogeneity in effects was statistically significant (and the Q statistic was very high at 306.42) and of large magnitude (i.e., the I^2 value was 78%). These results were expected and suggested that the total group of studies contained a mix of program effects and should be subdivided somehow in an effort to identify potential moderators of outcomes. Put another way, could we find a way to determine if certain study features were associated with better ASP outcomes?

We had hypothesized that two variables would explain the different outcomes across studies. These variables were (a) the outcome areas being assessed and (b) whether ASP staffs were following four evidence-based practices for developing young people's social skills. When we divided the total group of studies according to these variables, the results supported our hypotheses. The Q and I^2 tests at this point indicated that the heterogeneity of effects present in our grouping of studies was generally statistically nonsignificant and of low magnitude. Inspection of the mean effects for programs using evidence-based practices were statistically significant (i.e., between 0.14 and 0.37) in all six outcome areas (e.g., problem behaviors, drug use, academic performance), whereas programs not following evidence-based practices did not yield significant mean effects in any of the six areas. In other words, we were able to reduce the variability of effects obtained in our total group of 66 studies in line with our hypothesized variables to present a possible explanation of why some investigators of ASPs had obtained better results than others. However, the analyses were not finished.

In an individual experiment it is possible to think of possible rival explanations for the findings. Perhaps the results would differ for other participants or if the procedures were varied. In a meta-analysis, an important question is whether other study features might also account for heterogeneity in effects; however, the meta-analyst can test these other possibilities by rerunning the analyses using other potentially relevant variables. Thus, in the present instance we examined the possible influence of different methodological variables (e.g., type of design) and characteristics of the participants (i.e., age and gender), outcome measures (i.e., validity and reliability), and programs (i.e., duration and setting) by grouping the studies according to these variables and recalculating Q and I^2 tests. The results indicated that none of these other variables provided a reasonable alternative explanation for our findings.

CONCLUSION

Similar to other methodological approaches, there are conditions that limit the applicability of a meta-analysis. There is no magic number for how many studies are necessary, and the number of participants in the reviewed studies is also important. For example, the findings from a meta-analysis based on 10 studies involving a total of 200 participants will not be as compelling as an analysis of 50 studies involving several thousand individuals. A meta-analyst must also depend on the information provided in the original reports, and

useful MS quan anay; skills set meta analy.

invariably there is always some missing information of potential interest. Reviews of both clinical and preventive interventions have indicated that frequently a considerable amount of basic data relating to the participants and the interventions are never provided in the original research reports (Durlak, Celio, Pachan & Schellinger, 2009). If too many original studies lack information on matters relating to participants' age, ethnic status, or aspects of adjustment or fail to specify what procedures were used in the intervention, these variables cannot be examined sufficiently in a meta-analysis.

The limitations relevant to meta-analysis should not detract from its valuable positive features. Whenever studies begin accumulating in a particular area, there is a need to take stock of this information, and meta-analysis is one useful method for doing so. Meta-analysis is ideally suited for aggregating data across different type of studies and then summarizing a body of literature in terms of its impact, limitations, and future implications. It can alert readers to what works, what does not, and where more attention should be devoted to exploring key constructs and issues.

Relatively few meta-analyses have appeared in community research outlets as is evident in the volume by Jason et al. (2004). The intent of this chapter has been to clarify the main steps of a meta-analysis to encourage others to apply this research strategy to their interests or, at the very least, to become critical consumers of relevant meta-analyses when they appear.

REFERENCES

American Psychological Association. (2010). *Publication manual of the American Psychological Association* (6th ed.). Washington, DC: Author.

Bem, D. J. (1995). Writing a review article for *Psychological Bulletin*. *Psychological Bulletin, 118*, 172–177. doi:10.1037/0033-2909.118.2.172

Cooper, H., & Hedges, L. V. (Eds.). (1994). *Handbook of research synthesis*. New York, NY: Russell Sage Foundation.

Drotar, D. (2000). Reviewing and editing manuscripts for scientific journals. In D. Drotar (Ed.), *Handbook of research in pediatric and child clinical psychology* (pp. 409–424). New York, NY: Kluwer Academic/Plenum.

Durlak, J. A. (2000). How to evaluate a meta-analysis. In D. Drotar (Ed.), *Handbook of research in pediatric and clinical child psychology* (pp. 395–407). New York, NY: Kluwer Academic/Plenum.

Durlak, J. A. (2003). Basic principles of meta-analysis. In M. Roberts & S. S. Ilardi (Eds.), *Methods of research in clinical psychology: A handbook* (pp. 196–209). Malden, MA: Blackwell. doi:10.1002/9780470756980.ch10

Durlak, J. A. (2009). How to select, calculate, and interpret effect sizes. *Journal of Pediatric Psychology, 34*, 917–928.

Durlak, J. A., Celio, C. I., Pachan, M. K., & Schellinger, K. B. (2009). Sometimes it is the researcher, not the research, that goes "off the rails": The value of clear, complete, and precise information in scientific reports. In D. Streiner & S. Sidani (Eds.), *When research studies go off the rails: Why it happens and what you can do about it* (pp. 361–368). New York, NY: Guilford Press.

Durlak, J. A., Meerson, I., & Ewell-Foster, C. (2003). Meta-analysis. In J. C. Thomas & M. Hersen (Eds.), *Understanding research in clinical and counseling psychology: A textbook* (pp. 243–267). Mahwah, NJ: Erlbaum.

Durlak, J. A., Weissberg, R. P., & Pachan, M. (2010). A meta-analysis of after-school programs that seek to promote personal and social skills in children and adolescents. *American Journal of Community Psychology, 45,* 294–309. doi: 10.1007/s10464-010-9300-6

Duval, S., & Tweedie, R. (2000). Trim and fill: A simple funnel-plot-based method of testing and adjusting for publication bias in meta-analysis. *Biometrics, 56,* 455–463. doi:10.1111/j.0006-341X.2000.00455.x

Galvan, J. L. (2004). *Writing literature reviews.* Glendale, CA: Pyczak.

Hedges, L. V., & Olkin, I. (1985). *Statistical methods for meta-analysis.* New York, NY: Academic Press.

Higgins, J. P., Thompson, S. G., Deeks, J. J., & Altman, D. G. (2003). Measuring inconsistency in meta-analyses. *BMJ, 327,* 557–560. doi:10.1136/bmj.327.7414.557

Hunter, J. E., & Schmidt, F. L. (2004). *Methods of meta-analysis* (2nd ed.). Thousand Oaks, CA: Sage.

Jason, L. A., Keys, C. B., Suarez-Balcazar, Y., Taylor, R. R., Davis, M., Durlak, J., & Isenberg, D. (Eds.). (2004). *Participatory community research: Theories and methods in action.* Washington, DC: American Psychological Association.

Lipsey, M. W., & Wilson, D. B. (2001). *Practical meta-analysis.* Thousand Oaks, CA: Sage.

Mahoney, J. P., & Zigler, E. F. (2006). Translating science to policy under the No Child Left Behind Act of 2001: Lessons from the national evaluation of the 21st-century community learning centers. *Journal of Applied Developmental Psychology, 27,* 282–294.

Oxman, A. D. (1994). Checklists for review articles. *BMJ, 309,* 648–651.

Rosenthal, R. (2001). *Meta-analytic procedures for social research* (rev. ed.). Newbury Park, CA: Sage.

Smith, M. L., & Glass, G. V. (1977). Meta-analysis of psychotherapy outcome studies. *American Psychologist, 32,* 752–760.

Sternberg, R. J. (1991). Editorial. *Psychological Bulletin, 109,* 3–4. doi:10.1037/h0092473

Sternberg, R. J., Hojjat, M., Brigockas, M. G., & Grigorenko, E. L. (1997). Getting in: Criteria for acceptance of manuscripts in Psychological Bulletin. *Psychological Bulletin, 121,* 321–323. doi:10.1037/0033-2909.121.2.321

Wolf, F. M. (1986). *Meta-analysis: Quantitative methods for research synthesis.* Beverly Hills, CA: Sage.

III

METHODS INVOLVING CHANGE OVER TIME

8

TIME-SERIES ANALYSIS IN COMMUNITY-ORIENTED RESEARCH

BETTINA B. HOEPPNER AND RAE JEAN PROESCHOLD-BELL

Behaviorally oriented community researchers, such as Glenwick and Jason (1980; 1993), have for years argued for the inclusion of time-series types of data to document changes in how individuals interact with their communities over time as well as how community-level phenomena change over time (Biglan, Ary, & Wagenaar, 2000). In this chapter, we discuss what time-series data are and why they are useful. Ever so briefly, and for the sake of completeness, we then describe the statistical model that is used in time-series analysis (TSA) before moving on to how serial dependence is typically dealt with in applied community research. Our statistical description is not intended to be a full definition of the more technical details involved in TSA. Rather, our intent is to provide a point of reference for how the approach discussed in this chapter fits within the larger field of TSA.

The interested reader is encouraged to refer to introductory texts on TSA (e.g., Chatfield, 2004; Glass, Willson, & Gottman, 1975; Yaffee & McGee, 2000) for further clarification. Readers who are not interested in the statistical issues can skip over the Statistical Background section without loss of continuity. In the Research Design Issues section, we highlight the opportunities time-series designs offer to applied researchers and discuss specific design issues that are unique to time-series studies. To illustrate the whole process, we present a detailed applied example from our own research experience. Finally, we provide a summation of the benefits and drawbacks of time-series designs as well as offer some thoughts of why these designs may be underused despite repeated calls for this type of research in community research.

STATISTICAL BACKGROUND

What Are Time-Series Data?

What then are time-series types of data? Time-series data arise when a single *unit* has been described by a series of observations over time. The unit of interest is defined by the researcher. It can be a single person but, more interesting to community researchers, it also can be a clinic, school, district, or country. The *observations* then are meaningful summaries of the unit of interest at a particular point in time. Total number of clients, students' average performance on standardized math tests, or proportions of intake patients reporting a particular symptom all are examples of summary variables that could be used to describe the unit of interest at a particular time.

To monitor trends over time, the same type of summary information is collected at regular intervals. The resulting time-series data can then be analyzed to test whether the unit of interest is changing in a systematic fashion over time. For example, by recording quarterly math test scores, a school may notice a decline in overall math performance. By comparing the observed trends before and after a specific date, the time-series data also can be used to test whether an organizational change or other event affected existing trends. Such comparisons take into account differences in both overall levels (e.g., whether average math scores were higher before or after the date of interest) and slopes (e.g., whether there are different trends before or after the date of interest, which show that math scores may have declined before implementing a new curriculum but are now increasing). Together, they render a more complete account of how the community of interest is changing over time or how its development may have been impacted by specific events.

How Are Time-Series Data Analyzed?

Time-series data are typically, though not necessarily, analyzed using TSA. The reason that TSA may be necessary is that repeated observations from the same unit of interest are not independent from each other. Traditional statistical tests such as regression and analysis of variance make the assumption of independence of errors. If this assumption is violated, Type I and Type II error rates are impacted.

In TSA, the dependence of errors that arises when the same unit of interest is observed multiple times is called *serial dependence* or *autocorrelation*. More technically, autocorrelation is defined as the correlation of observations at particular temporal distances from one another within the same series. The idea is that, in general, observations made 3 days apart will be similarly related to each other regardless of whether the days in question are Days 3 and 6 or Days 2 and 5.

There are two types of serial dependence that, if ignored, can lead to two different errors in using inferential tests. As an illustration, consider the two lines in Figure 8.1. In both panels, the linear relationship between the two variables is the same (i.e., intercept = 5, slope = 0.1), but the dependent variable has different types of autocorrelation. It is important to notice the more haggard appearance of the series in the figure's Panel A (negative autocorrelation, with consecutive observations tending to be on opposite sides of the true trend) versus the smoother appearance of the series in Panel B (positive autocorrelation, with consecutive observations tending to be on the same side of the true trend). A simple linear regression would result in accurate parameter estimates for intercept and slope in both cases but would overestimate standard errors for the negatively autocorrelated series (Panel A), leading to an increased Type II error rate, and underestimate standard errors for the positively autocorrelated series (Panel B), leading to an increased Type I error rate. In psychological research, positive autocorrelation tends to be more common.

In TSA, the serial dependence of the data is modeled so that statistical hypothesis tests can be validly conducted. Depending on the complexity of the data and the accuracy with which the serial dependence needs to be modeled, this process can be either simple or complex. In applied community research, the focus tends to be on fairly basic questions, such as whether there was an increase over time or whether trends changed after the intervention occurred. For such questions, basic models for the serial dependence suffice. In other fields, however, the greater interest lies in predicting future observations based on what researchers know of past trends rather than in knowing what occurred during the past period. This process is called *forecasting* and is often of interest in econometrics or engineering, for example. For this purpose, it becomes very important to model the serial dependence as accurately as possible because such modeling accuracy will result in more accurate predictions.

In other research, forecasting may not be of interest, but the nature of the serial dependence itself may be of interest because it provides insight into the underlying mechanism of the observed phenomenon. In smoking cessation research, for example, the serial dependence of the number of cigarettes smoked every 6 hours may shed light on whether the underlying mechanism is habit strength or nicotine depletion in the body (Velicer, Redding,

(A)

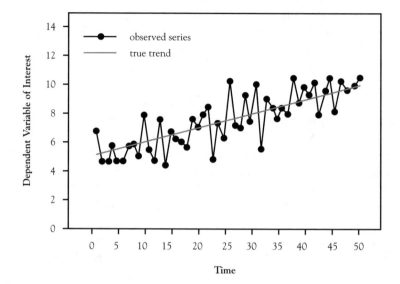

(B)

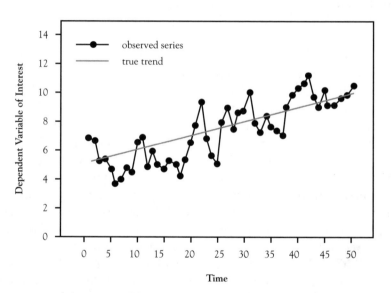

Figure 8.1. Two (simulated) time series consisting of 50 observations each are graphed. In both series, the dependent variable's "true" intercept is 5 (i.e., when time = 0, the dependent variable = 5), and the slope is 0.1 (i.e., for each consecutive observation, the dependent variable increases by 0.1). In Panel A, the series has a negative autocorrelation ($r = -.60$), whereas in Panel B, the series has a positive autocorrelation ($r = .60$).

Richmond, Greeley, & Swift, 1992). In this case as well, the accuracy with which the serial dependence is modeled becomes very important.

How Is Serial Dependence Modeled?

In TSA, repeated observations are theorized to follow an underlying autoregressive integrated moving-average (ARIMA) model of order (p, d, q), where p, d, and q are integers that refer to the complexity of each of three explicitly differentiated types of variance in the time series. Specifically, the ARIMA model distinguishes between autoregressive (AR, described by p) and moving-average (MA, described by q) processes and describes the degree to which the series is not stationary (d), which would complicate the estimation of model parameters. The actual definition of *stationary* is somewhat technical, but includes, for example, a constant mean.

If a series is not stationary, it is *differenced*, which means that instead of using the actually observed values, the differences $(Y_t - Y_{t-1})$ between successive observations are used instead. The AR terms describe the dependency among successive observations (e.g., the relatedness of yesterday's depression severity to today's or the relatedness of last Tuesday's clinic visits to this Tuesday's clinic visits). Each AR term has an associated correlation coefficient that describes the magnitude of the dependency. For example, a model with two AR terms $(p = 2)$ is one in which an observation is predicted by two previous observations in which the size of the effect is estimated for each term separately. By contrast, an MA process is one that is defined by a linear combination of current and previous random shocks (Yaffee & McGee, 2000). A *random shock* is a random or unexpected event that has subsequent effects on the variable of interest over time (e.g., the effect of a fight with a sibling on subjective well-being). The MA terms in the ARIMA model describe the persistence of a random shock from one observation to the next. A model with two MA terms $(q = 2)$ is one in which an observation depends on two preceding random shocks.

A series' ARIMA model is identified by examining the pattern of autocorrelations and partial autocorrelations of the observed data (Glass et al., 1975). This process is complex and is described in considerable detail in typical textbooks on TSA (e.g., Chatfield, 2004; Glass et al., 1975; Yaffee & McGee, 2000). Unfortunately, trained experts' accuracy in identifying ARIMA models correctly using the procedure laid out in the classic text by Glass et al. (1975) does not exceed 30% (Velicer & Harrop, 1983), and despite continued efforts to create computer-driven model-identification algorithms (Ong, Huang, & Tzeng, 2005; Schwarz, 1978), there continues to be a lack of reliable, nonsubjective, and readily available model identification procedures.

What Does One Do With Serial Dependence in Community Research Data?

As noted previously, in community research the interest commonly lies in removing serial dependence so that hypothesis tests about general trends in the observed data can be correctly conducted. To this end, two approaches have been proposed for community research. Simonton (1977) proposed modeling the first AR parameter only, with the rationale that typically serially dependent data in psychological research rarely require more complex structures. Similarly, in the general transformation approach (Velicer & McDonald, 1984), the focus is also on the AR parameters in which the first five terms are modeled on the basis of the rationale that mathematically it can be shown that an AR model always can be represented as an MA model of infinite length and vice versa (Box & Jenkins, 1976; Glass et al., 1975). The rationale for five modeled AR terms, with AR terms six through infinity indicated as zero, is that in social science research, the error terms of recent rather than distant past observations tend to be correlated with current observations. Simulation studies have shown that both approaches perform well in estimating mean level differences in interrupted time-series (ITS) designs (Harrop & Velicer, 1985; Velicer & Colby, 2005; Velicer & Harrop, 1983).

How Does One Interpret Time-Series Data?

After the serial dependence has been removed, TSA becomes a simple regression model from a statistical point of view. The interpretation of the model effects is a little bit different, however, because (a) in TSA the independent variable is time, and (b) there is only one unit of observation, which can be a single patient or participant or can be a unit representative of a larger population, such as a clinic, school, state, or country. It is important to recall that in simple linear regression, a multitude of observations from different persons are used to control for measurement error in the measured variables. The same principle applies in TSA, except that multiple observations are used instead of multiple people. Because observations are from a single unit, there is no variance due to individual differences, and thus the model has more statistical power.

Also, as with simple linear regression, the relationship between the independent and dependent variables is described across a range of values of the independent variable. In regular regression, this range of the independent variable is implicitly defined by the selection of the sample. For example, the relationship between depression and family functioning could be studied either in patients diagnosed with depression (i.e., tighter range of higher depression scores) or high school students (i.e., lower and wider range of depression scores). It is over this range of values that findings can be generalized. In TSA, the range of values of the independent variable, time, is chosen explicitly. Findings apply to this chosen time frame.

What Are Interrupted Time-Series Designs?

The ITS design is a special case of a time series in much the same way as the ANOVA is a special case of a regression; instead of a continuous predictor, a categorical predictor is used. In ITS designs, this categorical predictor is the absence or presence of an intervention in which the time before the implementation of an intervention is compared with the time after. Although the onset of the intervention can be determined by the researcher, clearly the individual observations cannot be randomized to the *pre* versus *post* conditions, thus making the design quasi-experimental.

[handwritten marginalia: absence shorter]

RESEARCH DESIGN ISSUES

There are primarily two sources of time-series data: archival data and prospectively collected data. Both types of data offer important research opportunities. They also both have unique challenges.

Using Archival Data for Time-Series Studies

Although archival data limit a researcher in many ways, they lend themselves well to TSA because they are by definition collected in a way suitable for TSA. Specifically, they represent meaningful summaries of the population of interest and are collected at regular intervals. As an example, consider Monitoring the Future data and government publications. Pampel and Aguilar (2007) used these data to understand youth smoking. They used TSA to test which type of explanation (e.g., cigarette pricing, tobacco advertising) best explained fluctuations in youth smoking over a 26-year time interval.

Archival data are also available on a smaller scale. Clinics and counseling centers routinely collect data about patients and clients, which can then be used to understand trends over time. For example, university counseling center staff commonly perceive that the levels of psychopathology and symptom severity among university counseling center client populations are increasing. This anecdotal observation can be tested empirically through the use of archival intake data (Hoeppner, Hoeppner, & Campbell, 2009).

Archival data also can lead to ITS design questions in which the effect of a particular incident on the variable of interest is tested. For example, in July 2003, Maine implemented a new policy to control the state's psychotropic medication costs by Medicaid programs and Medicare Part D plans. Using an ITS design to examine archival data, Lu, Soumerai, Ross-Degnan, Zhang, and Adams (2010), showed that Maine's new prior authorization policy resulted in a marked decrease in the rates of initiation of bipolar treatments. Similarly, the impact of terrorist attacks (e.g., 9/11, the Oklahoma City bombing) on suicide rates on local, state, and national levels can be tested (Pridemore, Trahan, & Chamlin, 2009).

Collecting Time-Series Data Prospectively

Archival data are not always available, particularly not when the effect of a new intervention is to be tested. At that point, a researcher may want to design a time-series study. We already mentioned two important characteristics of time-series data, namely, that (a) each observation represents a meaningful representation of the unit (e.g., clinic, school) of interest and (b) data are collected at regular intervals. Regular intervals are needed because time is modeled continuously in TSA, which means that the metric in which time is measured matters. If data are collected haphazardly—sometimes every week, then only every other week, then multiple times per week—the researcher needs to choose a metric for modeling these data over time. If this metric is weekly, then there will be much missing data for those time periods when data were collected only every other week. If the researcher decides to model time in biweekly intervals, then the separate observations conducted per week or within a week are collapsed into a smaller number of data points, which is not desirable. So, clearly, it is advantageous to collect the data in the interval or metric in which time is to be modeled in the analysis.

Depending on the setting of the study, collecting data at regular intervals may be hard. Such data collection requires stable and supportive partners. It is asking a lot of research partners to give you access to their resources (e.g., potential participants, space, staff to help recruit). It is asking even more to have them commit to providing those resources for multiyear periods, which is likely required if you are to collect data at enough preintervention as well as postintervention time points for adequate statistical power with time-series designs. In a study that involved two clinics for 2 years, we asked our clinic partners to sign memoranda of understanding with us regarding our data collection plans; however, it is not clear whether these memoranda of understanding could be enforced, and even if they could be, they would be damaging to our researcher–provider relationships, which extend beyond a single study. Instead, we tried to create pathways for good communication. We also sought to foster goodwill by occasionally bringing bagels and flowers and also by celebrating the midpoint of data collection with clinic staff.

Statistical Power

Many factors affect statistical power, but just like in all other designs, it is the sample size that matters the most. The difference in TSA is that the sample size is not the number of participants one enrolls but rather the number of observations one records. Thus, in designing a TSA study, it is important to maximize the number of temporal observations. Two options exist: either extend the length of the study or increase the frequency with which observations are made, depending on the phenomenon under study. For example, if pain following the removal of wisdom teeth was studied, it would make sense to increase the sample size by increasing the frequency of sampling within the hours following extraction because that is when the phenomenon under study is changing, rather than prolonging the study for several days. By contrast, offering free nicotine replacement therapy to patients in a clinic would likely have a gradual, long-term impact on clinic-wide smoking rates, and thus it would make sense to extend the observation period. Thus, determining the sample size (i.e., number of observations) in a TSA study requires an approximate understanding of how the variable of interest changes over time so that a temporally appropriate sampling frequency and length can be chosen.

Generalizability and Validity

Keep in mind that the goal of the analysis is to estimate a trend over a specified period of time. The degree to which the unit under study is representative of the larger population of interest is the degree to which the results of the analysis can be generalized. Meanwhile, the study's validity depends on how representative each observation is of the unit under study. If that unit happens to be a single person, this is not an issue. If the unit of interest, however, is a clinic or school, for example, one could either describe the unit of interest in absolute terms (e.g., total number of students enrolled per year, percentage of patients with a certain disease per month) or one could estimate these values by sampling (e.g., average awareness of recommendations for health behaviors sampled by a random survey of 30 students). This choice has a great impact on the findings' validity but little impact on the analysis. The TSA treats each observation equally, regardless of whether it is based on a comprehensive census or a sampled estimate. The only statistical impact the definition of each observation has on the analysis is that a sampled value may have greater fluctuations as a result of chance than an absolute value might have, and the fewer random fluctuations there are in a time series, the greater the statistical power.

Another consideration in determining the frequency and length of data collection is cyclical patterns or seasonality. For example, a researcher who was interested in seeing whether intake rates at a college counseling center would be impacted by a specific event might collect data on a weekly basis before (e.g., May–August) and after the event (e.g., September–December). The researcher would see a huge upward trend in intake rates, but that would merely be an artifact of the seasonal trend underlying college student client intake rates, which increase in the fall regardless of a specific event. To disentangle the effects of a potential intervention impact on intake rates from a seasonal upward trend in intake rate, the researcher would have to start collecting data 1 year prior to the intervention to be evaluated to capture the annual pattern. Thus, in designing a time-series study, an understanding of the cyclical or seasonal patterns impacting the data to be collected is necessary so that the data collection can accommodate these patterns.

Finally, depending on the length of the study, it is important to keep track of societal and policy changes that may impact the dependent variable. For example, if one's variable of interest is student achievement, changes in educational policies at the local, state, and national levels are important to note. In our study of knowledge of hepatitis C among persons with HIV, we kept track of changes in state resources directed toward hepatitis C. At one point during the study, the state hired a hepatitis C resource coordinator. We then tracked her efforts to determine whether at any point during our study they were designed to impact people with HIV in our study area. They were not, but had they been, it would have made it difficult to tease apart whether changes in hepatitis C knowledge were due to our intervention or the resource coordinator's efforts. We would have explored that further by examining our dependent variable by the timing of her hire. Therefore, dates are particularly important to track.

APPLIED EXAMPLE: PROGRAM EVALUATION OF A COMMUNITY INTERVENTION

To help the reader further understand the usefulness of time-series designs in community interventions, we now describe an example of an evaluator's decision-making process from the beginning of intervention research funding (for more detail, see Proeschold-Bell et al., 2010).

Using Theory to Guide Intervention Goals

In 2003, the Duke Center for Health Policy and the Piedmont HIV Healthcare Consortium received funding from the U.S. Department of

Health and Human Services through the Healthy Communities Access Project to improve the health of people coinfected with HIV and hepatitis C and to prevent hepatitis C infection among people with HIV. The overarching goal of the federally funded Healthy Communities Access Project was to create sustainable community-level change to foster health. Unlike in many research initiatives, the Healthy Communities Access Project grantees were to focus explicitly on systems-level rather than individual-level changes. Accordingly, rather than selecting an individual-level theory, we adhered to a socioecological framework (McLeroy, Bibeau, Steckler, & Glanz, 1988) when designing our intervention. This framework is a public health theory that proposes that health behavior change is a function of multiple levels of influence emanating out from the individual, rather like concentric circles radiating out from an innermost circle that represents the individual. The individual's health is influenced by the individual's own beliefs and values (intrapersonal level); by the beliefs and behaviors of close significant others (interpersonal level); by community norms and resources (community level); by institutional rules, regulations, and ethos (institutional level); and by civic policies, environments, and structures (policy level; McLeroy et al., 1988).

We had two primary intervention goals. The first was to increase the knowledge that people with HIV have about hepatitis C. Because both hepatitis C and HIV are blood-borne viruses, they share transmission routes. More than 30% of people with HIV in the United States are estimated to also have hepatitis C infection (Verucchi, Calza, Manfredi, & Chiodo, 2004), yet their understanding of hepatitis C transmission, treatment, and preventive behaviors is lacking (Proeschold-Bell et al., 2010). Our second goal was to increase the proportion of people with HIV who know their hepatitis C status. Until recently, HIV medical providers were too consumed with treating HIV and opportunistic infections to worry about slow-acting viruses such as hepatitis C. However, mortality from opportunistic infections has dramatically decreased with the availability of highly active antiretroviral therapy (Lima, Harrigan, & Bangsberg, 2009), and hepatitis C-related liver disease has emerged as a serious cause of mortality among people with HIV (Bica et al., 2001). Despite this fact, not all infectious disease clinics routinely tested for hepatitis C in 2003 and not all people with HIV who were tested for hepatitis C were told their status.

Using the socioecological framework, we selected multiple levels on which to intervene. At the intrapersonal level, we offered HIV–hepatitis C trainings directly to people with HIV and conducted a hepatitis C media campaign designed to reach people with HIV. At the interpersonal level, we created and facilitated support groups for people with HIV–hepatitis C coinfection and provided case management to people with coinfection. At the community level, we enhanced community health resources through providing HIV–hepatitis C trainings for HIV medical providers as well as HIV nonmedical providers such as social workers and addictions counselors. We also created a resource guide to connect people with coinfection to area resources. At the institutional level, we changed the HIV clinic system by creating a face sheet to be printed and inserted in the front of the patient's chart the day of the patient's appointment. This sheet included information on the date of the last hepatitis C test and the test result. Thus, we intervened at four of the five socioecological framework levels.

Evaluating the Success of the Community-Level Intervention

Choosing an evaluation design for this set of interventions was a challenge. Our intervention was essentially a community-level intervention aimed at six counties. We did not have the resources to intervene or collect data in enough communities to conduct a randomized controlled trial. We considered finding a community to serve as a comparison group, but past experience in local HIV research had taught us that adjacent communities were different in important ways, including health care and transportation access, from our intervention community. We would always suspect that any differences found between intervention and comparison communities were due to community differences rather than to our intervention. We were at a loss for what to do until we talked to a community psychologist who had recently read *Experimental and Quasi-Experimental Designs for Generalized Causal Inference* by Shadish, Cook, and Campbell (2002) and who recommended considering a TSA.

The ITS design that we used appealed equally to our team's researchers and interventionists. The researchers liked its strong causal inference. They also appreciated the fact that ITS would not require data collection from a comparison community that was gaining little from the project and might be hesitant to participate in data collection. The interventionists liked the fact that the research design would allow them to intervene with all people with HIV; in their past experience, they had been uncomfortable with having to hold back potentially beneficial services from control group participants.

We took a significant risk in this particular evaluation in that we assessed hepatitis C knowledge at the patient level, whereas we intervened directly with very few patients. We expected our intervention efforts at other levels of the socioecological framework to impact the knowledge of individual patients; however, with most of the intervention activities being one step removed from individuals, it might have been safer to assess provider knowledge and provider reports of communication with patients. Future projects might consider collecting data on outcomes at multiple levels.

Designing the Data Collection Plan

Logistically, it was feasible to use an ITS design. It was going to take many months to flesh out and institute our multilevel intervention, and yet the research team was fully staffed and could implement data collection in time to attain numerous (15) preintervention time points. The two area infectious disease clinics were willing to support a day of data collection in their clinics every other week for 2 years. Finding space to conduct private interviews was a challenge in both clinics and was made possible only through the community contacts of hired intervention staff who talked adjacent departments into allowing us to use their space. Our research budget was also large enough to sustain 1.1 full-time equivalent interviewers for 2 years for the data collection effort as well as to provide compensation to research participants.

We collected data every 2 weeks in the Duke Infectious Disease Clinic for 2 years. This gave us 15 preintervention time points and 40 postintervention time points. As a result of staff turnover and the administrative wishes of the Lincoln Early Intervention Clinic, we were unable to collect any preintervention data at their clinic. However, we discovered through analysis of our interviews that 100% of the Lincoln Early Intervention Clinic patients also had participated in an interview held at the Duke Infectious Diseases Clinic. Because these clinics' patients were not unique, we decided to analyze data from the Duke Infectious Diseases Clinic only.

With respect to statistical power, our sample size proved adequate in that we found significant changes across time. However, because statistical power in ITS is based on number of time points rather than number of interviews, it would have been preferable to have had more than 15 preintervention time points. With regard to response rates, our interview day response rates were sustained throughout the 2 years, we suspect, by the $10 interview compensation.

Data Management Issues Prior to Analysis

To illustrate how data from an ITS design can be analyzed, we focus on hepatitis C knowledge as the dependent variable. The data set is included in the web appendix for this chapter (http://pubs.apa.org/books/supp/Jason-Glenwick). The reader can examine it to see how it is set up and to run the code provided later in this section.

The goal of this analysis was to test whether there were changes in a clinic's patient population's average hepatitis C knowledge following a community-wide intervention. As discussed earlier, the outcome variable was sampled on the patient level at which the date of interview was noted for each patient. The starting database contained one row per interview, with some patients interviewed multiple times but most not.

As a first step, we calculated average hepatitis C knowledge scores by averaging the individual scores obtained within a biweekly interval. A decision had to be made on how to handle patients who had completed the knowledge test multiple times. In this case, we thought that it made sense to include patients interviewed at multiple times in multiple biweekly scores because their learning (or lack thereof) would be reflective of the clinic's patient population knowledge at that time.

The new data set contained one row per biweekly average in which the average knowledge score was one variable and the date of the last day of the biweekly interval was the second variable. (We also kept data on the total number of participants per each biweekly average, and the standard deviations and standard errors for each biweekly interval, but these served only descriptive purposes and were not used in the TSA). On the basis of the date variable, we created a dummy variable for before and after the start of the intervention; all biweekly intervals occurring before September 1 were coded as 0 and all biweekly intervals after this date were coded as 1. Then we inserted rows with missing values for all biweekly intervals during which interviews were not conducted because of staffing issues. We noted that the total intervention period spanned 55 biweekly intervals/observations, but we had observations for only 38 observations. The data were now in equally spaced sequential order.

Analyzing the Data

To analyze the data, we used the AUTOREG procedure in SAS 9.2 in which we used the Durbin–Watson statistic (Ansley, Kohn, & Shively, 1992) to test the statistical significance of different lags of the AR terms. We did not expect any seasonal trends and thus did not test the corresponding lag. In fact, we expected autocorrelations to be minimal given that we were estimating the clinic's patient population's average hepatitis knowledge through largely independent patient samples. To be on the safe side, and in line with the general transformation approach (Velicer & McDonald, 1984), we tested the first five lags for significant AR terms, using the following syntax:

```
proc autoreg;
        model hcv = intv / dw=5 dwprob;
    run;
```

Here, *hcv* is the name of the biweekly hepatitis C knowledge score, and *intv* is the name of the dummy-coded intervention effect. The output lists the estimated AR terms for Lags 1 through 5 and the estimated probabilities for negative and positive autocorrelation separately. In this case, we found no statistically significant autocorrelation. Had we found significant autocorrelation, we would have identified the relevant AR terms and then refitted the same model. For example, if only the first AR term was statistically significant for either positive or negative autocorrelation, we would model that autocorrelation using the following syntax:

```
proc autoreg;
            model hcv = intv / nlag=1;
    run;
```

The new output would now list two regression results: (a) the parameter estimates before the AR term was modeled and (b) the new model in which the AR term is included, appropriately labeled *final model estimation*. It is this second set of results that would be reported in a paper.

In our case, as there was no autocorrelation, it was not necessary to model any AR terms. This lack of autocorrelation afforded us some modeling freedom; we were now free to use weighted regression. The AUTOREG procedure does not allow for weighting, but other procedures in SAS do. Because we no longer had to worry about autocorrelation, we were free to use other procedures assuming independence of errors and were able to weigh each biweekly score by the number of patient interviews that were used to create it, thereby giving more weight to the data points that were more reflective of the clinic population.

Dissemination of Findings

During the dissemination of findings stage, all project staff, researchers and interventionists alike, valued the graphs generated. For example, Figure 8.2 depicts mean hepatitis C knowledge across time with a line indicating the start of the intervention. One can see that there was a decreasing trend in hepatitis C knowledge prior to the start of the intervention, that there was an increase in patient knowledge after the start of the intervention, and that patient knowledge decreased again, although at a reduced rate, during the intervention period. The decreasing trend in knowledge postintervention may have been due to patients forgetting what they had learned about hepatitis C, whose transmission patterns are easily confused with HIV. Had we created graphs throughout the project, we suspect it would have provided staff with a feeling of accomplishment to see the progress of data collection representing biweekly periods of effort on their part as well as the outcomes related to their work.

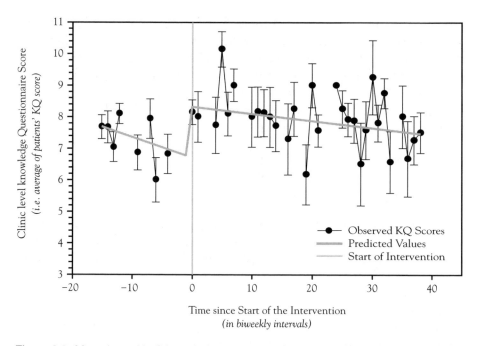

Figure 8.2. Mean hepatitis C knowledge scores per biweekly interval. Standard errors around the mean are represented by error bars. The predicted values are displayed in gray. KQ = knowledge questionnaire. From "An Interrupted Time Series Evaluation of a Hepatitis C Intervention for Persons With HIV," by R. J. Proeschold-Bell, B. B. Hoeppner, B. Taylor, S. Cohen, R. Blouin, B. Stringfield, and A. Muir, 2011, *AIDS and Behavior, 15,* p. 1728. Copyright 2011 by Springer. Adapted with permission.

BENEFITS AND DRAWBACKS OF TIME-SERIES ANALYSIS

The great strength of the time-series design is that it can be used in situations in which experimental control is not possible, which is often the case in community-based research. The ITS, in particular, eliminates many threats to validity, as described in detail by Cook and Campbell (1979). Consider, for example, the presence of a preexisting trend that is unrelated to the intervention under study. If researchers simply collected data on a sample before the start of the intervention and again at a time point after the start of the intervention and then compared the means, they would conclude that the intervention was effective because the postintervention mean was higher. The increase in means, however, may have been due to a preexisting trend, which was unaffected by the intervention. In an ITS design, differences in both the means and the slopes of the trends before and after the intervention would be tested by examining the main effect of the dichotomous pre–post time variable and the interaction term with time (a detailed description of how to specify and interpret design matrices is given by Huitema & McKean, 2000). The researchers would conclude correctly that there was an increasing trend over time but that this trend was not affected by the intervention. Excitingly, in ITS designs, a researcher is not limited to examining mean level or linear slope differences but also can explore different types of changes, such as delayed effects, decaying treatment effects, or evolutionary effects in which performance first decreases as a result of novelty and then increases and surpasses previous performance. (for a more detailed description of different intervention effects, see Velicer & Fava, 2003).

Time-series designs are vulnerable to other threats to validity that cannot be statistically controlled, but they can be avoided using careful data collection methods. Such threats to validity include changes in instrumentation (i.e., using different ways of measuring the outcome of interest before vs. after the start of the intervention such that observed effects may be attributable to the way of measuring instead of representing intervention effects) and interactions with sampling selection (e.g., sampling subpopulations of the population of interest that are particularly high or low on the outcome such that changes in outcome could merely represent regression to the mean). Other threats to validity cannot be avoided, but they can be tested for. For example, changes in the composition of the unit of observation (e.g., nonrandom shifts in the demographic makeup of the population of interest) might occur, which, if present, would be an alternative explanation for any observed effects rather than the presence of the intervention.

The greatest weakness of the time-series design is that the data are from a single unit of interest. Thus, the conclusions drawn from a TSA are only generalizable to the extent to which this unit of interest is representative of the population of interest. For example, if a single clinic is examined, the generalizability of the results hinges on how representative each observation was of this clinic and how representative the observed clinic was of other clinics. Replications across multiple sites strengthen the generalizability of the results but also may be prohibitively costly or not feasible.

WHY TIME-SERIES ANALYSIS MAY BE UNDERUSED BY COMMUNITY-ORIENTED RESEARCHERS

There are multiple reasons why TSA is underused by community-oriented researchers. On a very pragmatic level, community-oriented researchers may simply not be trained to think in terms of time-series designs. A typical graduate program in psychology, for example, emphasizes research methodology that is primarily based on cross-sectional data (e.g., regression, ANOVA, factor analysis). In recent years, there has been an increased focus on longitudinal research methodology, but that focus has been almost exclusively on panel-type data in which many participants are assessed over a very limited number of time points (e.g., two to four as opposed to dozens or hundreds of time points as would be done in TSA). Only the occasional graduate program offers an elective course on TSA, which is not of interest to all students. This lack of training in TSA results in researchers who are unfamiliar with it and thus unlikely to use it in their research and also in reviewers who do not know how to evaluate and review a TSA study, which makes it harder to publish such studies in applied psychological research journals. Even a required heading such as "Participants" in the American Psychological Association's journals and other journals emphasizes the focus on person-level studies and makes it difficult to describe a time-series study adequately within this focus.

A further barrier is the mathematical complexity of the TSA literature. Even seasoned statisticians can be scared away by the complex equations and models that time-series specialists are examining in the primary literature, and even introductory level TSA textbooks are more mathematically complex than the average applied psychological researcher is comfortable with. For the purposes of applied community-oriented research, this level of detail is likely not necessary. Community-oriented researchers are likely to be mostly interested in removing serial dependence in order to proceed with ordinary hypothesis testing about differences in levels and slopes before and after an intervention. In contrast, accurate ARIMA model identification and concomitant issues are mostly relevant to forecasting and research questions that are interested in fine-grained processes. TSA textbooks, though, tend not to be written for community-oriented researchers, and thus, this point gets lost.

Finally, there is the issue of cost. A study design that includes hundreds of time points appears prohibitively costly at first glance, at least, when one is thinking of panel-type longitudinal data. Importantly, however, archival time-series data often are collected for administrative and other purposes and could easily be used for TSA studies with minimal cost. Even when designing a time-series study to collect data, it is important to keep in mind that it is not individual people for whom follow-up needs to be arranged, which is the costly part of panel-type data, but rather the clinic that is the unit of interest.

CONCLUSION

Time-series designs in general are potentially very useful for researchers interested in community-level phenomena, just as ITS designs in particular are potentially useful for the evaluation of community-level interventions. There are many reasons why these designs are currently underused by community researchers, but most of the reasons have to do with knowledge and training rather than barriers to accessing archival data or collecting original data appropriate to time-series designs. We hope that this chapter encourages researchers to consider using such designs. In the chapter, we have attempted to convey a few key practical points, such as the need for equal spacing of time intervals and considerations regarding the number of time points before and after an intervention. With this knowledge, researchers can partner with a statistician skilled in TSA to use this design for either intervention evaluation purposes or for greater understanding of community phenomena across time.

REFERENCES

Ansley, C. F., Kohn, R., & Shively, T. S. (1992). Computing p values for the generalized Durbin–Watson and other invariant test statistics. *Journal of Econometrics, 54*, 277–300. doi:10.1016/0304-4076(92)90109-5

Bica, I., McGovern, B., Dhar, R., Stone, D., McGowan, K., Scheib, R., & Snydman, D. R. (2001). Increasing mortality due to end-stage liver disease in patients with human immunodeficiency virus infection. *Clinical Infectious Diseases, 32,* 492–497. doi:10.1086/318501

Biglan, A., Ary, D., & Wagenaar, A. C. (2000). The value of interrupted time-series experiments for community intervention research. *Prevention Science, 1*(1), 31–49. doi:10.1023/A:1010024016308

Box, G. E. P., & Jenkins, G. M. (1976). *Time-series analysis: Forecasting and control* (Rev. ed.). San Francisco, CA: Holden Day.

Chatfield, C. (2004). *The analysis of time series* (6th ed.). Boca Raton, FL: CRC Press.

Cook, T. D., & Campbell, D. T. (1979). *Quasi-experimentation: Design and analysis issues for field studies.* Chicago, IL: Rand McNally.

Glass, G. V., Willson, V. L., & Gottman, J. M. (1975). *Design and analysis of time series experiments.* Boulder: Colorado Associate University Press.

Glenwick, D. S., & Jason, L. A. (Eds.). (1980). *Behavioral community psychology: Progress and prospects.* New York, NY: Praeger.

Glenwick, D. S., & Jason, L. A. (1993). Behavioral approaches to prevention in the community: An historical and theoretical overview. In D. S. Glenwick & L. A. Jason (Eds.), *Promoting health and mental health with children, youth, and families* (pp. 3–13). New York, NY: Springer.

Harrop, J. W., & Velicer, W. F. (1985). A comparison of alternative approaches to the analysis of interrupted time-series. *Multivariate Behavioral Research, 20*(1), 27–44. doi:10.1207/s15327906mbr2001_2

Hoeppner, B. B., Hoeppner, S. S., & Campbell, J. F. (2009). Examining trends in intake rates, client symptoms, hopelessness, and suicidality in a university counseling center over 12 years. *Journal of College Student Development, 50,* 539–550. doi:10.1353/csd.0.0090

Huitema, B. E., & McKean, J. W. (2000). Design specification issues in time-series intervention models. *Educational and Psychological Measurement, 60*(1), 38–58. doi:10.1177/00131640021970358

Lima, V. D., Harrigan, R., & Bangsberg, D. R. (2009). The combined effect of modern highly active antiretroviral therapy regimens and adherence on mortality over time. *Journal of Acquired Immune Deficiency Syndromes, 50*, 529–536. doi:10.1097/QAI.0b013e31819675e9

Lu, C. Y., Soumerai, S. B., Ross-Degnan, D., Zhang, F., & Adams, A. S. (2010). Unintended impacts of a Medicaid prior authorization policy on access to medications for bipolar illness. *Medical Care, 48*(1), 4–9. doi:10.1097/MLR.0b013e3181bd4c10

McLeroy, K. R., Bibeau, D., Steckler, A., & Glanz, K. (1988). An ecological perspective on health promotion programs. *Health Education Quarterly, 15*, 351–377.

Ong, C.-S., Huang, J.-J., & Tzeng, G.-H. (2005). Model identification of ARIMA family using genetic algorithms. *Applied Mathematics and Computation, 164*, 885–912. doi:10.1016/j.amc.2004.06.044

Pampel, F. C., & Aguilar, J. (2007). Changes in youth smoking, 1976–2002: A time-series analysis. *Youth & Society, 39*, 453–479. doi:10.1177/0044118X07308070

Pridemore, W. A., Trahan, A., & Chamlin, M. B. (2009). No evidence of suicide increase following terrorist attacks in the United States: An interrupted time series analysis of September 11 and Oklahoma City. *Suicide and Life-Threatening Behavior, 39*, 659–670. doi:10.1521/suli.2009.39.6.659

Proeschold-Bell, R. J., Blouin, R., Reif, S., Amana, A., Rowland, B., Lombard, F., . . . Muir, A. J. (2010). Hepatitis C transmission, prevention, and treatment knowledge among patients with HIV. *Southern Medical Journal, 103*, 635–641. doi:10.1097/SMJ.0b013e3181e1dde1

Schwarz, G. (1978). Estimating the dimensions of a model. *Annals of Statistics, 6*, 461–464. doi:10.1214/aos/1176344136

Shadish, W., Cook, T. D., & Campbell, D. (2002). *Experimental and quasi-experimental designs for generalized causal inference.* New York, NY: Houghton Mifflin.

Simonton, D. K. (1977). Cross-sectional time-series experiments: Some suggested statistical analyses. *Psychological Bulletin, 84*, 489–502. doi:10.1037/0033-2909.84.3.489

Velicer, W. F., & Colby, S. M. (2005). A comparison of missing-data procedures for ARIMA time series analysis. *Educational and Psychological Measurement, 65*, 596–615. doi:10.1177/0013164404272502

Velicer, W. F., & Fava, J. L. (2003). Time series analysis. In J. Schinka & W. F. Velicer (Eds.), *Research methods in psychology* (1st ed., Vol. 2, pp. 581–606). New York, NY: Wiley.

Velicer, W. F., & Harrop, J. W. (1983). The reliability and accuracy of time series model identification. *Evaluation Review, 7*, 551–560. doi:10.1177/0193841X8300700408

Velicer, W. F., & McDonald, R. P. (1984). Time series analysis without model identification. *Multivariate Behavioral Research, 19*(1), 33–47. doi:10.1207/s15327906mbr1901_2

Velicer, W. F., Redding, C. A., Richmond, R. L., Greeley, J., & Swift, W. (1992). A time series investigation of three nicotine regulation models. *Addictive Behaviors, 17*, 325–345. doi:10.1016/0306-4603(92)90039-X

Verucchi, G., Calza, L., Manfredi, R., & Chiodo, F. (2004). Human immunodeficiency virus and hepatitis C virus coinfection: Epidemiology, natural history, therapeutic options and clinical management. *Infection, 32*(1), 33–46. doi:10.1007/s15010-004-3063-7

Yaffee, R., & McGee, M. (2000). *Introduction to time series analysis and forecasting with applications of SAS and SPSS.* San Diego, CA: Academic Press.

9

SURVIVAL ANALYSIS IN PREVENTION AND INTERVENTION PROGRAMS

CHRISTIAN M. CONNELL

Community research is grounded in the use of rigorous methods to address real-world problems and social issues, and determining the effectiveness of community-based programs is a central aspect of this work as evidenced by Tolan, Keys, Chertok, and Jason (1990, p. 3). Often, the goal of such programs is to delay or reduce the occurrence of a specific negative event (e.g., initiation of substance use, recidivism of delinquent behavior) or to expedite the occurrence of a specific positive event (e.g., returning home from an out-of-home placement, obtaining employment). Three questions may guide research and evaluation related to such outcomes: What is the likelihood that a given event will occur among individuals or program participants? When is the event most likely to occur? What factors, such as intervention condition or participant characteristics, alter the likelihood or timing of the event for individuals? *Survival analysis* is a statistical method to answer these types of questions that offers significant advantage over other methods.

Survival analysis is a family of related data-analytic methods that provide a range of strategies for studying the likelihood and timing of events (Allison, 1995). Because there are a variety of distinct approaches to this method, using different types of data or emphasizing different statistical estimates, the question of "what is survival analysis?" is not a simple one to answer. A defining

147

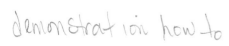
demonstration how to

feature of these various methods, however, is the focus on time until an event occurs as the primary outcome of interest (Kleinbaum & Klein, 2005). Other data-analytic approaches also may seem suited to answering questions related to the likelihood and timing of a particular event but present some limitations. Logistic regression, for example, could be used to identify factors associated with likelihood of experiencing a specified event but cannot directly address the question of timing without use of arbitrary cut points (e.g., likelihood of experiencing the event within x months). Similarly, linear regression might be used to examine factors associated with timing, treating duration to event as a continuous dependent variable, but this approach raises questions about how to treat individuals who do not experience the event during the study period (referred to as *censoring*, as is described later). Possible solutions such as discarding cases that do not experience the event or replacing missing data on time to event with a specified value (e.g., the latest possible event time) introduce potential biases regarding timing of event occurrence (Allison, 1995). Survival analysis provides an appropriate and flexible solution to these and other challenges related to the analysis of time-to-event data.

This chapter provides an overview of survival analytic methods and discusses key differences among popular survival methods (e.g., discrete time survival analysis, Kaplan–Meier methods, Cox proportional hazard methods). In addition, simulated data from a hypothetical evaluation of an intervention program to reduce recidivism rates in a juvenile justice sample are used here to demonstrate the application of these various techniques and methods. For those interested in a more detailed exploration of survival analysis methods, a number of accessible texts are available (e.g., Allison, 1995; Kleinbaum & Klein, 2005; Singer & Willett, 2003).

METHODOLOGICAL REQUIREMENTS

Three methodological requirements need to be satisfied to ensure that relevant data are being collected to conduct survival analysis: operationalization of the target event (i.e., the dependent variable for analyses), identification of a relevant time point to begin observations, and selection of an appropriate metric for measuring the duration of time until the occurrence of the event (Allison, 1995; Singer & Willett, 2003). Each is described in the sections that follow.

Defining the Target Event

Operationalization of a target event involves defining criteria that reflect the qualitative transition from one state to another that may occur

148   CHRISTIAN M. CONNELL

within a given sample or population (Allison, 1995). Target events must be clearly defined with states that are discrete and exhaustive of the range of possible statuses a person can occupy (Singer & Willett, 2003; Wright, 2000). Potential target events include outcomes such as onset or initiation of a particular risk behavior, recurrence of a behavior or condition following intervention, or exit from or termination of a particular setting or program as well as more positive events, such as obtaining employment following job training. Finally, events may be the sort an individual can experience only once (e.g., initiation of sexual activity) or may be repeatable (e.g., experiencing maltreatment). *recidivism, births, age @ first OH drink*

gender

Identifying a Starting Point

In addition to defining the target event, researchers also need to define the starting point at which they begin measuring time to event for the sample. The starting point must be a point at which all individuals in the sample are still at risk of experiencing the target event (Singer & Willett, 2003). Researchers typically use one of three methods to identify the starting point for survival analyses: (a) begin at birth, (b) begin at a precipitating event that defines entry to the study, or (c) select an arbitrary point that is not related to event occurrence. Identification of a meaningful starting point may be dictated by the nature of the target event being studied.

Birth is a relatively easy way to "start the clock" when measuring time to event. Birth is essentially the method whenever age is selected as the metric with which to measure time to event. Studies that focus on initiation of normative events or developmental milestones would likely begin measuring time from this perspective.

For many research questions, birth may not be an appropriate starting point. This is the case, for example, when studies focus on a target event that is anticipated for only a subset of the population. In such instances, the researcher first must specify the risk population and then select an appropriate means by which to define the onset of risk for that population. If a researcher was interested in studying the effects of a particular program to reduce rates of recidivism among youths in the juvenile justice system, for example, a more appropriate starting point would be after a particular precipitating event such as initial contact with police or release from a juvenile detention facility.

There may be some instances in which it is difficult to select a particular point at which to begin measuring time to event occurrence. In such instances, the researcher may elect to specify an arbitrary point at which to begin measuring time as long as that point would not be expected to relate to the risk of event occurrence. One example of this type of approach is the selection of randomization to treatment or control group within an intervention trial as the starting point for measurement. As long as assignment to condition is random, there is little chance that such an assignment would be directly related to the likelihood of event occurrence.

Selecting a Metric for Measuring Time

Finally, a researcher needs to determine how time duration will be measured and whether it will be measured in continuous units or discrete time intervals. This decision is guided by the research question's specific focus as well as by the nature of the target event and the feasibility of gathering precise information about its occurrence. Continuous measures of event duration require that the researcher know precisely when an event occurs for study participants. Such precision often requires intensive data collection and data management support to obtain reliable information from participants in survey studies or access to large administrative databases that track dates of event occurrence for studies using official records of events (e.g., recidivism data in juvenile justice samples).

If such precision is not possible or practical to implement in a particular study, discrete or interval-based methods of measuring time may be preferred. Discrete methods track event duration in larger intervals of time that do not permit a more specific estimation of event occurrence. For example, a researcher collecting student survey data may ask respondents to indicate the age at which they had their first alcoholic beverage. The metric for alcohol initiation would be in years because the methods do not provide data on more precise measures of when the event took place.

Continuous time data have a number of advantages over discrete data methods. First, discrete data are likely to result in a significant number of ties in event time (i.e., many individuals in the sample will have the same event duration), and some powerful survival methods (e.g., Cox proportional hazards modeling, Kaplan–Meier analyses) require the assumption that ties are infrequent. Another advantage of continuous time data is the flexibility they provide the researcher, in that it is relatively easy to convert continuous time to different metrics or even to discrete or interval units. Thus, one must weigh the demands of collecting continuous measures of time against the benefits resulting from such data.

CENSORED DATA

Measuring time to event is further complicated by the issue of censoring, which occurs when the duration to event occurrence is not known for a subset of participants in the study sample. Censoring is present if one cannot determine either when the risk of event occurrence begins or, more commonly, whether or when an individual experiences the target event. Thus, although censored cases cannot be used to calculate time to event occurrence, they do provide valuable information about nonoccurrence while individuals are at risk. The phenomenon of censoring, although not unique to survival analysis, is a common feature of the statistical method and may result from a number of potential causes. The two primary distinctions in censoring are whether it is left or right censored and whether the censoring mechanism is informative or noninformative (Allison, 1995; Gruber, 1999; Singer & Willett, 2003).

Left censoring occurs when some individuals within a given sample experience the event of interest prior to the observation period. One might encounter left censoring, for example, in a study of alcohol initiation among high school students because a subset of the sample is likely to have initiated use prior to high school entry. Right censoring is more commonly encountered in survival analysis and occurs when the target event is not observed for a participant at the conclusion of the study observation period. This may occur for one of three reasons: A participant may never experience the target event or experience it after the observation period for the study has ended; a participant may experience a competing event that prevents him or her from experiencing the target event; or a participant may be lost to follow-up or attrition from the study (Clark, Bradburn, & Altman, 2003; Gruber, 1999).

Survival analysis methods were developed in response to the challenges of measuring duration with right-censored cases present. Left censoring poses a greater challenge to most survival methods. Singer and Willett (2003) suggested that most left-censored cases arise from difficulties in operationalizing the beginning of time for a population, an issue that may be particularly challenging in the case of potentially repeatable events (e.g., studies of re-maltreatment, an area in which colleagues and I have used survival analytic methods; Connell, Bergeron, Katz, Saunders, & Tebes, 2007; Connell et al., 2009). In these cases, Singer and Willett suggested the study's origin be redefined, linking the beginning of the observation period to a precipitating event (e.g., an index event that occurs after the start of the observation period for a study).

The distinction between informative and noninformative censoring is whether the cause of censoring is independent of the risk of event occurrence (Allison, 1995; Singer & Willett, 2003). Noninformative censoring occurs when the particular mechanism for censoring is under the control of the researcher or directly impacted by the design of a study (e.g., censoring is the result of the end of data collection and unrelated to specific characteristics of censored participants). Conversely, informative censoring occurs when the mechanism for censoring is linked in a systematic way to the target event of interest (i.e., is under the control of the target event or the participant in some way). Study attrition, for example, could result in informative censoring if those individuals who are at the greatest risk of experiencing the target event are, as a result of the target event, also most likely to be lost to follow-up and fail to have the event observed (e.g., if substance abuse relapse is also associated with increased risk of not having follow-up data on relapse occurrence). In such cases, censoring may bias researchers' estimates of event duration. Researchers need to take careful steps to minimize the possibility of informative censoring and make realistic assessments about the assumption of noninformative censoring for a given study.

TYPES OF SURVIVAL ANALYSIS

A number of different types of survival analysis methods exist, including nonparametric, semiparametric, and fully parametric procedures as well as methods for handling different types of data (e.g., discrete vs. continuous measures of time). Nonparametric methods (e.g., life table, Kaplan–Meier methods) are most appropriate when the primary focus of analysis is on estimating time-to-event duration, although some comparisons among categorical predictor variables (referred to as *covariates*) also may be conducted through these methods (Allison, 1995; Gruber, 1999). Because these methods are nonparametric, they can tolerate a relatively small sample size (determined by the number of uncensored cases; Gruber, 1999). The key difference between these two methods is in the handling of time during the observation period. Life table methods are based on discrete time analysis and divide the observation window for a study into intervals of equivalent duration (e.g., a 2-year observation window may be subdivided into 24 monthlong intervals to track rate of event occurrence). *Kaplan–Meier analyses*, also known as the *product-limit estimator method*, structure the survival data into intervals of unequal duration by measuring the time between successive events in the sample (Kleinbaum & Klein, 2005). Thus, Kaplan–Meier methods are most appropriate for continuous time data because many ties in event duration are likely to result in interval-based measures of time. Both methods allow for simple comparisons of survival time across groups.

Semiparametric methods, such as the Cox proportional hazard model (Cox & Oakes, 1984), provide a stronger multivariate framework for integrating both continuous and categorical covariates into estimation of risk for event occurrence (Bradburn, Clark, & Altman, 2003; Kleinbaum & Klein, 2005). The primary focus for these methods is on the testing of regression models to determine the nature of the relationship between hypothesized covariates and the rate of target event occurrence (Gruber, 1999). In addition, there are *parametric survival analytic methods* (e.g., parametric Cox proportional hazard models, accelerated failure time models). These methods are beyond the scope of the current chapter but are briefly described in the advanced survival analytic methods section of the web appendix to this chapter (http://pubs.apa.org/books/supp/Jason-Glenwick) and discussed in greater detail in other sources (Bradburn, Clark, & Altman, 2003; Tabachnick & Fidell, 2007).

SUMMARY STATISTICS OF SURVIVAL ANALYSIS

The primary statistics used to describe survival data are two related functions—the survival function, $S(t)$, and the hazard function, $h(t)$. To calculate these functions, information regarding how many individuals are at risk of experiencing the event, how many individuals do experience the event, and how many individuals are censored at a given time is needed. Both functions are described in the sections that follow, with additional information on their calculation included in the web appendix.

Survival Function

The *survival function* represents the probability that an individual will survive from the time origin (i.e., time = 0) to a specified later time. Survival is generally cumulative over time, ranges from 1 to 0, and is nonincreasing. In other words, the probability of survival begins at 1 and can only decrease as individuals experience the target event over time; if everyone in the study experienced the event of interest, $S(t)$ would eventually reach 0. Cumulative survival may be plotted on a graph to depict the decline in the probability of survival over time, although it is also common to subtract the cumulative survival rate from 1 and plot it as an increasing function representing the rate of event occurrence over time.

Hazard Function

The *hazard function* represents the potential to experience the target event at a particular moment or interval of time, given survival up to that time. The hazard function is relatively simple to conceptualize in discrete time survival models (e.g., the life table method). For these models, the hazard function represents the probability that an individual will experience the target event in a specified time period given that he or she did not experience the event during a prior interval. For survival analysis using continuous time measures, hazard becomes somewhat more complicated because the likelihood of event occurrence during a given time is very low because time consists of an infinite number of instants. The hazard function for continuous time is expressed with a limit that changes as time from one instant to the next approaches 0. Thus, in continuous time, the hazard function is expressed as a rate, rather than a probability, and ranges from 0 to infinity. Unlike survival, hazard may increase or decrease over time as the likelihood of event occurrence rises or falls.

HYPOTHETICAL CASE EXAMPLE

To demonstrate the various approaches to survival analysis that have been described, I now turn to a hypothetical case example. These data were generated using the Monte Carlo function in Mplus 6.0 (Muthén & Muthén, 2010) to simulate data that might be observed in a hypothetical quasi-experimental evaluation of an intervention to reduce recidivism rates among first-time juvenile offenders; all analyses were completed using SPSS 17.0.2 (PASW Statistics, 2009). In the hypothetical study, 200 cases were assigned to either a treatment or comparison condition following an initial court disposition; participants were enrolled in the study over a 6-month period and followed until the study's conclusion at the end of a 1-year period. Thus, all participants had follow-up data for at least a 6-month period, and those who entered the study earlier in the enrollment period potentially had data for a period of up to 1 year. It is important to note that alternative designs (e.g., enrollment throughout the observation period, uniform follow-up time for all participants) are also acceptable but would differ in terms of how censoring would be defined and calculated. Additional information on data setup is provided in the web appendix.

Life Table Survival Analysis

The life table method provides a way to examine overall rates of survival and hazard over time and to compare these rates across groups. The key feature of the method is the use of an interval-based approach to measuring time. For demonstration purposes I have divided the yearlong follow-up period for the hypothetical example into 26 two-week intervals, beginning at Week 0. The results of the life table analysis are presented in Table 9.1. Details on the calculation of table columns are provided in the life table analysis section of the web appendix.

The data from the last two columns of the life table are used to generate the survival and hazard plots, respectively (see Figure 9.1). The top half

TABLE 9.1
Life Table for Juvenile Justice Recidivism Study Data (Overall Survival)

Interval start time	No. entering interval	No. withdrawing during interval	No. exposed to risk	No. of terminal events	Proportion terminating	Proportion surviving	Cumulative proportion surviving	Hazard rate
0	N = 200	0	200.0	23	0.115	0.885	0.885	0.061
2	177	0	177.0	25	0.141	0.859	0.760	0.076
4	152	0	152.0	17	0.112	0.888	0.675	0.059
6	135	0	135.0	16	0.119	0.881	0.595	0.063
8	119	0	119.0	7	0.059	0.941	0.560	0.030
10	112	0	112.0	8	0.071	0.929	0.520	0.037
12	104	0	104.0	8	0.077	0.923	0.480	0.040
14	96	0	96.0	5	0.052	0.948	0.455	0.027
16	91	0	91.0	5	0.055	0.945	0.430	0.028
18	86	0	86.0	2	0.023	0.977	0.420	0.012
20	84	0	84.0	4	0.048	0.952	0.400	0.024
22	80	0	80.0	4	0.050	0.950	0.380	0.026
24	76	0	76.0	3	0.039	0.961	0.365	0.020
26	73	1	72.5	1	0.014	0.986	0.360	0.007
28	71	5	68.5	3	0.044	0.956	0.344	0.022
30	63	8	59.0	1	0.017	0.983	0.338	0.009
32	54	8	50.0	2	0.040	0.960	0.325	0.020
34	44	4	42.0	2	0.048	0.952	0.309	0.024
36	38	6	35.0	1	0.029	0.971	0.301	0.014
38	31	5	28.5	2	0.070	0.930	0.279	0.036
40	24	4	22.0	1	0.045	0.955	0.267	0.023
42	19	4	17.0	1	0.059	0.941	0.251	0.030
44	14	3	12.5	0	0.000	1.000	0.251	0.000
46	11	5	8.5	0	0.000	1.000	0.251	0.000
48	6	1	5.5	0	0.000	1.000	0.251	0.000
50	5	5	2.5	0	0.000	1.000	0.251	0.000

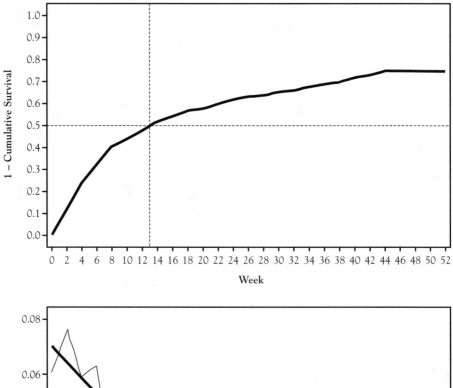

Figure 9.1. Life table estimates of survival (1 − cumulative survival) and hazard functions.

of the figure represents one minus the cumulative survival rate and provides an indication of the cumulative rate of event occurrence over the 52-week study. The steepness of the curve corresponds to the hazard rate, which is depicted in the bottom half of the figure. That is, as risk of event occurrence increases, the survival curve rises more steeply, and as risk declines, the survival curve begins to level off. The primary focus of this example is to estimate the median survival time until recidivism occurs; median survival time occurs at the point at which the curve crosses the survival rate of 0.5—approximately 13 weeks in this hypothetical example. The hazard plot depicts the hazard rates for each interval of the study. Because hazard plots tend to be somewhat erratic, particularly as interval lengths decrease, it is sometimes useful to add a smoothed curve to the hazard plot to capture the overall trajectory of the hazard function over time (Clark et al., 2003; Luke & Homan, 1998); in this case a Lowess curve was fit to the estimated hazard data. Inspection of the hazard plot further confirms that risk of recidivism is highest immediately following the index court disposition and declines over time, a common pattern in studies of this nature.

The life table method also provides a method of making simple comparisons in survival rates across groups, referred to as *factors* in statistical analysis programs such as SPSS. When a factor such as treatment condition is compared using the life table method, separate tables are calculated for each condition, and the median survival time for each group is compared using a Wilcoxon statistic. Because time was measured continuously in the present example, however, these comparisons are made using the Kaplan–Meier method, which provides additional statistics with which to make these comparisons, as demonstrated in the next part of this case example.

Kaplan–Meier Survival Analysis

The Kaplan–Meier method also produces a life table, but the intervals in the table are based on the time between successive event occurrences rather than a uniform discrete interval (Allison, 1995; Kleinbaum & Klein, 2005). Excerpts of the life table for the case example are presented in Table 9.2. As with discrete time survival models, separate tables are created for each level of the factor. Because each individual in a given condition is used to generate a time interval, the life table includes as many rows as participants for each condition. The cumulative proportion of individuals surviving in each group is estimated, along with a standard error at the end of each interval involving an event occurrence. In cases in which ties occur, survival is calculated at the end of the period. As with other survival methods, Kaplan–Meier analyses may be used to generate survival and hazard plots.

TABLE 9.2
Portion of Survival Table Results From Kaplan–Meier Analysis of Treatment
Comparisons for Juvenile Justice Recidivism Study Data

| | | | | Cumulative proportion surviving at the time | | No. of cumulative events | No. of remaining cases |
	Tx	Time	Status	Estimate	SE		
0	1	1	1	—.	—.	1	94
	2	1	1	.979	.015	2	93
	3	2	1	.	.	3	92
	4	2	1	.958	.021	4	91
	87	276	0	.	.	73	8
	88	299	1	.183	.047	74	7
	89	303	0	.	.	74	6
	93	330	0	.	.	74	2
	94	347	0	.	.	74	1
	95	359	0	.	.	74	0
1	1	1	1	.990	.009	1	104
	2	3	1	.981	.013	2	103
	3	4	1	.971	.016	3	102
	4	5	1	.962	.019	4	101
	90	281	0	.	.	66	15
	91	287	1	.322	.052	67	14
	92	287	0	.	.	67	13
	103	357	0	.	.	67	2
	104	361	0	.	.	67	1
	105	362	0	.	.	67	0

Note. For treatment condition (Tx), 0 = comparison and 1 = intervention. Dashes represent breaks in the full table. SPSS only calculates the estimate for the last incident when ties occur for time to outcome; the output includes a "." for the other rows.

A primary interest in using the Kaplan–Meier method with this hypothetical case example is to compare survival times across the treatment and comparison conditions. The results of these comparisons are presented in Table 9.3 and Table 9.4. Median survival time is the preferred estimate of event duration because survival time data are frequently skewed, which may bias the mean estimate (Allison, 1995). Survival times may be compared across groups using the log-rank or Mantel–Cox statistic (Cox, 1972; Mantel, 1966). The log-rank test compares expected versus observed event occurrence results over failure times across the entire survival function and is evaluated against a chi-square distribution (Kleinbaum & Klein, 2005; Wright, 2000). Statistical packages also provide alternative tests of median survival comparisons, including the Breslow, or generalized Wilcoxon,

TABLE 9.3
Kaplan–Meier Estimates of Survival Times by Treatment Condition for Juvenile Justice Recidivism Study Data

Tx	M Estimate	SE	Lower bound	Upper bound	Mdn Estimate	SE	Lower bound	Upper bound
			95% CI				95% CI	
0	127.738	13.621	101.041	154.436	76.0	17.720	41.268	110.732
1	178.161	14.287	150.158	206.163	137.0	39.123	60.319	213.681
Overall	154.293	10.089	134.518	174.067	90.0	13.081	64.360	115.640

Note. For treatment condition (Tx), 0 = comparison and 1 = intervention. CI = confidence interval.

statistic (Breslow, 1970) and the Tarone–Ware statistic (Tarone & Ware, 1977). These tests differ in the extent to which they weight events that occur earlier or later in a study observational period and are discussed in greater detail elsewhere (Kleinbaum & Klein, 2005; Wright, 2000). Here, all three tests indicate a statistically significant difference between the survival times for the treatment and comparison groups, suggesting that participation in the intervention condition does reduce overall rates of recidivism among the hypothetical study sample. The median time to recidivism for those in the treatment condition is 137 days compared with only 76 days in the comparison group—a 2-month difference.

Nonparametric survival analyses, such as the life table and Kaplan– Meier methods, provide a useful framework for estimating survival functions and making simple comparisons across categorical predictors. These methods also have been extended to incorporate more complex predictors (e.g., continuous covariates, time-varying predictors) but require additional data preparation to set up a discrete-time survival model using a person–period data structure in which individuals in the study sample have multiple lines of data representing each time period in which they were in the risk set for the study (Keiley & Martin, 2005; Singer & Willett, 2003). The Cox proportional

TABLE 9.4
Comparison of Survival Time Estimates by Treatment Condition Outcomes for Kaplan–Meier Analysis

Statistical test	χ^2	df	p
Log-rank (Mantel–Cox)	6.493	1	.011
Breslow (generalized Wilcoxon)	6.933	1	.008
Tarone–Ware	6.860	1	.009

hazard model, or Cox regression model, is the preferred method for incorporating continuous predictors and testing full multivariate models of survival data (Allison, 1995), as demonstrated in the final set of analyses in the hypothetical case example.

Cox Proportional Hazard Survival Analysis

In contrast to nonparametric methods that emphasize comparison of survival time across conditions, Cox proportional hazard modeling emphasizes the effect of specified covariates on the hazard function using a regression framework (Bradburn, Clark, & Altman, 2003). Covariates may be either categorical or continuous, and the resulting beta coefficients are exponentiated to produce a hazard ratio that is interpreted in a similar manner to an odds ratio in a logistic regression model. A hazard ratio that is significantly greater than 1 indicates increasing hazard as the value of the covariate increases, resulting in decreased likelihood of survival (i.e., survival duration will be shorter). Conversely, a hazard ratio that is significantly less than 1 (i.e., between 0 and 1) indicates decreasing hazard as the value of the covariate decreases (i.e., survival duration will be longer) for a given value. A hazard ratio of 1 indicates no difference in hazard between values of the covariate.

An important assumption of the Cox model is that hazard ratios are proportional over time (i.e., that the value of the hazard ratio is constant over time). A number of methods for testing this assumption have been described in the statistical literature, including examination of cumulative hazard function plots and various statistical tests (Allison, 1995; Bradburn, Clark, Love, & Altman, 2003; Kleinbaum & Klein, 2005). Additional detail on methods for testing this assumption and addressing potential violations are provided in the web appendix to this chapter in the Cox Proportional Hazard Survival Analysis section.

For the hypothetical example, gender and total risk scores are entered in the first block, followed by treatment condition (the primary focus of the model) in the second block. Cox regression models use a partial likelihood estimation method and produce a log-likelihood statistic that can be compared across nested models (e.g., blocks within a hierarchical regression model) by comparing the difference between $-2*$log-likelihood values on a chi-square distribution (Singer & Willett, 2003). Omnibus tests of model fit are presented in Table 9.5; one can see that Model 1 (covariates) significantly improves model fit over a model with no covariates and that the addition of treatment condition in Model 2 further improves model fit.

Hazard ratios for the Cox regression models are presented in Table 9.6. Individual betas and standard errors are estimated for model covariates and tested for statistical significance against a Wald statistic. The estimated betas

TABLE 9.5

Chi-Square Results From Cox Proportional Hazard Models of Recidivism Intervention Study

Model	−2 Log likelihood	Overall score			Change from previous model		
		X^2	df	p	X^2	df	p
1	1305.921	40.698	2	.000	40.220	2	.000
2	1290.362	56.214	3	.000	15.558	1	.000

Note. Model 1 = covariates only; Model 2 = covariates and treatment condition.

are also exponentiated to obtain the hazard ratio associated with the covariate. For categorical covariates the ratio is interpreted relative to a selected reference category (e.g., the effect of being male on hazard relative to the effect of being female); for continuous covariates the ratio is interpreted as the effect on hazard associated with a one-unit change in the value of the covariate. On the basis of the results of Model 2, the model that includes gender and total risk covariates as well as the treatment effect of central interest, one can see that each has a significant effect on hazard for recidivism. Males are more than twice as likely to recidivate as females after adjusting for risk score and treatment effects, and higher scores on the total risk score are similarly associated with increased likelihood of recidivism. One can also see a significant preventive effect on recidivism associated with the hypothetical treatment condition; specifically, over time, youths enrolled in the treatment condition are approximately half as likely to recidivate as youths enrolled in the comparison condition after controlling for the effects of gender and total risk score. As with other survival methods, a range of plots can be created to graphically depict comparison results (see Figure 9.2).

TABLE 9.6

Hazard Ratios from Cox Proportional Hazard Models of Recidivism Intervention Study

Model	Covariate	B	SE	Wald	df	p	Exponentiated (B)
1	Gender (male)	0.48	0.20	5.91	1	.02	1.62
	Risk	0.54	0.09	33.81	1	.00	1.72
2	Gender (male)	0.74	0.21	12.62	1	.00	2.09
	Risk	0.57	0.09	39.21	1	.00	1.76
	Treatment	−0.71	0.18	15.71	1	.00	0.49

Note. Model 1 = covariates only; Model 2 = covariates and treatment condition.

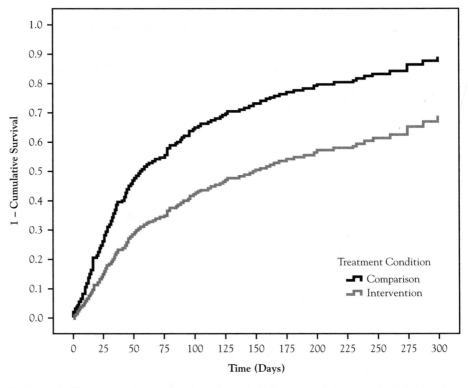

Figure 9.2. Cox regression estimates of survival (1 − cumulative survival) for treatment condition controlling for effects of gender and total risk score.

CONCLUSION

In this chapter, I have highlighted the range of methodological options of survival analysis, including applications for discrete or continuous measures of time as well as applications that reflect nonparametric, semiparametric, and parametric methods. Survival analysis can be an important tool for researchers and program evaluators interested in examining event occurrence in the context of prevention and intervention programs or services. The various survival methods offer a flexible method for assessing the likelihood that individuals will experience a given target event, determining when that likelihood is greatest, and evaluating the effects of predictors or covariates on the likelihood or timing of event occurrence. Although other analytic methods are available to assess these types of outcomes (e.g., logistic regression of event occurrence, linear regression of time to event), survival analytic methods were specifically developed to address the issue of censoring, which occurs when time to event occurrence is not known for some individuals in a given study.

As demonstrated in the hypothetical case example, survival analysis encompasses a number of different methods and techniques. Additional applications and advanced features of the survival model are described in the web appendix to this chapter. Each presents a certain set of assumptions and data requirements, incorporates a different set of statistical tests, and emphasizes different aspects of the analytic outcomes (e.g., median duration, survival rate, or hazard ratios). Given the flexibility of the analytic method, it is incumbent on the researcher to ensure that proper methods are being used to answer the specific research questions being investigated and that key assumptions and requirements are being addressed appropriately.

Survival analysis generally has been underused in the social sciences relative to other disciplines (e.g., medical and public health research), but the approach represents an important statistical tool for researchers and evaluators interested in studying program outcomes. The primary focus on occurrence and timing of events and on the relationship of covariates and predictors to these outcomes fits well within the context of other longitudinal methods for studying program effects or risk and protective processes associated with the occurrence of both normative and nonnormative outcomes for individuals. Furthermore, the graphical depiction of survival and hazard estimates and the use of hazard ratios to interpret effects of covariates can make intuitive sense to both researchers as well as the lay community. It is hoped that this chapter can provide a foundation for greater use of these methods in longitudinal research and program evaluation contexts.

REFERENCES

Allison, P. D. (1995). *Survival analysis using the SAS System: A practical guide.* Cary, NC: SAS Institute.

Bradburn, M. J., Clark, T. G., & Altman, D. G. (2003). Survival analysis Part II: Multivariate data analysis—An introduction to concepts and methods. *British Journal of Cancer, 89,* 431–436. doi:10.1038/sj.bjc.6601119

Bradburn, M. J., Clark, T. G., Love, S. B., & Altman, D. G. (2003). Survival analysis Part III: Multivariate data analysis—Choosing a model and assessing its adequacy and fit. *British Journal of Cancer, 89,* 605–611. doi:10.1038/sj.bjc.6601120

Breslow, N. (1970). A generalized Kruskal–Wallis test for comparing K samples subject to unequal patterns of censorship. *Biometrika, 57,* 579–594. doi:10.1093/biomet/57.3.579

Clark, T. G., Bradburn, M. J., & Altman, D. G. (2003). Survival analysis Part I: Basic concepts and first analyses. *British Journal of Cancer, 89,* 232–238. doi:10.1038/sj.bjc.6601118

Connell, C. M., Bergeron, N., Katz, K. H., Saunders, L., & Tebes, J. K. (2007). Re-referral to child protective services: The influence of child, family, and case characteristics on risk status. *Child Abuse & Neglect, 31,* 573–588. doi:10.1016/j.chiabu.2006.12.004

Connell, C. M., Vanderploeg, J. J., Katz, K. H., Caron, C., Saunders, L., & Tebes, J. K. (2009). Maltreatment following reunification: Predictors of subsequent child protective services contact after children return home. *Child Abuse & Neglect, 33,* 218–228. doi:10.1016/j.chiabu.2008.07.005

Cox, D. R. (1972). Regression models and life tables (with discussion). *Journal of the Royal Statistical Society. Series B (Methodological), 34,* 187–220.

Cox, D. R., & Oakes, D. (1984). *Analysis of survival data.* London, England: Chapman & Hall.

Gruber, F. A. (1999). Tutorial: Survival analysis—A statistic for clinical, efficacy, and theoretical applications. *Journal of Speech, Language, and Hearing Research, 42,* 432–447.

Keiley, M. K., & Martin, N. C. (2005). Survival analysis in family research. *Journal of Family Psychology, 19,* 142–156. doi:10.1037/0893-3200.19.1.142

Kleinbaum, D. G., & Klein, M. (2005). *Survival analysis: A self-learning text* (2nd ed.). New York, NY: Springer.

Luke, D. A., & Homan, S. M. (1998). Time and change: Using survival analysis in clinical assessment and treatment evaluation. *Psychological Assessment, 10,* 360–378. doi:10.1037/1040-3590.10.4.360

Mantel, N. (1966). Evaluation of survival data and two new rank order statistics arising in its consideration. *Cancer Chemotherapy Reports. Part 1, 50,* 163–170.

Muthén, L. K., & Muthén, B. O. (2010). *Mplus user's guide* (6th ed.). Los Angeles, CA: Muthén & Muthén.

PASW Statistics. (2009). *SPSS for Windows* (Rel. 17.0.2). Chicago, IL: SPSS.

Singer, J. D., & Willett, J. B. (2003). *Applied longitudinal data analysis: Modeling change and event occurrence.* New York, NY: Oxford University Press.

Tabachnick, B. G., & Fidell, L. S. (2007). *Using multivariate statistics* (5th ed.). Boston, MA: Pearson Education.

Tarone, R. E., & Ware, J. (1977). On distribution-free tests for equality of survival distributions. *Biometrika, 64,* 156–160. doi:10.1093/biomet/64.1.156

Tolan, P., Keys, C., Chertok, F., & Jason, L. (Eds.). (1990). *Researching community psychology.* Washington, DC: American Psychological Association. doi:10.1037/10073-000

Wright, R. E. (2000). Survival analysis. In L. G. Grimm & P. R. Yarnold (Eds.), *Reading and understanding more multivariate statistics* (pp. 363–407). Washington, DC: American Psychological Association.

IV

METHODS INVOLVING CONTEXTUAL FACTORS

10

MULTILEVEL MODELING: METHOD AND APPLICATION FOR COMMUNITY-BASED RESEARCH

NATHAN R. TODD, NICOLE E. ALLEN, AND SHABNAM JAVDANI

The desire to understand the interplay between settings and individual behavior and attitudes is central to community-based research (e.g., Bronfenbrenner, 1979). *Multilevel modeling* (MLM, also known as *hierarchical linear modeling*) is a regression-based method that simultaneously examines how characteristics of the individual and the setting may predict individual attitudes and behavior (e.g., Snijders & Bosker, 1999). Community researchers have recognized the potential of this method to capture context and to investigate multiple levels of analysis beyond the individual (Luke, 2005; Shinn & Rapkin, 2000). For example, MLM allows the researcher to understand how characteristics of both an individual (e.g., individual socioeconomic status [SES]) and a group (e.g., the average SES of a school classroom) may predict an individual-level outcome (e.g., academic success). In community-based research, MLM has been used to examine the effects of neighborhoods (e.g., Garner & Raudenbush, 1991), schools (e.g., Khoury-Kassabri, Benbenishty, Astor, & Zeira, 2004), religious organizations (e.g., Schwadel, 2002), and collaborative efforts (e.g., Allen, 2005) on individual attitudes and behavior. Thus, MLM can be used to examine community-level phenomena.

167

In addition to its capacity to expose the effects of setting-level characteristics (e.g., a supportive school climate), MLM has other important features attractive to community researchers, such as assessing longitudinal
change. Given that many community researchers are interested in examining change or in testing the effectiveness of community-based interventions
over time, MLM is an attractive methodology. It has been used to examine
the impact of systems change efforts over time (e.g., Javdani, Allen, Todd,
& Anderson, 2011) and to delineate specific intervention outcomes that
emerge over time, such as in the work of Olson, Jason, Davidson, and Ferrari
(2009). Furthermore, MLM can be used to examine outcomes that are not
measured on a continuous scale, such as binary (e.g., present/absent) or other
logistic outcomes such as proportions and rates (Javdani et al., 2011). Thus,
MLM has great potential to address questions of interest to community
researchers by examining individual and setting effects, change over time,
and logistic outcomes.

In this chapter, we blend a conceptual and practical treatment of MLM
to equip the reader with the basic information and skills necessary to use
MLM. Building on the work of Shinn and Rapkin (2000) and Luke (2005),
we focus on when and how to use MLM to understand individual- and setting-
level effects for continuous outcomes (for longitudinal applications of MLM,
see Singer & Willett, 2003). The first section provides the foundational concepts of MLM, and the second presents an applied example of MLM. The web
appendix to this chapter (http://pubs.apa.org/books/supp/Jason-Glenwick)
includes extensions of MLM to logistic outcomes and further instructions on
using SAS to conduct MLM.

describe

CONCEPTUAL FOUNDATIONS OF MULTILEVEL MODELING

This section provides a user-friendly introduction to the foundational
concepts and issues that are needed to understand and use MLM. As with
any method, MLM has unique terminology and concepts that may seem
abstract and confusing. The goal of this section is to explain these concepts,
relating MLM to other statistical procedures that may be more familiar, such
as multiple regression. In addition, these concepts are illustrated with examples and a few definitional equations. In statistics, equations are the most
concise way to represent a concept, communicating the exact workings of a
method. However, equations may be opaque, and thus concrete examples
and explanations are also given throughout to explain these concepts.
Finally, as with any method, there are unresolved issues in the MLM literature; these issues are briefly raised but should be investigated more fully by
those using MLM.

Excellent chapter

Nested Data

Nested data occur when smaller units are contained in a larger unit. Just as young birds (smaller unit) share the same nest (the larger unit) as their siblings, there are many instances in which data have a nested structure. For example, individuals (smaller unit) can be nested in a setting (larger unit). This type of nesting can be illustrated by students nested in classrooms, religious participants nested in religious organizations, or prisoners nested in prisons. The main idea is that individuals share a common nest and that there are many nests. However, the concept of nesting is more general than individuals nested in settings, and *units* can be defined in flexible ways. Community researchers are often interested in nested types of data structures in which individuals (or other units) are nested in settings. Nested data provide a statistical challenge because individuals in the same group (e.g., students in the same classroom) may be more similar to one another than to members of another group (e.g., to students in different classrooms).

For example, if a classroom has a misbehaving student who continually disrupts the learning environment, it is possible that students in that classroom will have lower achievement scores than students from other classrooms where there is no systematic disruption. This similarity is called *dependence*, in that knowing something about the group to which someone belongs (e.g., classroom membership) provides information about the individual (e.g., achievement scores). Ordinary least squares linear regression is not appropriate to use with nested data because of this dependence. Specifically, dependence produces correlated error terms, thereby violating an important assumption of ordinary regression (i.e., that error is random, not systematic). However, MLM is able to include this dependence in the statistical model, provides accurate parameter estimates, and has emerged as an effective method for use with nested data.

Levels, Centering, and Aggregation

A nested data structure in which there are multiple individuals nested in a setting (e.g., employees in a law firm) along with multiple settings (multiple law firms) provides the type of data used in MLM. To be clear about this structure, MLM uses the language of *levels* to describe the smaller (e.g., lawyers) and larger (e.g., law firms) measurement units. Namely, Level I refers to something that is measured about the smaller unit (e.g., individual self-efficacy or individual productivity), and Level II refers to something measured about the larger unit (e.g., relational climate of the law firm, average productivity of the firm). How Level I and Level II variables are formed remains a central issue in MLM. When Level I is the individual, Level I *centering* ✱

variables are about the individual, such as gender, race, personal productivity, or personal attitudes. Level I variables can be formed by what is referred to as *centering*.

Similar to centering variables in ordinary least squares regression, centering in MLM refers to how individual observations are centered around the mean of their group (i.e., group-mean centering: $[X_{ij} - \overline{X}_{.j}]$) or around the mean of all the observations (i.e., grand-mean centering: $[X_{ij} - \overline{X}_{..}]$). In this notation, X_{ij} is the score on an independent variable for the *i*th individual (i.e., a particular individual) in the *j*th group (i.e., a particular group). $\overline{X}_{.j}$ is the mean, or average, of X for group *j*, whereas $\overline{X}_{..}$ is the mean for all participants across all groups. For example, if a lawyer's score on a Level I variable such as personal productivity (X_{ij}) is subtracted from the average productivity in their law firm ($\overline{X}_{.j}$) and this is done for all individuals from all the law firms in the sample, this is group-mean centering. Thus, an individual lawyer's score is relative to the mean of his or her firm (i.e., he or she may have higher productivity relative to the average of his or her firm).

If instead, a lawyer's score on personal productivity is subtracted from the mean of all individuals in the sample ($\overline{X}_{..}$), this is grand-mean centering. Thus, an individual lawyer's score is relative to the sample as a whole across all individuals in all firms. Both group- and grand-mean centered variables are Level I variables. There are additional considerations for centering time in longitudinal applications of MLM (Singer & Willett, 2003) and for centering dummy-coded variables (Raudenbush & Bryk, 2002). What is important in all these cases is to understand how centering influences the interpretation of the variables. Such consequences of group- and grand-mean centering are discussed later.

Level II variables can be formed in multiple ways. One helpful distinction is to consider if the Level II variable is formed by aggregating (i.e., combining) information from individuals in a group or is instead formed without using any individual-level information. The first type of Level II variable, called an *aggregated variable*, is usually formed by taking the mean, or average, of all individuals in a group, represented as $\overline{X}_{.j}$. For example, the average productivity of a law firm may be used as a Level II aggregated variable to represent law firm productivity. In short, aggregated variables use information from individuals within a group to characterize the group. In contrast, extra individual Level II variables can be formed without using information from individuals (Shinn & Rapkin, 2000). For example, such variables as square footage, the quality of technology, organizational policies, or the amount of green space surrounding a firm are all Level II variables that do not depend on individual-level characteristics but can be directly assessed at the setting level.

How to Know When to Use Multilevel Modeling

The decision to use MLM rests on a number of factors. To illustrate, consider individuals (Level I) nested in an organization (Level II). First, if there is a nested data structure, it is likely that there is dependence in the data that needs to be modeled using MLM. Second, MLM is necessary to use when there is unexplained variance in the dependent variable at both the individual (Level I) and group (Level II) levels. Remember that variance is the standard deviation squared and captures the degree of deviation or spread around a mean. For example, if the dependent variable is productivity, the unexplained variance is simply the variance around the mean of productivity within each group. This is an example of Level I unexplained variance. However, MLM is also concerned with unexplained variance in the dependent variable at Level II.

To illustrate, consider 30 law firms. Each law firm has a score for average productivity. Plotting each of these 30 scores in a histogram would create a distribution of group means, and this distribution of group means would itself have a mean and variance. This variance around the group means is the unexplained variance in the dependent variable at Level II. The more similar the law firms are to one another on average productivity, the smaller the Level II unexplained variance. The greater the difference in average productivity between law firms, the larger the Level II variance. MLM is thus used when groups (e.g., law firms) are sampled from a population of groups (e.g., all law firms in Chicago) and when it is expected that the groups have different means on the dependent variable. Importantly, one can then pose substantive questions to explain variance at both the individual and setting levels, as discussed below.

To summarize, MLM should be used when people within groups are more similar to one another than to people in other groups. This implies that groups themselves will be different on the dependent variable and that unexplained variance will be both at Level I and Level II. Concretely, the intraclass correlation (ICC, ρ_I) is a statistic that provides an index of the variability in the dependent variable that can be explained at the group level (Snijders & Bosker, 1999). Another interpretation is that the ICC indexes how similar people are within their group and the degree of difference between groups. The ICC is computed by taking the Level I (i.e., σ^2) and Level II (i.e., τ^2) components of variance to form a ratio of Level II unexplained variance to the total unexplained variance $\rho_I = \dfrac{\tau^2}{\tau^2 + \sigma^2}$.

Therefore, the ICC is an index of how much of the unexplained variance is due to group membership. The larger the ICC, the greater the justification for using MLM. If there are no differences between the groups on the

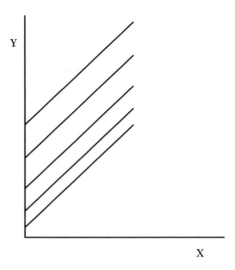

Figure 10.1. Random intercept model. Example of association between independent (*X*) and dependent (*Y*) variables, with each line representing the association within five different groups.

dependent variable, then there is no Level II variance and the ICC would be zero and regular regression could be used. There is no agreed-on value for how large the ICC needs to be to use MLM; however, even if there is only a small amount of group-level variance (i.e., $\rho_I \geq .05$), it may be justifiable to use MLM. If mean productivity was the same across firms, the ICC would be zero. However, if mean productivity across firms was different (i.e., some firms were more productive on average than others) the ICC would be larger.

In addition to the ICC, descriptive plots are helpful in examining if groups are different on the dependent variable. As shown in Figure 10.1, the mean on the dependent variable for each group is the place where the regression line for each group crosses the y-axis. This is called the *intercept* for each group. Moreover, the larger the difference in the group intercepts, the larger the ICC will be. Considering the ICC in concert with the descriptive plots helps to determine if MLM is appropriate to use.

Hypotheses Tested by Multilevel Modeling

The language of levels can then be extended to formulate hypotheses at the individual and group levels. For example, at the individual level it may be hypothesized that within each group the independent variable of individual self-efficacy has a positive association with the dependent variable of individual productivity. These are within-group hypotheses. In contrast, at the group level it could be hypothesized that the independent variable of relational climate has a positive association with the dependent variable of average productivity in a law firm such that more positive relational climates are associated with greater average productivity. These are between-groups hypotheses. MLM allows for the concurrent examination of within- and between-groups associations. Schwadel (2002) provided a good example from research with individuals nested in religious congregations. He used personal income (i.e., Level I) and average congregational income (i.e., Level II aggregated variable) to predict personal involvement in church finance committees. He found a positive within-group association at Level I, indicating that greater personal income predicted greater personal involvement in financial congregational committees. In contrast, he found a negative between-groups association at Level II, with greater average congregational income predicting lower average participation in financial committees. This suggests that people with more income participate more frequently in financial roles (Level I), however, the more affluent the congregation, the lower the average involvement in finance committees (Level II). This difference between effects at different levels highlights the *ecological fallacy*, which occurs when associations at one level (e.g., individual) are incorrectly assumed to be the same at other levels of analysis (e.g., group). MLM provides the conceptual and methodological tools to simultaneously examine how phenomena may operate differently at different levels of analysis, a longstanding interest in community research.

In addition to within-group and between-groups hypotheses, it is possible to examine how a group-level variable (i.e., Level II) will predict something about the individual (i.e., Level I). These are called *contextual hypotheses* regarding how the setting influences the individual. For example, an independent variable of relational climate (i.e., Level II) may predict individual productivity (i.e., Level I). Finally, Level I and Level II units may also statistically interact. These cross-level interactions refer to how settings may moderate individual-level associations. Such cross-level hypotheses examine how associations may be different in different settings. For example, in high-disorder neighborhoods, the Level I association between relationship quality and personal distress was negative, whereas in low-disorder neighborhoods, there was no Level I association (Cutrona, Russell, Hessling, Brown, & Murry, 2000). Thus, neighborhood disorder is the Level II moderator such that the Level I link between relationship quality and personal distress depends on or interacts with a feature of the setting. In sum, MLM enables a community researcher to examine within-group, between-groups, contextual, and cross-level hypotheses.

The Multilevel Model

MLM is based on a relatively straightforward model that can be generalized to address within-group, between-groups, contextual, and cross-level hypotheses. Exhibit 10.1 presents the foundational multilevel model. Familiarity with this model and with the meaning of each component of the model is crucial for understanding and interpreting MLM results. In this section, we explain each of these components and describe how MLM works. For illustration, consider students (Level I) nested in schools (Level II) in which the researcher is interested in how the independent variables of student IQ and average student IQ in each school may predict the dependent variable of student academic achievement.

First, MLM defines a *hierarchical model* in which the independent variables are separated into Level I student (student IQ) and Level II school (average student IQ of each school) effects, separating Levels I and II to reflect the hierarchical structure of the data with students nested in schools (see Exhibit 10.1, Model a). In MLM, the dependent variable (e.g., individual academic achievement), Y_{ij}, is measured at Level I. The Level I model is analogous to a standard multiple regression equation, where X_{ij} is the independent variable (student IQ) that predicts the dependent variable Y_{ij}. The intercept term β_{0j} is called the *group-dependent intercept*. This intercept term indicates that schools may have different averages on the dependent variable (e.g., schools have different average academic achievement). The Level II model is a regression equation predicting the school average on the dependent variable (e.g., average academic achievement, β_{0j}) from other school-level variables (e.g., average school IQ, ($\bar{X}_{.j}$). Thus, what would typically be the intercept in a standard regression model is also modeled.

Importantly, the hierarchical model works to separate the unexplained variance at Level I (R_{ij}) and at Level II (U_{0j}), thus accounting for the nested structure of the data. Inclusion of the U_{0j} in the Level II model denotes a random intercept, which means that groups have different averages on the dependent variable. The hierarchical model is very helpful in organizing the variables according to their levels. The next step is to create one model, called the *linear mixed model*, that contains both Level I and Level II predictors. A linear mixed model is formed by combining the Level I and Level II hierarchical models through algebraic substitution. For example, in Exhibit 10.1, Model a, $\gamma_{00} + \gamma_{01}(\bar{X}_{.j}) + U_{0j}$, is substituted for β_{0j} (the intercept) and γ_{10} is substituted for β_{1j} (a given slope), resulting in a linear mixed model that contains both individual-level (γ_{10}) and group-level (γ_{01}) effects. With both Level I and Level II effects included in one model, they can be estimated simultaneously. This is the logic of MLM.

EXHIBIT 10.1
Summary of Multilevel Models

(a) Foundational Multilevel Model

Hierarchical Model:

Level I: Individual Level:
$$Y_{ij} = \beta_{0j} + \beta_{1j}(X_{ij}) + R_{ij}$$
Level II: Group Level:
$$\beta_{0j} = \gamma_{00} + \gamma_{01}(\bar{X}_{.j}) + U_{0j}$$
$$\beta_{1j} = \gamma_{10}$$

Linear Mixed Model:
$$Y_{ij} = \gamma_{00} + \gamma_{10}(X_{ij}) + \gamma_{01}(\bar{X}_{.j}) + U_{0j} + R_{ij}$$

(b) Group-Mean Centered Model

Hierarchical Model:

Level I: Individual Level:
$$Y_{ij} = \beta_{0j} + \beta_{1j}(X_{ij} - \bar{X}_{.j}) + R_{ij}$$
Level II: Group Level:
$$\beta_{0j} = \gamma_{00} + \gamma_{01}(\bar{X}_{.j}) + U_{0j}$$
$$\beta_{1j} = \gamma_{10}$$

Linear Mixed Model:
$$Y_{ij} = \gamma_{00} + \gamma_{10}(X_{ij} - \bar{X}_{.j}) + \gamma_{01}(\bar{X}_{.j}) + U_{0j} + R_{ij}$$
Where:
$$\gamma_{10} = \beta_w$$
$$\gamma_{01} = \beta_b$$
$$\beta_c = \gamma_{01} - \gamma_{10}$$

(c) Cross-Level Interaction Model

Hierarchical Model:

Level I: Individual Level:
$$Y_{ij} = \beta_{0j} + \beta_{1j}(X_{ij}) + R_{ij}$$
Level II: Group Level:
$$\beta_{0j} = \gamma_{00} + \gamma_{01}(\bar{Z}_{.j}) + U_{0j}$$
$$\beta_{1j} = \gamma_{10} + \gamma_{11}(\bar{Z}_{.j}) + U_{1j}$$

Linear Mixed Model:
$$Y_{ij} = \gamma_{00} + \gamma_{10}(X_{ij}) + \gamma_{01}(\bar{Z}_{.j}) + \gamma_{11}(X_{ij})(\bar{Z}_{.j}) + U_{0j} + U_{1j}(X_{ij}) + R_{ij}$$

(d) Grand-Mean Centered Model

Hierarchical Model:

Level I: Individual Level:
$$Y_{ij} = \beta_{0j} + \beta_{1j}(X_{ij} - \bar{X}_{..}) + R_{ij}$$
Level II: Group Level:
$$\beta_{0j} = \gamma_{00} + \gamma_{01}(\bar{X}_{.j}) + U_{0j}$$
$$\beta_{1j} = \gamma_{10}$$

Linear Mixed Model:
$$Y_{ij} = \gamma_{00} + \gamma_{10}(X_{ij} - \bar{X}_{..}) + \gamma_{01}(\bar{X}_{.j}) + U_{0j} + R_{ij}$$
Where:
$$\gamma_{10} = \beta_w$$
$$\gamma_{01} = \beta_c$$
$$\beta_b = \gamma_{01} + \gamma_{10}$$

Note. Within-group effect = β_w, between-group effect = β_b, and contextual effect = β_c. The level I error term is R_{ij}. The level II error terms are U_{0j} and U_{1j}. From *Hierarchical Linear Models: Applications and Data Analysis Methods* (p. 140), by S. W. Raudenbush and A. S. Bryk, 2002, Thousand Oaks, CA: Sage Publications. Copyright 2002 by Sage Publications. Adapted with permission.

Connecting Models to Hypotheses

Now that basic concepts and the multilevel model have been described, the next step is to connect MLM to specific research hypotheses. A random intercept, U_{0j}, is included in all of these models to allow for group differences on the dependent variable. Thus, these are called *random intercept models* in which it is assumed that the ICC is nonzero and that there is variance at Level II (e.g., schools). Hypotheses about within-level effects ask if Level I variables (e.g., student IQ) predict the dependent variable (e.g., individual educational attainment) and are entered in the Level I model. To estimate within-group effects, the association between the individual-level independent and dependent variables within each school is computed and then averaged across groups to form the average slope parameter γ_{10}, which is the average direction and strength of association between the individual-level independent and dependent variables (e.g., a slope of .80 indicates a positive association between student IQ and student academic achievement). Hypotheses about between-groups effects refer to the school-level associations between independent (e.g., average student IQ of each school) and dependent (e.g., average student achievement of each school) variables and are entered in the Level II part of the model. For example, β_{0j} represents average student achievement, whereas $\overline{X}_{.j}$ is average student IQ in each school. To estimate between-groups effects, the association between the school-level independent and dependent variables is calculated. Thus, the parameter γ_{01} shows the direction and strength of association for the school-level variables, such as the association between the average student IQ of each school and average academic achievement. In sum, within-group effects test student-level associations between these variables, whereas between-groups effects test school-level associations.

Hypotheses about contextual effects focus on how, in our current example, the school may influence the student. A contextual effect shows how much additional variance in the dependent variable (i.e., student academic success) can be explained by knowing what school someone belongs to, over and above individual characteristics. For example, after controlling for individual differences in student IQ, how does school IQ predict individual student achievement? The contextual effect is not the same as the between-groups effect because the between-groups effect is the association between school means (i.e., average student IQ and average student achievement within each school). The contextual effect shows how a school may be influential over and above characteristics of the individual.

A major issue in MLM is how to construct the Level I and Level II models to test between-groups and contextual hypotheses. The main debate involves how to interpret Level II estimates on the basis of the centering of

Level I variables. Although there are other opinions, consensus is growing that the following types of centering lead to particular interpretations (Enders & Tofighi, 2007; Raudenbush & Bryk, 2002). First, as displayed in Exhibit 10.1, Model b, group-mean centering of Level I variables leads to testing hypotheses about between-groups effects for the Level II variable. If group-mean centering is used, this separates within-group and between-groups effects, examining individual- and group-level associations separately. For example, group-mean centering separates the effect of a given student's IQ relative to the average IQ in his or her school (the within effect) from the association between average IQ and average academic success (the between effect). Second, as displayed in Exhibit 10.1, Model d, grand-mean centering of Level I variables leads to the testing of contextual hypotheses for the Level II variable. Now, the interpretation of the Level II variable is how the setting influences the individual over and above the individual-level effect. For example, how does average school IQ influence the individual student's academic performance over and above the individual student's IQ? The only difference between Models b and d is in the centering of X_{ij}.

Cross-level interaction hypotheses are examined by adding a random slope to the model. Although the random intercept model allows for different groups (e.g., neighborhoods) to have different means on the dependent variable, the random slope model allows for different groups to have different slopes characterizing the association between independent and dependent

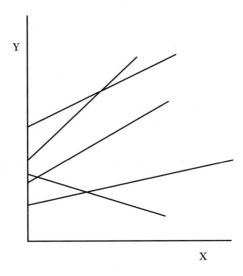

Figure 10.2. Random slope model. Example of different associations between independent (X) and dependent (Y) variables, with each line showing different slopes for five different groups.

variables, such as different associations in different neighborhoods, as illustrated in Figure 10.2, in which five different groups have different slopes. For example, consider individual relationship quality as a Level I independent variable predicting personal distress. As we noted previously, Cutrona et al. (2000) found no association between relationship quality and personal distress in low-disorder neighborhoods, whereas a positive association between relationship quality and personal distress was present in high-disorder neighborhoods. Thus, the degree of neighborhood disorder moderated the link between relationship quality and personal distress.

This cross-level effect is present in the Level II equations in Exhibit 10.1, Model c, in which a regression equation is now constructed to predict the group-dependent slope, β_{1j}. A random effect for the slope (U_{1j}) in the cross-level interactive model allows for the slopes to be different in different Level II groups. One can then use a group-level variable (i.e., $\overline{Z}_{.j}$) to predict the slopes. When the linear mixed model is formed through substitution, a cross-level interaction is present between the individual (X_{ij}) and group level ($\overline{Z}_{ij}$) variables. As shown in Exhibit 10.1, Model c, the interaction itself is formed by taking the raw, uncentered variable multiplied by the Level II variable (e.g., $[X_{ij}][\overline{Z}_{.j}]$). If this effect, γ_{11}, is significant, the group variable moderates the individual-level associations, meaning that slopes are different in particular types of groups.

These cross-level interactions are of particular interest to community researchers because they show how a setting may moderate individual-level associations. Hypotheses about the protective effects of a setting are in fact tested by examining cross-level interactions in which an association between a risk factor (e.g., poor relationship quality) and outcome (e.g., personal distress) is attenuated in a particular type of setting (e.g., low-disorder neighborhoods). For example, the association between poor relationship quality and personal distress may be present in high-disorder neighborhoods and not present in low-disorder neighborhoods. Thus, a low level of disorder in a neighborhood may protect against the negative influence of poor relationship quality. Analytically, to understand the nature of cross-level interactions, follow-up analyses examine the individual-level associations in different types of groups to elucidate how the associations are different. For example, one could follow up by examining associations separately in low- versus high-disorder neighborhoods. Overall, cross-level interactions show how settings may produce different individual-level associations.

Power: A Perennial Issue in Multilevel Modeling

It is important to have large enough samples at Level I (i.e., enough individuals in each group) and Level II (i.e., enough groups) to have adequate statistical power to detect significant effects. Determining the appropriate sample size for adequate power in MLM is more complex than in regression or analysis of variance because MLM estimates fixed and random effects at Level I and Level II. Scherbaum and Ferreter (2008) provide a nice review of these issues as well as power tables to help in selecting sample sizes. They note that increasing the number of Level II units may have the greatest impact on increasing power and that detecting cross-level interactive effects requires different considerations, citing literature recommending a minimum of 30 groups and 30 observations per group to detect cross-level interactions. Finally, Hedeker, Gibbons, and Waternaux (1999) provide power tables for longitudinal applications of MLM.

SUMMARY OF THE STEPS IN USING MULTILEVEL MODELING

The following steps illustrate the process of using MLM. First, the research questions and hypotheses should be clearly articulated to ensure that MLM can be used to address these questions. In addition, the data collection strategy should ensure that enough Level I units will be nested in enough Level II units to have enough power to detect significant effects. Second, a statistical program should be selected for analysis, such as SAS, HLM, SPSS, or R. Each program has strengths and weaknesses, and the selection may rest on personal preference and experience. For example, we use SAS because we had experience with SAS for other analyses. Selecting a program is important because this may influence the third step, setting up the data file, described in the example that follows. However, regardless of which program is selected, each will test the same linear mixed model from Exhibit 10.1. Once the data are collected, preliminary analyses are used to determine if MLM is appropriate by calculating the ICC and examining descriptive plots to assess if groups have different averages on the dependent variable. Third, the research hypotheses should be connected to the associated multilevel model (e.g., models from Exhibit 10.1) to determine which type of centering to use and what variables to include in the model. Next, variables should be centered appropriately. Hypotheses can then be tested. These steps are illustrated in the sections that follow, with further information in the web appendix to this chapter.

APPLYING THE MULTILEVEL MODELING APPROACH

This section provides a practical example of applying the multilevel modeling approach. The research questions and data set are described first, followed by steps to conduct preliminary analyses and to test hypotheses.

Description of Illustration Research Questions and Data Sets

Community researchers have long been interested in how religious settings may affect individuals (e.g., Kloos & Moore, 2000), and this illustration uses MLM to examine individuals nested within religious congregations (for a full analysis, see Todd & Allen, 2010). For this example, we investigate social justice (SJ) prioritization in religious congregations. SJ prioritization is a continuous dependent variable representing the priority members place on having SJ activities sponsored and supported by their religious congregation. Our research questions for this example focus on which individual and congregational variables may predict individual SJ prioritization and which congregational variables may moderate individual-level associations. Specifically, we examine how bridging social capital (i.e., the degree of congregational partnerships with other congregations) at both the individual (i.e., personal perception of degree of congregational partnerships) and congregational (i.e., average within each congregation of the degree of congregational partnerships) levels may predict SJ prioritization. These analyses examine within-group, between-groups, and contextual effects. Second, we examine if the theological orientation of the congregation (i.e., whether the congregation is theologically liberal or conservative) moderates the association between frequency of religious attendance and SJ prioritization. This is tested by examining a cross-level interaction. We use a data set that was collected by Dudley (1991; available online at http://www.thearda.com) and contains 5,123 individuals nested within 62 Christian congregations.

Step 1: Preliminary Analyses

Step 1 includes preliminary analyses such as creating the data file, centering variables, constructing descriptive plots, examining the ICC, and computing individual- and group-level descriptive statistics.

Creating the Data File and Centering Variables

Before preliminary analyses can be conducted, the data file needs to be constructed in a particular manner depending on which statistical program one has selected. See the web appendix to this chapter for a description of how to set up the data set using SAS and Online Table 10.1 for an example data file structure. In addition, group- and grand-mean centered variables should be created for every participant. For this example, individual-level group- and grand-mean centered variables are labeled *groupCvariable* and *grandCvariable*, respectively. Group-level congregational variables are labeled *grpMvariable*, such as *grpMbridge*. See the web appendix to this chapter for variable names and descriptions.

Descriptive Plots

Descriptive plots are examined to determine if congregations have different mean levels of SJ prioritization (i.e., different intercepts) and to see if Level I associations are different in different congregations (i.e., different slopes). If there are different intercepts, a random intercept should be included in the model. If the slopes are different, a random slope should be included. A helpful plot to examine consists of separate regression lines for each congregation. For example, the association between individual bridging and SJ prioritization is shown in Online Figure 10.1, found in the web appendix to this chapter, in which each regression line is for a different congregation. In such a plot, the intercept for each regression line is the mean on the dependent variable (i.e., SJ prioritization), whereas the slope for each line is the association between individual bridging and SJ prioritization. Here, congregations appear to have different intercepts; moreover, there appear to be different associations between individual bridging and SJ prioritization because the regression lines for each congregation are not parallel. The SAS code for generating such plots is provided in the web appendix to this chapter. As the old adage goes, a picture is worth a thousand statistical tests, especially in MLM.

Intraclass Correlation

Computing the ICC complements these descriptive plots by providing an index of the amount of variance explained at the congregational level. A large ICC suggests differences between groups on the dependent variable and justifies including a random intercept in the model. For these data, the ICC for the outcome of SJ prioritization is .095. This indicates that 9.5% of the variance on the outcome is explained by the congregation. Taken in conjunction with the descriptive plots, it appears that a random intercept is appropriate to be included in the model because congregations have different average SJ prioritization. Thus, because there is unexplained variance at the congregational level, MLM should be used (see the web appendix to this chapter for how to compute the ICC).

Individual and Group Descriptive Statistics

Finally, basic descriptive statistics, such as means, standard deviations, and correlations, should be examined. For individual associations, compute the correlation between variables for all participants, as usual. Next, construct a Level II data set in which each row is a congregation and then compute the group-level correlations. Such a data set and the associated SAS code is provided in the web appendix to this chapter. Descriptive statistics for both levels can then be presented in a table, as displayed in Online Table 10.2, in the web appendix.

Step 2: Testing Hypotheses

Step 2 includes how to connect specific hypotheses to models, to conduct follow-up tests for cross-level interactions, and to extend multilevel modeling to multilevel logistic regression.

Connecting Hypotheses to Models and Significance Testing

For this example, we are interested in testing within-group, between-groups, contextual, and cross-level hypotheses to understand how characteristics of individuals and religious congregations predict individual SJ prioritization. We likely have adequate power to test these hypotheses, given the large number of congregations and individuals. To connect each of these hypotheses to the MLM, we examine Exhibit 10.1. For example, to test within-group and between-groups hypotheses that bridging predicts SJ prioritization, we use Model b from Exhibit 10.1 and include both groupCbridge and grpMbridge variables in the model. For the contextual hypothesis that congregational bridging predicts SJ prioritization over and above individual-level bridging, we use Model d and enter the grand-mean centered variable grandCbridge with grpMbridge. It is important to remember that a random intercept is included in all of these models. To test if congregational theological orientation (i.e., grpMtheol) moderates the association between frequency of religious participation (e.g., relfreq) and SJ prioritization, we use Model c and examine if the cross-level interaction (i.e., relfreq*grpMtheol) is significant while also including a random intercept and slope. It is crucial to connect one's hypothesis to the associated linear mixed model in Exhibit 10.1, which is then used by one's statistical program to estimate the significance for each of the variables in the model. Specifically, for each variable in the model, a slope is estimated and tested, with a p value provided by the program. The slope indicates the strength and direction of association between the predictor and the outcome while controlling for all other variables in the model, and the p value indicates significance. One must examine the variables that test one's hypothesis. Online Table 10.3 includes the information one reports for a multilevel analysis: Model 1 tests within-group and between-groups effects; Model 2, a contextual effect; and Model 3, a cross-level effect. As indicated in this table, we found within-group, between-groups, and contextual effects for bridging predicting SJ prioritization. The supplemental materials show how to run these models in SAS.

Follow-Up Tests for Cross-Level Interactions

Follow-up analyses need to be conducted to understand the nature of significant cross-level interactions. For example, we found a cross-level interaction between frequency of religious participation and congregational theological orientation; therefore, the theological orientation (i.e., liberal or conservative) of the congregation moderates the association between frequency of religious attendance and SJ prioritization. To understand this moderation, we conduct separate regressions for people in theologically conservative and liberal congregations. First, we classify congregations as liberal or conservative by using a median split by congregational theological orientation, coding congregations as conservative or liberal. Because congregational theological orientation was the moderator, we classify congregations rather than individuals. We then examine the association between frequency of religious participation and SJ prioritization separately in liberal and conservative congregations using regular regression. In this example, the slope is significant and positive in liberal congregations and nonsignificant ($p > .05$) in conservative congregations. A plot of the regression lines for each group is very helpful in understanding the moderation, and is presented in Online Figure 10.2, found in the web appendix to this chapter.

General Extensions: Multilevel Logistic Regression and Control Variables

For the interested reader, a section in the web appendix describes multilevel logistic regression and our applied example in predicting SJ participation, a dichotomous outcome. A more general extension for both continuous and dichotomous outcomes is the inclusion of control variables. As with regular multiple regression, it is possible to enter variables as controls, meaning that significant effects for independent variables are over and above the variance that is explained by control variables. In MLM, variables can be used as statistical controls at Level I and Level II. In other work, we control for individual demographics, such as age, and also control for Level II variables, such as the denomination of the congregation (Todd & Allen, 2010). A few demographic variables are included in the web appendix data to use as controls.

CONCLUSION: BENEFITS AND DRAWBACKS OF MULTILEVEL MODELING

MLM provides a powerful, flexible, and statistically robust tool to examine multiple levels of analysis. Research that aims to understand the influence of various settings on human behavior can benefit from this methodology because it maps well onto the conceptualizations and questions often pursued by community researchers. In addition, MLM can be extended to different types of outcomes, to higher levels of nesting (e.g., students nested in classrooms nested in schools, where school is Level III), and to multiple hypotheses relevant to community researchers. However, one of the main drawbacks of MLM is collecting enough nested data to have adequate power for testing hypotheses. There may be limited resources to obtain the desired number of Level II settings, or in some cases, the Level II units are limited by the phenomenon of interest, such as having only 21 domestic violence coordinating councils in one state (Javdani et al., 2011). Another drawback is the complexity of the models, which makes the mechanics of statistical estimation more challenging; violations of assumptions can occur at both Level I and Level II, and altering one parameter in a model has the potential to alter the findings. Thus, MLM needs to be conducted with care and humility, driven by theory in both hypothesis testing and interpretation. Overall, though, MLM promises to be a vital methodology for community researchers who seek to understand how context and social ecology matter in the lives of individuals and groups.

REFERENCES

Allen, N. E. (2005). A multilevel analysis of community coordinating councils. *American Journal of Community Psychology*, 35, 49–63. doi:10.1007/s10464-005-1889-5

Bronfenbrenner, U. (1979). *The ecology of human development*. Cambridge, MA: Harvard University Press.

Cutrona, C. E., Russell, D. W., Hessling, R. M., Brown, P. A., & Murry, V. (2000). Direct and moderating effects of community context on the psychological well-being of African American women. *Journal of Personality and Social Psychology*, 79, 1088–1101. doi:10.1037/0022-3514.79.6.1088

Dudley, C. S. (1991). From typical church to social ministry: A study of the elements which mobilize congregations. *Review of Religious Research*, 32, 195–212. doi:10.2307/3511206

Enders, C. K., & Tofighi, D. (2007). Centering predictor variables in cross-sectional multilevel models: A new look at an old issue. *Psychological Methods*, 12, 121–138. doi:10.1037/1082-989X.12.2.121

Garner, C. L., & Raudenbush, S. W. (1991). Neighborhood effects on educational attainment: A multilevel analysis. *Sociology of Education*, 64, 251–262. doi:10.2307/2112706

Hedeker, D., Gibbons, R. D., & Waternaux, C. (1999). Sample size estimation for longitudinal designs with attrition: Comparing time-related contrasts between two groups. *Journal of Educational and Behavioral Statistics*, 24, 70–93.

Javdani, S., Allen, N. E., Todd, N. R., & Anderson, C. J. (2011). Examining systems change in the response to domestic violence: Innovative applications of multilevel modeling. *Violence Against Women, 17*, 359–375.

Khoury-Kassabri, M., Benbenishty, R., Astor, R. A., & Zeira, A. (2004). The contributions of community, family, and school variables to student victimization. *American Journal of Community Psychology, 34*, 187–204. doi:10.1007/s10464-004-7414-4

Kloos, B., & Moore, T. (2000). The prospect and purpose of locating community research and action in religious settings. *Journal of Community Psychology, 28*, 119–137. doi:10.1002/(SICI)1520-6629(200003)28:2<119::AID-JCOP2>3.0.CO;2-5

Luke, D. A. (2005). Getting the big picture in community science: Methods that capture context. *American Journal of Community Psychology, 35*, 185–200. doi:10.1007/s10464-005-3397-z

Olson, B., Jason, L. A., Davidson, M., & Ferrari, J. R. (2009). Increases in tolerance within naturalistic, intentional communities: A randomized, longitudinal examination. *American Journal of Community Psychology, 44*, 188–195. doi:10.1007/s10464-009-9275-3

Raudenbush, S. W., & Bryk, A. S. (2002). *Hierarchical linear models: Applications and data analysis methods* (2nd ed.). Thousand Oaks, CA: Sage.

Scherbaum, C. A., & Ferreter, J. M. (2008). Estimating statistical power and required sample sizes for organizational research using multilevel modeling. *Organizational Research Methods, 12*, 347–367. doi:10.1177/1094428107308906

Schwadel, P. (2002). Testing the promise of churches: Income inequality in the opportunity to learn civic skills in Christian congregations. *Journal for the Scientific Study of Religion, 41*, 565–575. doi:10.1111/1468-5906.00137

Shinn, M. B., & Rapkin, B. (2000). Cross-level analysis without cross-ups. In J. Rappaport & E. Seidman (Eds.), *Handbook of community psychology* (pp. 669–695). New York, NY: Kluwer Academic. doi:10.1007/978-1-4615-4193-6_28

Singer, J. D., & Willett, J. B. (2003). *Applied longitudinal data analysis: Modeling change and event occurrence*. New York, NY: Oxford University Press.

Snijders, T., & Bosker, R. (1999). *Multilevel analysis: An introduction to basic and advanced multilevel modeling*. Thousand Oaks, CA: Sage.

Todd, N. R., & Allen, N. A. (2010, December 23). Religious congregations as mediating structures for social justice: A multilevel examination. *American Journal of Community Psychology*. Advance online publication. doi: 10.1007/s10464-010-9388-8

11

EPIDEMIOLOGIC APPROACHES TO COMMUNITY-BASED RESEARCH

LEONARD A. JASON, NICOLE PORTER, AND ALFRED RADEMAKER

Epidemiology has traditionally been described as the study of the distribution and determinants of disease, particularly problematic behaviors (e.g., tobacco use) or social conditions (e.g., poverty, crime) in populations (Gordis, 2000). In addition to summarizing information about the distribution of these types of illnesses or conditions, epidemiologic methods allow investigators to make inferences about the importance of (a) individual (e.g., sex, age, race), social contextual (e.g., family, neighborhood, community), and environmental (e.g., racial discrimination) risk factors (Torres-Harding, Herrell, & Howard, 2004) and (b) at times, causal factors, such as smoking with respect to cancer. However, even if the specific cause of an illness or social condition is not known, epidemiologists can uncover associa-

We appreciate the funding provided by the National Institute of Allergy and Infectious Diseases (AI49720 and AI055735). We also appreciate the help of many individuals: Judith Richman, Renee Taylor, Susan Torres-Harding, Lynne Wagner, Caroline King, Sharon Song, Karina Corradi, Mary Gloria Njoku, Molly Brown, Meredyth Evans, Abby Brown, Valerie Anderson, Jessica Hunnell, Athena Porter, Nancy Bothne, David Lipkin, Fred Friedberg, Dachao Liu, Andy Plioplys, Morris Papernik, and Karen Jordan. In addition, we are particularly appreciative of the many national and international myalgic encephalopathy and chronic fatigue syndrome activists and organizations that have collaborated with our research group.

diagnostic unreliable

insight highlight

187

tions between risk factors and social conditions that can lead to important community-level interventions.

For example, in one of the first epidemiologic studies, John Snow in the mid 1800s found that the closer one lived to a polluted source of water, the higher the prevalence of cholera cases (Snow, 1856). Snow concluded that the polluted water caused cholera, even though the scientists and physicians of that time had no knowledge that bacteria caused the illness. This demonstrated that associating a disease (cholera) with exposure to a risk factor (the contaminated water) could lead to life-saving public health interventions (e.g., separating drinking water from sewage), even if the exact cause of the disease (e.g., cholera) was not known.

One of the more successful epidemiologic efforts has involved the reduction of tobacco use. Ubiquitous in the 1950s and 1960s, tobacco use began to change with the release of the Surgeon General's 1964 report indicating the dangers of tobacco use (U.S. Public Health Service, 1964). For the first time, most smokers realized that smoking shortens human life; causes lung cancer and other forms of cancer; and exacerbates heart disease, emphysema, bronchitis, and a number of other illnesses. Much of this evidence was based on a number of well-controlled longitudinal epidemiologic studies, such as the Framingham Heart Study, involving 5,209 men and women between the ages of 30 and 62 from the town of Framingham, Massachusetts, in the late 1940s (Yach, 2010). After the release of the Surgeon General's report, the U.S. Public Health Service, the American Cancer Society, and other national and local agencies launched campaigns to spread the word about the dangers of smoking. Slowly, over the next few decades norms began to change, and even tobacco commercials on television were terminated. Antismoking television commercials were enormously effective in changing the attitudes of people toward cigarettes, and levels of tobacco use significantly decreased over time.

Epidemiologists measure the effect on disease of exposure to various risk factors (Rothman, 2002), and this often takes the form of relative measures (e.g., risks, odds, hazards). Community theorists and interventionists sometimes rely on community respondents to provide estimates of risk factors and markers of either illness or health, and epidemiological methods try to reduce bias among such interviewees to reduce inaccurate estimates. An important goal of this type of research is to ensure that an appropriate sample has been obtained so that the results can be generalized to the population of interest. The epidemiologist is faced with the basic problem that the number of known cases of an illness or problem is almost always outweighed by those cases that remain undiscovered. If one studies a minority of cases, particularly if they are unrepresentative of the population of cases, this can lead to an inaccurate view of the disease. In this chapter, we provide a brief overview of basic epidemiologic methods and then explore how unintentional bias can be reduced to accurately include samples having the illness or condition under investigation and to exclude those not having the illness or condition.

HOW ONE DOES THE APPROACH

Epidemiologic studies may be designed in a number of different ways depending on the nature of the research question, the availability of financial resources to conduct the study, and the availability of accessible data sources. Some epidemiologic studies are more descriptive, for example, elucidating the distribution of a particular disease across different ethnic, economic, and gender categories. Other epidemiologic studies focus on biological frameworks, examining either physiological (e.g., high cholesterol in relation to heart disease) or family history data (e.g., whether a family history of schizophrenia is related to mental disorders).

One main distinction in epidemiologic research methods is that between retrospective and prospective designs. Both types compare two or more groups when assessing the relationship between exposure to a risk factor and outcome. *Retrospective* studies select the groups to be compared on the basis of disease outcome and then look backward in time at each person's records to compare the groups on exposure factors that may be related to the outcome. *Prospective* studies, also called *natural history studies*, select nondiseased groups to be compared on the basis of exposure and then follow the participants forward to compare the groups on disease outcome. Retrospective studies are sometimes referred to as *case control studies*, whereas prospective studies are frequently termed *cohort studies*.

Another epidemiologic design—one not requiring looking backward or forward within a person's life cycle—is the *cross-sectional* study. A *prevalence* study, which is a special case of a cross-sectional design, seeks to determine the prevalence of a condition, that is, the proportion of individuals in a defined population who have the condition. There are no hypothesis-driven comparison groups in a prevalence study, and the study's goal is to determine the rate, or prevalence, of the condition as well as how individual and community risk factors might be related to these rates. In contrast, incidence is a measure of the risk of developing some new condition within a specified period of time (e.g., new cases of cancer each year). Space limitations preclude discussion of incidence research in the present chapter. For further details, the interested reader is referred to Coggon, Rose, and Barker (1997).

One way to conduct a prevalence study is to conduct a community survey. In a community survey, the population of interest is generally defined by geographic boundaries and population size. To conduct a community survey-type prevalence study, a random sample of the community is sampled, and for each individual in the sample, a determination is made as to whether the condition is present. The prevalence rate is the proportion of sample individuals with the condition divided by the sample size. Because the sample was randomly selected from the larger community, the community prevalence may be inferred to be the sample prevalence.

Sample selection is clearly an important issue for epidemiologists conducting community surveys to determine prevalence (Torres-Harding et al., 2004). To avoid systematic bias, every person in a population of interest should have a known nonzero probability of selection into the sample (Levy & Lemeshow, 1999). There are many methods used to accomplish this goal, including random digit dialing from a list of telephone exchanges, systematically visiting homes in a community to interview a random sample of individuals, and using archival registries. With about 20% of households having access only by cell phone and with more individuals screening their phone calls, using telephones to identify random samples of participants is becoming more challenging for investigators. Certainly, in the future, more studies will generate samples using the Internet and other social media outlets. For example, Knowledge Networks (http://www. knowledgenetworks.com/knpanel/KNPanel-Design-Summary.html) is a nationwide online panel that consists of about 50,000 adult members (ages 18 and older) who have agreed to be interviewed and includes persons living in cell-phone-only households. This data base is representative of the entire U.S. population and is available to researchers to generate samples.

When estimating the prevalence of a condition, one needs to define an outcome variable representing the description of that condition. Outcome variables can be broadly or narrowly defined, and how such variables are specified can have important consequences. For example, defining the homelessness outcome variable as *any episode* of homelessness over a 6-month period versus 6 months of *continuous homeless* will have important implications for the prevalence of homelessness when one tries to estimate the prevalence of homelessness. Cantwell (1996) argued, with respect to outcome definition in general, that the most valid criteria specify which reliable instrument to use, what type of informants to interview, and how to determine the presence and severity of the condition. As an example, it might be necessary to specify a certain number and type of symptoms that should be present to make a particular diagnosis. Also, standardized procedures should be used for determining whether a particular symptom or condition is severe enough to qualify as one of the symptoms or conditions required for the diagnosis.

Definition of prevalence outcome variables for a condition is strongly related to the diagnostic criteria for that condition. Sources of variance can be divided into the following five categories: subject variance, occasion variance, information variance, observation variance, and criterion variance

(Jason & Choi, 2008). *Subject variance* occurs when patients have different conditions at different times. For example, a patient may have acute alcohol intoxication on admission to a hospital but develop delirium tremens several days later. *Occasion variance* occurs when patients are in different stages of the same condition at different times. An example is a patient with multiple sclerosis who was in remission during one period of illness and symptomatic during another. *Information variance* occurs when clinicians have different sources of information about their patients. For example, one clinician may regularly question patients about areas of functioning and symptoms that another clinician does not assess. *Observation variance* occurs when clinicians presented with the same signs and symptoms differ in what they detect and perceive. An example of this type of variance is disagreement among clinicians as to whether a patient is irritable or depressed. *Criterion variance* occurs when there are differences in the formal inclusion and exclusion criteria that clinicians use in reaching diagnostic conclusions. An example includes discordance as to whether difficulty concentrating is a necessary criterion for the identification of severe fatigue.

Criterion variance accounts for the largest source of diagnostic unreliability. Therefore, improvement in diagnostic reliability is primarily dependent on reducing criterion variance as a source of unreliability. Criterion variance is most likely to occur when operationally explicit criteria do not exist for diagnostic categories. When diagnostic categories lack reliability and accuracy, the validity (i.e., usefulness) of a diagnostic category is inherently limited by its reliability. One consequence of this is that different studies addressing the prevalence of a given condition may actually not be looking at the same condition because of variability across studies in diagnostic criteria. This may also explain a wide variance in prevalence estimates when several studies published by independent investigators attempt to determine a condition's prevalence.

Low reliability of routine diagnostic procedures poses a significant epidemiologic problem with respect to the estimation of prevalence rates of a variety of disorders and conditions. If these basic psychometric properties of the dependent variable are not established, the entire scientific enterprise is vulnerable, including the estimation of prevalence rates for a condition. As an example, both the first and second editions of the American Psychiatric Association's official nomenclature, the *Diagnostic and Statistical Manual of Mental Disorders* (DSM–I, DSM–II), were predominantly composed of largely unreliable, purely clinical descriptions of psychiatric disorders (Leckliter & Matarazzo, 1994). Epidemiologic estimates of the prevalence of mental disorders in the populations thus suffered as a result of the low rates of interrater reliability, which were primarily due to problems with criterion variance. With the development of the Feighner criteria, which were operationally explicit criteria for the then 16 diagnostic categories of the *DSM–II*, there was an immediate and dramatic improvement in interrater diagnostic reliability (Helzer et al., 1977), and ultimately, there were better estimates of the prevalence of mental disorders in the United States.

By the 1970s, researchers in the field of psychiatric epidemiology and diagnostics also recognized that the provision of operationally explicit, objective criteria was not enough to guarantee that clinicians would know how to elicit the necessary information from a clinical interview to permit them to apply it to the reliable criteria. These concerns led to the development of a series of structured interview schedules, such as the Structured Clinical Interview for *DSM–IV* Axis 1 (First, Spitzer, Gibbon, & Williams, 1995). The benefit of structured interview schedules is that they ensure that clinicians in the same or different settings conduct clinical interviews and examinations that maximize the accuracy of clinical diagnosis. Structuring and standardizing the questions asked by each interviewer and using structured interview schedules increase the likelihood that relevant clinical material is elicited. Thus, structured interview schedules serve to remove as much as possible the unreliability in the resulting psychiatric diagnosis introduced by differences in the way clinicians elicit clinical information. Together, the provision of operationally explicit, objective criteria and standardized interviews has been found to significantly improve the reliability of clinical diagnosis for a number of psychological and psychiatric conditions.

Tucker (1998), however, warned that in contemporary practice, the focus tends to be on the mere presentation of symptoms, without regard to either their antecedents or consequences. In emphasizing and focusing on a predetermined set of symptoms, the views of the patient can be dismissed, and additional sources of important information, such as the report of family and friends, tend to be ignored. Meaningful distinctions among patients within the same diagnostic categories are also likely to be disregarded. For example, in the evaluation of subjective experiences (e.g., complaints of pain, fatigue), self-reported symptoms cannot be effectively interpreted without careful consideration of the antecedents, consequences, overall context, and fluctuations in intensity over time (i.e., the patient's story).

A final consideration is the use of polythetic criteria (i.e., sets of criteria in which not all the criteria need to be present to make a diagnosis). As an example, to diagnose chronic fatigue syndrome (CFS), a patient has to have only four out of eight specific symptoms (Fukuda et al., 1994). Although three of these symptoms (i.e., postexertional malaise, memory or concentration problems, unrefreshing sleep) are generally considered to be critical and cardinal characteristics of the illness, a patient might not have any of these three and still have four other symptoms, thereby receiving a diagnosis of CFS. It has been argued (Tucker, 1998) that although standardized diagnostic criteria are needed for research, the use of polythetic criteria derived by expert committees (as is the case with CFS) may not be methodologically sound. For example, the use of polythetic criteria may result in the creation of two very different groups of patients within the same diagnostic category or of similar groups in different diagnostic categories.

APPLYING THE APPROACH TO A COMMUNITY-RELATED RESEARCH PROJECT

CFS is an extremely debilitating illness, with patients being more functionally impaired than those with type 2 diabetes mellitus, congestive heart failure, multiple sclerosis, and end-stage renal disease (J. S. Anderson & Ferrans, 1997; Buchwald, Pearlman, Umali, Schmaling, & Katon, 1996). In spite of this, many studies indicate that patients with this illness have experienced disrespectful treatment by providers in the health care system. For example, J. S. Anderson and Ferrans found that 77% of individuals with CFS reported negative experiences with health care providers. Green, Romei, and Natelson (1998) reported that 95% of individuals seeking medical treatment for CFS reported feelings of estrangement, and 70% believed that others uniformly attributed their CFS symptoms to psychological causes. It is clear that some medical professionals do not consider CFS to be a legitimate illness (Barsky & Borus, 1999) or believe it to be a variant of depressive disorder (Abbey, 1993).

If medical personnel believe that CFS is a relatively rare disorder and that it is primarily caused by psychiatric explanations, then physicians might minimize or misinterpret the physical complaints of patients with CFS, leading to the mistrust and lack of communication that has been reported between patients and medical personnel. It is important that the prevalence of this disorder be estimated in a manner that is understandable (i.e., the population of interest is well defined) and believable (i.e., appropriate epidemiologic methodology has been used). Accurate sampling and measurement have been at the heart of the debate between researchers and community members surrounding this illness. Among the basic issues under dispute have been the prevalence of CFS and the rates of CFS comorbidity with other disorders.

In the 1990s, the Centers for Disease Control (CDC) conducted an epidemiologic study on the prevalence of this illness, with physicians in U.S. cities identifying patients having unexplained fatigue-related symptoms and then referring those patients to the study to determine whether they met criteria for CFS (Gunn, Connell, & Randall, 1993). Using data from this study, the CDC estimated the prevalence of CFS in the United States to be from 4.0 to 8.7 per 100,000 people (Reyes et al., 1997). If these estimates were correct, that would have indicated that there were about 20,000 individuals with CFS in the United States. Subsequently, the perception that CFS was a relatively uncommon disorder was used to justify not allocating financial resources for its research and treatment. These low prevalence numbers, however, contrasted sharply with the interest expressed in information about this disorder. For example, the high rates of telephone calls to the CDC seeking information about this illness, up to 3,000 per month, suggested that this disorder might have been more common than had been reported (McCluskey, 1993). In addition, the fact that more than 20,000 people in the country were members of the largest CFS self-help organization suggested that the real prevalence numbers might be higher than the CDC's projections.

Concerns about the sampling practices used in these early prevalence studies led some to believe that the true prevalence of this disorder had been severely underestimated. Prevalence data were collected in either primary care or hospital-based settings, thus restricting their samples to individuals who had access to health care resources. In particular, people of ethnic minority status may have been excluded because they tend to have differential access to health care (Richman, Flaherty, & Rospenda, 1994). Some persons with CFS, because of skepticism and lack of understanding on the part of medical professionals, may have pursued alternative health care treatments. In addition, studies relying on physician referral may have underestimated the prevalence of CFS because some physicians might not have diagnosed the illness as a result of their belief that it was not a legitimate disorder.

Because of concerns over sampling issues in the CDC's epidemiologic study, a randomly selected community-based prevalence study was initiated at DePaul University in an effort to address past methodological problems (Jason et al., 1999). Telephone calling and screening was the primary method of recruitment of adults (i.e., 18 years or older) into the study. A random sample of listed and unlisted telephone numbers stratified to represent several neighborhoods in Chicago was selected using procedures developed by Kish (1965). This prevalence study involved a two-phase design developed by Shrout and Newman (1989). This design (a) first screens all individuals in a defined population using a brief screening tool for the disorder (Phase 1) and (b) then provides a definitive diagnosis by a thorough medical and psychiatric examination for a certain proportion of screen positives and screen negatives (Phase 2). The data obtained in this process are then used to estimate the overall population prevalence.

When this design was applied in the DePaul prevalence study, 18,675 individuals were screened in the initial random sample. Of these 18,668 adults, 9,715 were White, 3,691 African American, 3,447 Latino, and 1,614 of other ethnic origins. (Seven cases were not included because fatigue-related information was missing.) In addition, 780 (4.2%) reported chronic fatigue (i.e., 6 or more months of fatigue). Of these, 408 had both chronic fatigue and the occurrence of four or more symptoms (which were required for a CFS diagnosis). These 408 persons were defined as screen positives, with the remaining 18,260 defined as screen negatives (seven individuals were not included because fatigue-related information was missing). This completed Phase 1 of the two-phase design. In Phase 2, 166 of the 408 screen positives and 47 of the 18,260 screen negatives were provided a comprehensive physical examination by an independent physician. Structured psychiatric interviews were also obtained. All of the participants in Phase 2 were classified as having either CFS, idiopathic chronic fatigue (meaning that there were not enough symptoms for the participant to be diagnosed with CFS), chronic fatigue explained (meaning that the chronic fatigue was explained by medical or psychiatric reasons), or controls (meaning not having 6 or more months of fatigue; for more details, see Jason et al., 1999). Table 11.1 illustrates the numeric breakdown of participants as they progressed through both phases of the investigation.

From the data in Table 11.1, the point prevalence (i.e., the proportion of people in a population who have a disease or condition at a particular time) of CFS and its standard error were estimated according to the methods and notation described by Shrout and Newman (1989). Computational details and the data set to compute these estimates are located in the web appendix to this chapter (http://pubs.apa.org/books/supp/Jason-Glenwick). The way in

TABLE 11.1

Frequency Data at Various Diagnostic Stages for Participants Screening Positive and Negative for Chronic Fatigue Syndrome-Like Illness

Diagnostic stage	Screened positive	Screened negative
Completed initial screening, Phase 1[a]	408	18,260
Selected for Phase 2 evaluation	408	199
Completed physician review, Phase 2	166	47
Final diagnosis		
Chronic fatigue syndrome	32	0
Idiopathic chronic fatigue	45	1
Chronic fatigue explained[b]	89	2
No fatigue	0	44

Note. Chronic fatigue explained = chronic fatigue explained by medical or psychiatric reasons. From "A Community-Based Study of Chronic Fatigue Syndrome," by L. A. Jason, J. A. Richman, A. W. Rademaker, K. M. Jordan, A. V. Plioplys, R. R. Taylor, . . . S. Plioplys, 1999, *Archives of Internal Medicine, 159,* p. 2132. Copyright 1999 by the American Medical Association. Reprinted with permission. [a]Seven cases were not included because fatigue-related information was missing. [b]Nineteen participants had melancholic depression; three had bipolar disorders; four had anorexia nervosa or bulimia nervosa; seven had psychotic disorders; 25 had drug or alcohol related disorders; and 33 had medical explanations for their fatigue.

which prevalence estimates were calculated is explained in the formula that follows. (The notation that was used is in the web appendix and Excel spreadsheet.) Shrout and Newman's notations are in parentheses. The prevalence of CFS, which is the number to be estimated, is represented by P (p). The total number of respondents screened in Phase 1 (18,668) is N (N_t). The proportion of screened positives (408/18,668 = .0219) is PI (π), and the proportion of screened negatives (18,260/18,668 = .9781) is $1 - PI$ ($1 - \pi$). The proportion of screened positives evaluated in Phase 2 who were diagnosed with CFS (32/166 = .1928) is L1 (λ_1), and the proportion of screened negatives evaluated in Phase 2 who were diagnosed with CFS (0/47 = 0.0) is L2 (λ_2) This information was then used in the following formula to obtain the estimate of the prevalence P:

$$P = L1 \times PI + L2 \times (1 - PI)$$
$$= .1928 \times .0219 + 0.0 \times .9781 = .0042 \tag{1}$$

Table 11.2 presents data on the point prevalence of CFS. The estimated prevalence rate for CFS was .42%, which was considerably higher than the rate reported in previous epidemiology studies. (Although only 32 out of 18,668 had CFS, this translated to 422 out of 100,000 using the formula provided.) Table 11.2 also presents prevalence estimates of CFS according to

TABLE 11.2
Prevalence Rates (± Standard Error) of Chronic Fatigue Syndrome (CFS)

Sociodemographic subcategory	No. of respondents	No. of cases	CFS prevalence rate
All	18,668	32	422 ± 70
Female	10,507	23	522 ± 103
Male	8,110	9	291 ± 91
White	9,715	15	318 ± 77
Latino	3,447	9	726 ± 227
African American	3,691	5	337 ± 145
Other	1,614	3	491 ± 258
18–29 years old	6,618	8	315 ± 103
30–39 years old	4,718	8	412 ± 138
40–49 years old	2,611	9	805 ± 249
50–59 years old	1,716	3	413 ± 229
60 years old and over	2,668	4	354 ± 168
Unskilled or semiskilled worker	4,232	8	436 ± 149
Skilled worker	3,415	11	701 ± 195
Professional	8,587	12	325 ± 87

Note. Cases are per 100,000 persons. From "A Community-Based Study of Chronic Fatigue Syndrome," by L. A. Jason, J. A. Richman, A. W. Rademaker, K. M. Jordan, A. V. Plioplys, R. R. Taylor, . . . S. Plioplys, 1999, *Archives of Internal Medicine, 159*, p. 2133. Copyright 1999 by the American Medical Association. Reprinted with permission.

sociodemographic subcategories of gender, ethnic identification, age, and socioeconomic status. The prevalence of CFS was substantially higher among females than males. Latino, African American, and other groups exhibited higher rates of CFS than did Whites, with Latino participants demonstrating the highest prevalence. Individuals in the 40- to 49-year-old age range exhibited the highest rates when compared with individuals in other age groups. With respect to socioeconomic status, the prevalence of CFS was highest among skilled workers and lowest among professionals.

The proportion of screened positives with completed evaluation in Phase 2 (166/408 = .4069) is F1 (f_1), and the proportion of screened negatives with completed evaluation in Phase 2 (47/18,260 = .0025) is F2 (f_2). The F1 and F2 are needed to calculate the standard error. The web appendix describes how to calculate the standard error as well as 95% confidence intervals for prevalence. Although the overall prevalence of CFS was .42%, the standard error was 0.07% and the 95% confidence interval was 0.28% to 0.56%. The data observed in this survey could have arisen from any true prevalence rate between these two values. Prevalence rates from different subgroups may be compared to infer different levels of disposition toward having a disease. Risk ratios are typically calculated from cohort studies that have a longitudinal follow-up component during which the disease is manifested and measured. Prevalence studies do not have this follow-up period, so risk in its strictest definition may not be estimated. However, calculating a ratio of prevalence rates between subgroups will approximate risk ratios under assumptions of population stability. As Table 11.2 indicates, the CFS prevalence rate for Latinos was 726 per 100,000, whereas the CFS prevalence rate for Whites was 318 per 100,000. This would indicate that in this population, the risk ratio between these two subgroups was 726/318 or 2.3 or that Latinos were 2.3 times more likely to have CFS than Whites. The web appendix and data set also provide details on the estimation of prevalence rates of idiopathic chronic fatigue and CFS-like conditions, in the same way as was done for CFS.

These findings highlighted the limitations of prior CFS epidemiological studies that were based solely on samples recruited from hospitals or primary care providers. Only 10% of people with CFS in this sample had been diagnosed as such by a physician prior to participation in the study. Thus, the results directly contradicted both the previously reported prevalence rates and the perception that upper class White women were the primary people to have CFS.

These overall findings were subsequently corroborated by a CDC population-based prevalence study of fatigue-related disorders (Reyes et al., 2003). However, a few years later, the CDC (Reeves et al., 2005) recommended the use of specific instruments and cutoff points, which resulted in a broadened case definition. For example, a community-based study in Georgia that used the CDC's revised guidelines indicated that CFS prevalence estimates had escalated to more than 4 million Americans (Reeves et al., 2007). In a relatively brief period of time, the CDC's characterization of CFS had evolved from portraying the illness as a rare disorder, affecting about 20,000 individuals, to portraying it as one of the more common chronic illnesses in the nation.

Our research group was concerned that this broadening of the case definition might inappropriately lead to including cases that were actually primary affective disorders, such as major depression, and that this more heterogeneous CFS group would ultimately make it impossible to uncover biological markers for the illness. It is important to note that the new CDC's CFS estimated prevalence rates were 2.54%, which is comparable to the prevalence rate of major depressive disorders (Regier et al., 1988). Therefore, our group conducted a study to clarify this situation, collecting data from two distinct samples, one with CFS and the other with major depressive disorder. The study found that using the CDC's expanded case definition, 38% of the major depressive disorder group would have been misdiagnosed with CFS (Jason, Najar, Porter, & Reh, 2009).

These findings were used to focus increased attention on potential problems with the CDC's expanded CFS case definition. For example, when diagnostic categories lack reliability and accuracy, greater heterogeneity is introduced. If a case definition is too broad and cannot reliably identify those with an illness, the identification of biological markers will be compromised. In other words, if a diagnostic category includes both those with and without an illness, the biologic markers of those with the illness will not be consistently detected. Illnesses without biological markers are often referred to as *unexplained*, with researchers often seeking psychogenic explanations for the syndromes.

The study described here represents a cross-sectional design, but epidemiologic studies can also follow individuals over time in what are called natural history, or cohort, studies. Our research group at DePaul University attempted to recontact the 213 adults who were medically and psychiatrically evaluated from 1995–1997 in our original Wave 1 CFS epidemiology project (Jason et al., 1999). Wave 2 involved a 10-year follow-up study, which also encompassed a complete physical examination and a structured psychiatric assessment (Jason, Porter, Hunnell, Rademaker, & Richman, 2011).

In this study, we found that CFS rates were relatively stable over the decade from Wave 1 to Wave 2. This is in marked contrast to the CDC report of a tenfold increase in CFS over the past decade, an increase probably due to their expanded case definition. Of additional interest, those in the CFS group in the Jason, Porter, et al. (2011) study did not have higher levels of psychiatric comorbidity than did those in any of the other groups, suggesting that CFS is not a psychogenic illness.

As Kelly (2003) indicated, complex community interventions and phenomena can best be understood using multiple methodologies. In addition to the quantitative data we analyzed in our CFS natural history study, V. Anderson, Jason, Porter, and Cudia (2011) analyzed qualitative data using grounded theory, which involves reading interviews and identifying and categorizing context-dependent themes within them. Our findings supported Richman and Jason's (2001) perspective, which emphasized that a significant portion of the medical community still attributes psychiatric causes to CFS, whereas people with CFS largely attribute their illness to a currently unknown biological etiology. In conjunction with the quantitative results, our qualitative findings can give voice to a group of people who have been disbelieved and historically silenced. As indicated by V. Anderson et al., qualitative methods allow researchers to take a deeper look at the relationship of illness perception to power distribution, oppression, and privilege in society and ultimately to develop consciousness-raising strategies to disseminate the reality of the CFS experience to the general public. Our qualitative findings support the need for research on the self-perceptions of those with CFS as a way to better understand experiences of marginalization.

Epidemiologic studies can also gather information that can help explain genetic and biological factors associated with an illness, thereby providing basic information about the pathophysiology of disease. As part of our epidemiologic study of CFS, blood samples were collected and analyzed, and we are currently exploring differences in genetic and biological markers in our various sample groups. Past research by our group (Porter, Lerch, Jason, Sorenson, & Fletcher, 2010) uncovered findings compatible with a latent viral infection in various CFS subgroups. Such findings demonstrate the need for the continued study of viral exposure and other biological factors in individuals with CFS.

While using mixed methods in our natural history study of CFS, we have had an opportunity to collaborate with physicians, psychologists, psychiatrists, epidemiologists, biostatisticians, immunologists, economists, and computer scientists. The latter collaboration has involved a procedure called data mining, which uses neural networks to help determine the types of symptoms that may be most useful in accurately diagnosing CFS (Jason, Skendrovic, et al., 2011). Neural networks are computer simulations that attempt to mimic the processing technique used by the human brain, and we are now investigating how the network learns and what inputs the network determines to be the most effective way to classify people into diagnostic categories. Clearly, these types of multidisciplinary collaborations are essential to and compatible with the methodological pluralism that has been advocated in this volume.

We know that the phenomena we study interact in complex ways, and these dynamic systems (Hirsch, Levine, & Miller, 2007) often can only be understood at multiple levels in nonlinear ways. As an example, sometimes small inputs can result in large and unanticipated outcomes. Dynamic systems such as catastrophe theory models abrupt changes in behavior due to small changes in system parameters (Witkiewitz & Marlatt, 2004). Such theories might provide the conceptual foundations for more sophisticated methods to explain complex systems. Although the scientific community has been resistant to embracing such methods (Resnicow & Page, 2008), we probably will need to turn to these types of dynamic models to understand how the immune, endocrine, and nervous systems interact with each other (Broderick et al., 2010) as well as how more environmental and policy systems affect individuals with myalgic encephalopathy and CFS.

SUMMARY: BENEFITS AND DRAWBACKS OF THE EPIDEMIOLOGIC APPROACH

In this chapter, we have described several designs related to the conduct of population-based epidemiologic studies. Besides retrospective case-control studies and prospective cohort studies, the chapter's focus has been on cross-sectional epidemiologic studies, with the prevalence study as a particular example. Several issues concerning such studies warrant discussion. First, when attempting to obtain population-based prevalence estimates of a disease, it is important to ensure that the sample is composed of a representative and nonbiased group of individuals so that the results can be generalized to the population. Biased sampling may over- or underestimate the true prevalence rate; for example, using physician gatekeepers to identify cases of CFS results in higher than population-based estimates of disease frequency. If this bias occurs, it will impede efforts to both understand the nature of the condition and develop appropriate and effective social and community interventions.

Second, diagnostic definitions affect the prevalence rate, and tracking prevalence rates over time using different studies from the literature needs to be done with caution to ensure comparable case definition. As is evident with the case of CFS, if either too narrow or too broad case definitions are used by investigators, there will be large changes in prevalence rates for the illness. Most alarmingly, however, is that the use of a broadened case definition might misidentify true cases of the illness and overidentify cases that should not be included, thereby making it more difficult to have comparable samples across different investigative teams as well as to identify biological markers.

Finally, the design of cross-sectional surveys may need to accommodate for population size or disease rarity by using a two-phase screening and estimation design rather than a simple random sample. All individuals in a sample cannot be examined medically and psychiatrically given the expense of these procedures, so appropriate methods often need to be developed to screen for those individuals with the greatest chance of having the illness during an initial phase of the study. In addition, as illustrated in this chapter, proper statistical techniques need to be used to obtain accurate prevalence estimates, especially when such multistage sampling is used. These concepts and issues have been illustrated using a prevalence study of CFS, demonstrating how epidemiologic research can result in findings having significant implications and consequences for sizable groups within society.

REFERENCES

Abbey, S. E. (1993). Somatization, illness attribution and the sociocultural psychiatry of chronic fatigue syndrome. In B. R. Bock & J. Whelan (Eds.), *Chronic fatigue syndrome* (pp. 238–261). New York, NY: Wiley.

Anderson, J. S., & Ferrans, C. E. (1997). The quality of life of persons with chronic fatigue syndrome. *Journal of Nervous and Mental Disease, 185,* 359–367. doi:10.1097/00005053-199706000-00001

Anderson, V., Jason, L. A., Porter, N., & Cudia, J. (2011). *A natural history study of ME/CFS in the community: A qualitative analysis.* Manuscript submitted for publication.

Barsky, A. J., & Borus, J. F. (1999). Functional somatic syndromes. *Annals of Internal Medicine, 130,* 910–921.

Broderick, G., Fuite, J., Kreitz, A., Vernon, S. D., Klimas, N., & Fletcher, M. A. (2010). A formal analysis of cytokine networks in chronic fatigue syndrome. *Brain, Behavior, and Immunity, 24,* 1209–1217. doi:10.1016/j.bbi.2010.04.012

Buchwald, D., Pearlman, T., Umali, J., Schmaling, K., & Katon, W. (1996). Functional status in patients with chronic fatigue syndrome, other fatiguing illnesses, and healthy individuals. *The American Journal of Medicine, 101,* 364–370. doi:10.1016/S0002-9343(96)00234-3

Cantwell, D. P. (1996). Classification of child and adolescent psychopathology. *Journal of Child Psychology and Psychiatry, and Allied Disciplines, 37,* 3–12. doi:10.1111/j.1469-7610.1996.tb01377.x

Coggon, D., Rose, G., & Barker, D. J. P. (1997). *Epidemiology for the uninitiated.* (4th ed.). BMJ Publishing Group. Retrieved from http://resources.bmj.com/bmj/readers/epidemiology-for-the-uninitiated/epide

First, M. B., Spitzer, R. L., Gibbon, M., & Williams, J. B. W. (1995). *Structured clinical interview for DSM–IV axis disorders* (Patient ed.). New York, NY: New York State Psychiatric Institute, Biometrics Research Department.

Fukuda, K., Straus, S. E., Hickie, I., Sharpe, M. C., Dobbins, J. G., & Komaroff, A. (1994). The chronic fatigue syndrome: A comprehensive approach to its definition and study. *Annals of Internal Medicine, 121,* 953–959.

Green, J., Romei, J., & Natelson, B. J. (1998). Stigma and chronic fatigue syndrome. *Journal of Chronic Fatigue Syndrome, 5,* 63–95. doi:10.1300/J092v05n02_04

Gordis, L. (2000). *Epidemiology.* Philadelphia, PA: W. B. Saunders.

Gunn, W. J., Connell, D. B., & Randall, B. (1993). Epidemiology of chronic fatigue syndrome: The Centers for Disease Control study. In B. R. Bock & J. Whelan (Eds.), *Chronic fatigue syndrome* (pp. 83–101). New York, NY: Wiley.

Helzer, J. E., Robins, L., Taibleson, M., Woodruff, R., Reich, T., & Wish, E. (1977). Reliability of psychiatric diagnosis. *Archives of General Psychiatry, 34,* 129–133.

Hirsch, G. B., Levine, R. L., & Miller, R. L. (2007). Using system dynamics modeling to understand the impact of social change initiatives. *American Journal of Community Psychology, 39,* 239–253. doi:10.1007/s10464-007-9114-3

Jason, L. A., & Choi, M. (2008). Dimensions and assessment of fatigue. In Y. Yatanabe, B. Evengard, B. H. Natelson, L. A. Jason, & H. Kuratsune (Eds.), *Fatigue science for human health* (pp. 1–16). Tokyo, Japan: Springer.

Jason, L. A., Najar, N., Porter, N., & Reh, C. (2009). Evaluating the Centers for Disease Control's empirical chronic fatigue syndrome case definition. *Journal of Disability Policy Studies, 20*(2), 93–100. doi:10.1177/1044207308325995

Jason, L. A., Porter, N., Hunnell, J., Rademaker, A., & Richman, J. (2011). CFS prevalence and risk factors over time. *Journal of Health Psychology, 16,* 445–456. doi:10.1177/1359105310383603

Jason, L. A., Richman, J. A., Rademaker, A. W., Jordan, K. M., Plioplys, A. V., Taylor, R., . . . Plioplys, S. (1999). A community-based study of chronic fatigue syndrome. *Archives of Internal Medicine, 159,* 2129–2137. doi:10.1001/archinte.159.18.2129

Jason, L. A., Skendrovic, B., Furst, J., Brown, A., Weng, A., & Bronikowski, C. (2011). Data mining: Comparing the empiric CFS to the Canadian ME/CFS case definition. *Journal of Clinical Psychology.* Advance online publication. doi:10.1002/jclp.20827

Kelly, J. G. (2003). Science and community psychology: Social norms for pluralistic inquiry. *American Journal of Community Psychology, 31,* 213–217. doi:10.1023/A:1023998318268

Kish, L. (1965). *Survey sampling.* New York, NY: Wiley.

Leckliter, I. N., & Matarazzo, J. D. (1994). Diagnosis and classification. In V. B. Van Hasselt & M. Hersen (Eds.), *Advanced abnormal psychology* (pp. 3–18). New York, NY: Plenum Press.

Levy, P. S., & Lemeshow, S. (1999). *Sampling of populations* (3rd ed.). New York, NY: Wiley.

McCluskey, D. R. (1993). Pharmacological approaches to the therapy of chronic fatigue syndrome. In B. R. Bock & J. Whelan (Eds.), *Chronic fatigue syndrome* (pp. 280–297). New York, NY: Wiley.

Porter, N., Lerch, A., Jason, L. A., Sorenson, M., & Fletcher, M. A. (2010). A comparison of immune functionality in viral versus non-viral CFS subtypes. *Journal of Behavioral and Neuroscience Research, 8,* 1–8.

Reeves, W. C., Jones, J. J., Maloney, E., Heim, C., Hoaglin, D. C., Boneva, R., . . . Devlin, R. (2007). New study on the prevalence of CFS in metro, urban and rural Georgia populations. *Population Health Metrics, 5,* 5. doi:10.1186/1478-7954-5-5

Reeves, W. C., Wagner, D., Nisenbaum, R., Jones, J. F., Gurbaxani, B., Solomon, L., . . . Heim, C. (2005). Chronic fatigue Syndrome—A clinical empirical approach to its definition and study. *BMC Medicine, 3,* 19. doi:10.1186/1741-7015-3-19

Regier, D. A., Boyd, J. H., Burke, J. D., Jr., Rae, D. S., Myers, J. K., Kramer, M., . . . Locke, B. Z. (1988). One-month prevalence of mental disorders in the United States: Based on five epidemiological catchment area sites. *Archives of General Psychiatry, 45,* 977–986.

Resnicow, K., & Page, S. E. (2008). Embracing chaos and complexity: A quantum change for public health. *American Journal of Public Health, 98,* 1382–1389. doi:10.2105/AJPH.2007.129460

Reyes, M., Gary, H. E., Jr., Dobbins, J. G., Randall, B., Steele, L., Fukuda, K., . . . Reeves, W. C. (1997, February 21). Descriptive epidemiology of chronic fatigue syndrome: CDC Surveillance in four cities. *Morbidity and Mortality Weekly Report, Surveillance Summaries, 46,* 1–13.

Reyes, M., Nisenbaum, R., Hoaglin, D. C., Unger, E. R., Emmons, C., Randall, B., . . . Reeves, W. C. (2003). Prevalence and incidence of chronic fatigue syndrome in Wichita, Kansas. *Archives of Internal Medicine, 163,* 1530–1536. doi:10.1001/archinte.163.13.1530

Richman, J. A., Flaherty, J. A., & Rospenda, K. M. (1994). Chronic fatigue syndrome: Have flawed assumptions been derived from treatment-based studies? *American Journal of Public Health, 84,* 282–284. doi:10.2105/AJPH.84.2.282

Richman, J. A. & Jason, L. A. (2001). Gender biases underlying the social construction of illness states: The case of chronic fatigue syndrome. *Current Sociology, 49,* 15–29.

Rothman, K. J. (2002). *Epidemiology: An introduction.* Oxford, England: Oxford University Press.

Shrout, P. E., & Newman, S. C. (1989). Design of two-phase prevalence surveys of rare disorders. *Biometrics, 45,* 549–555. doi:10.2307/2531496

Snow, J. (1856). Cholera and the water supply in the South districts of London in 1854. *Journal of Public Health and Sanitary Review, 2,* 239–256. Retrieved from http://johnsnow.matrix.msu.edu/work.php?id=15-78-56

Torres-Harding, S. R., Herrell, R., & Howard, C. (2004). Epidemiological research: Science and community participation. In L. A. Jason, C. B. Keys, Y. Suarez-Balcazar, R. R. Taylor, M. I. Davis, J. A. Durlak, & D. H. Isenberg (Eds.), *Participatory community research: Theories and methods in action* (pp. 53–69). Washington, DC: American Psychological Association. doi:10.1037/10726-003

Tucker, G. J. (1998). Putting DSM–IV in perspective. *The American Journal of Psychiatry, 155,* 159–161.

U.S. Public Health Service, Office of the Surgeon General. (1964). *Smoking and health: Report of the Advisory Committee to the Surgeon General of the Public Health Service.* Washington, DC: Author.

Witkiewitz, K., & Marlatt, G. A. (2004). Relapse prevention for alcohol and drug problems. That was zen, this was tao. *American Psychologist, 59,* 224–235. doi:10.1037/0003-066X.59.4.224

Yach, D. (2010). From Framingham to the framework convention on tobacco control. *Progress in Cardiovascular Diseases, 53,* 52–54. doi:10.1016/j.pcad.2010.05.001

12

APPLYING GEOGRAPHIC INFORMATION SYSTEMS TO COMMUNITY RESEARCH

CORY M. MORTON, N. ANDREW PETERSON, PAUL W. SPEER,
ROBERT J. REID, AND JOSEPH HUGHEY

In this chapter, we explore the possibilities and applications of geographic information systems (GIS) in relation to the practice of community research. GIS is a combination of analytical tools allowing users to investigate spatial or geographic information. Without explicitly realizing it, people frequently analyze spatial information in their daily lives. Every time someone decides to take a shortcut from point A to point B or map out the best route to the airport to avoid traffic, the person is analyzing spatial information. GIS allows people to analyze this type of information in a detailed way. It can include information about the physical environment (e.g., buildings, roads) as well as information about the socioeconomic environment (e.g., unemployment rates, demographic profiles) and how individuals move through their environment (e.g., paths taken to work, the nearest alcohol retailer). The common feature is that the information has some geographic reference. For example, in the case of the physical environment, the geographic reference could be a street address, and in the case of the socioeconomic environment, the reference could be aggregated individual characteristics, as in unemployment rates in a zip code (Martin, 1991; Steinberg & Steinberg, 2006). The ability to analyze individual and group processes in context has long been a goal of community-based research.

GIS

explore potential uses

The Society for Community Research and Action has stated the follow- (SRA) ing as one of its four broad principles: "Human competencies and problems are best understood by viewing people within their social, cultural, economic, geographic, and historical contexts" (Society for Community Research and Action, n.d., para. 4). Luke (2005) examined the content of empirical articles published in the *American Journal of Community Psychology* and found that although researchers used contextual frameworks in their work, they rarely applied contextual methods to the examination of community phenomena, creating a disconnect between their theoretical orientation and their methods in terms of both data collection and analytic approach.

GIS has been used extensively over the past 2 decades to examine contextual impact on individual and group behavior. Investigations have focused on a range of topics, including environmental justice, disease diffusion, child abuse, food availability in poor communities, and alcohol and tobacco retailing (Coulton, Crampton, Irwin, Spilsbury, & Korbin, 2007; Morton, Peterson, Schneider, Smith, & Armstead, 2010; Verhasselt, 1993; Weitzman, Folkman, Folkman, & Wechsler, 2003). Although this work reflects diverse subject matter, there exists a common thread throughout, namely, the investigation of context and place. This investigation of place has been mainly concerned with seeking out spatial patterns in the distribution of some variable. Is child maltreatment concentrated in impoverished neighborhoods? Do tobacco companies selectively market to neighborhoods with certain racial profiles? The questions asked in an analysis using GIS seek to establish this pattern and make it visible through both mapping and statistical analysis.

The use of GIS focuses explicitly on context by using data and methods that place objects of interest within their particular context and spatial plane. It is hard to think about the context of community without recognizing the unique role of geography on the processes at play. GIS allows for modeling the combination of different types of variables affecting community life, including geographic, economic, and cultural variables. This chapter is intended to provide an introduction to GIS capabilities. Although the techniques for creating maps and conducting spatial analysis are beyond the scope of this introduction, we do present an example of a GIS application at the close of the chapter to illustrate the use of the technique in community-based research.

The Environmental Systems Research Institute's (2001) *Dictionary of GIS Terminology* defines a *geographic information system* as a collection of computer hardware, software, and geographic data for capturing, storing, updating, manipulating, analyzing, and displaying all forms of geographically referenced information. GIS is an "integrated system of components" (Maantay & Ziegler, 2006, p. 8) in which users combine contextual data from different sources and integrate both spatial and nonspatial data to arrive at conclusions to social problems. Although a common product of GIS is a map, GIS can also be used to complete spatial statistical analysis and to do much more than simple map making (Galati, 2006; Luke, 2005). Typically, GIS enables users to layer information to represent complex contextual relationships. Layering data is at the heart of GIS and can be thought of as stacking transparencies to get a picture of a series of relationships. Online Figure 12.1 in this chapter's web appendix (http://pubs.apa.org/books/supp/Jason-Glenwick) illustrates this. At the foundation the user has an image base (here an aerial photograph), followed by two more layers that add information about the area under review: the municipal boundaries and road network. Information is layered until the user has combined the features needed to elaborate on a research question. Notice that as the user layers different elements, different data types are also combined. For instance, the spatial data of where a neighborhood boundary is located (e.g., census tract) are combined with the nonspatial data of the median income within the neighborhood, and typically, geographic features have a multitude of nonspatial data ready for combination or layering (Maantay & Ziegler, 2006).

Integrating GIS into community-based research allows for a nuanced investigation of the role environmental and spatial attributes of an area play in terms of affecting individual or group processes. The growing recognition of the importance of place in determining behavior has provided an impetus for methodological techniques that use the spatial dimension of communities in the conceptual and analytical approach to solving community problems. To that end, this chapter serves as an introduction to GIS and its use in a community-based research project. To illustrate the ability to use GIS for community-level research, its functionality is broadly broken down into three activities: data sourcing, data representation, and data analysis. The following section describes each of these activities.

USING GEOGRAPHIC INFORMATION SYSTEMS

It should first be noted that although cartographic and geographic theory was used in the creation of GIS, GIS remains a platform that will accept the theoretical orientation of its user. That being said, one caveat has effects for the statistical analysis of any geographic information. This problem deals not with the conceptual model that users bring to their understanding of relationships but with the statistical analysis of those concepts. It is the problem of spatial autocorrelation, which "corresponds to what was once called the first law of geography: everything is related to everything else, but near things are more related than distant things" (Lee & Wong, 2001, pp.78–79). This means that in spatial analysis the assumption that observations are independent does not always hold. Therefore, statistical controls must be used to correct for the fact that objects located close together are related to one another because of proximity alone.

Data Sourcing

The unique feature of GIS is its ability to combine an almost endless array of data types in one place. As such, GIS may use primary data, secondary data, or a combination of the two. The U.S. Census Bureau provides a comprehensive collection of spatial and demographic data available at different levels of aggregation. From census data, one can investigate the distribution of socioeconomic and demographic characteristics at the neighborhood, county, and state levels and beyond. Most states collect and make available geographic information as well, such as the land use data and licensing information used in the application example in this chapter's web appendix. The data used in GIS are driven by the research question asked, and most endeavors that consider community context have an available geographic component that may be analyzed using GIS. The following example illustrates the flexibility and creativity that can be combined to help answer research questions using GIS.

Mason, Cheung, and Walker (2004) investigated how social networks and geography combine to influence substance use among urban-dwelling adolescents. This study used primary and secondary data collection methods to envision substance-using adolescents' safety and risk environments. Participants were asked to list the people and places that were either risky or safe and to provide an address or cross streets so the researchers could pinpoint the location using GIS. Additionally, the researchers used several secondary data sources: census data to create the spatial distribution of poverty in the neighborhoods where the adolescents lived; police reports to indicate the distribution of violent crime; and licensing data to plot the location of liquor stores. Positive resources, such as libraries and boys and girls clubs, were also included. Using an illustrative case study from their sample, Mason et al. (2004) were able to show that within walking distance of adolescents' homes, risk factors heavily outweighed protective factors. It was much easier to walk to a liquor store or a substance-using friend's home than it was to walk to a boys and girls club or to a nonsubstance- using friend's home. This investigation showed how using GIS and thinking spatially about adolescents' substance use behavior and environment may inform prevention efforts.

Additionally, Coombes, Jones, and Hillsdon (2010) investigated the relationship of physical activity to obesity prevention in Great Britain by combining surveys about the use of public green space with information about individual accessibility to green space using GIS. Coombes et al. postulated that easier access to public green space would encourage more frequent physical activity and thus have a community impact on rates of obesity. Their findings suggested that proximity to green space does indeed encourage activity and that individual weight increased as the distance to accessible green space increased (Coombes et al., 2010).

The implications of studies such as those of Mason et al. (2004) and Coombes et al. (2010) operate at both the individual and community levels. For example, knowledge of youths' substance use environment can inform treatment plans in which practitioners connect youths to prosocial network opportunities, such as after-school programs. Also illustratively, knowledge that access to green space may reduce obesity can inform public policy and siting strategies with respect to public parks or athletic fields.

Data Representation

The mapping features of GIS model the data in one of two ways, namely, either vector models or raster models. A *vector model* uses two-dimensional information about a geographic feature composed of points to form lines or polygons on a spatial plane. These points represent a specific location on a map with unique x and y coordinates, often latitude and longitude. They could represent the location of a school, motor vehicle accident, retail establishment, or a community pharmacy, as in Online Figure 12.2, represented by either a cross or a star. Later in the chapter, we discuss an application of GIS focusing on community pharmacies that retail products associated with disease: tobacco, alcohol, or lottery tickets. In Online Figure 12.2, pharmacies that retail no disease-promoting products are labeled with a cross, whereas those that carry any combination of tobacco, alcohol, or lottery tickets are labeled as disease-promoting pharmacies and identified with a star.

Vector models may also be used to combine a series of points, and this series of coordinates or points forms lines, represented when the points in a spatial plane are connected. Lines are used most often to represent street networks. Lines in GIS always have a direction, which is given by the order of coordinates indicating how the line should be formed (Clarke, 1999). Finally, polygons are line segments that are enclosed, forming an area as in the census tract boundaries in Online Figure 12.2. They generally represent a sort of boundary, as in county, census tract, election district, or tax parcel. Many spatial features may be thought of as polygons. Vector models allow for great precision because lines and polygons may be formed using an infinite number of points to create great detail in representation. Discrete data are best represented by the vector model, and the ability to have this type of data represented in a figure or map allows readers to easily ascertain patterns that could be lost in tables.

For example, Luke, Esmundo, and Bloom (2000) investigated the link between tobacco advertising, specifically outdoor billboards, and the socioeconomic profiles of neighborhoods. Their findings indicated that there was a targeted market campaign to neighborhoods with lower incomes and higher percentages of African American residents. Using a vector model to represent median family income by census block group and the location points for tobacco billboards, Luke et al. were able to show a clear pattern of targeted marketing activities. The example contained in this chapter also presents a vector model, as seen in Online Figure 12.2. In this investigation we investigated the siting strategies of pharmacies that sold addictive products (i.e., alcohol, tobacco, lottery tickets). Online Figure 12.2 shows Passaic County, New Jersey, divided into census tracts and visually illustrates that tracts with higher percentages of Latino residents were more likely to have a higher density of pharmacies retailing addictive products.

Raster models use a grid placed on a spatial plane to hold data about its features. Whereas vector models use points to represent data, raster models use an interconnected grid containing information within each square in the grid. As such, these models do not provide the precise location of features, only that the features are located within the grid (DeMers, 1997). The size of the squares within the grid can be thought of as the resolution of the model, as in pixels on a computer screen, and the smaller the size of the pixel, the higher the resolution and the greater the detail when viewing. Raster models are generally used to represent continuous data, such as terrain, temperature, and orthophotography. An example of a raster model is the satellite function of Google maps in which satellite images or aerial photography are georeferenced and then pieced together on a map.

Data Analysis

A wide range of data analysis can be completed using GIS. Here we concentrate on the analysis of discrete objects in space, focusing on three types of information about these entities that answer three questions: "What is it? Where is it? (description) and What is its relation to other entities? (decision making)" (Burrough & McDonnell, 1998, p. 163). These questions break down into the two basic categories of data analysis, that is, description and decision making.

As in other approaches to data analysis, one must first be concerned with describing one's data. GIS allows for description of points in space by attaching properties and location information to these discrete elements. As mentioned earlier, layering is a major foundation of GIS, and this is used in description through the ability to join layers together in both visual and tabular form. One can simply use this to describe an area (e.g., the number of people unemployed in a neighborhood or the name of a particular liquor store), perform simple arithmetical operations (e.g., the employment rate in a neighborhood or a count of the liquor stores in a neighborhood), or perform Boolean operations on the attributes allowing one to find specific combinations of data that fit research questions (e.g., identifying the liquor stores in a neighborhood with 600 square feet of retail space that also sold tobacco products).

The visual analysis associated with GIS is the map, and in terms of analyzing data this is the *thematic map*, which is a "specialized map that depicts the spatial distribution of one or more explicit themes" (Galati, 2006, p.156). Thematic maps allow users to depict relationships usually seen in tabular form on a geographic plane so that bivariate or multivariate relationships can be visualized. GIS allows for several types of thematic maps to be created: choropleth, graduated symbol, and dot density maps. Choropleth maps are also referred to as *graduated color maps* and use shading or color to represent values (ratios, proportions) within bounded regions. An example is the mapping of population density for counties in a state, with darker colors representing densely populated areas (see Online Figure 12.3 in this chapter's web appendix). *Graduated symbol maps* are similar in that the same type of relationship is represented, but instead of color they use a symbol to represent values (see Online Figure 12.4 in this chapter's web appendix). Generally these maps use a circle or a dot, going from smaller to bigger to represent progressively increasing values. Dot density maps are used to show the position of some attribute within a large area. For instance, one could map the population of municipalities within a county. Dots represent a user-identified quantity to portray the distribution of an attribute over a large space (see Online Figure 12.5 in this chapter's web appendix).

GIS allows for several options, from description to multivariate statistical analysis, for considering an entity's relationship with other entities. At the simplest level, the operations completed within GIS can be exported to an outside statistical package for analysis. However, the option exists in some GIS software packages to complete multivariate analysis within the GIS instead of exporting to another statistical package, especially if the analysis is concerned with the spatial nature of the data and using points for proximity, hotspot, or network analysis. These tools are used to show, respectively, the distance and relationship between two points, to identify areas where a certain activity is likely to cluster (e.g., crime in a city), or to identify the best route along a network (e.g., community access to a mental health clinic). We now turn to an example of the application of GIS in an applied community context, namely, predicting the density of community pharmacies.

GEOGRAPHIC INFORMATION SYSTEMS APPLICATION: PREDICTING THE DENSITY OF DISEASE-PROMOTING PHARMACIES

As part of a larger initiative in Passaic County, New Jersey, called Project C.O.P.E. (Communities Organizing for Prevention and Empowerment), we applied GIS in an analysis of the locations of community pharmacies in the target county to determine whether pharmacies that sold potentially harmful products (i.e., tobacco, alcohol, and lottery tickets) were more likely to be located in communities of color and those with less access to resources. The density of certain types of outlets, such as alcohol, is an important community-level factor that may contribute to health disparities, and community leaders in this county expressed an interest in studying the issue.

Community pharmacies play an important role in the U.S. health care system, filling prescriptions for patients and acting as a conduit for health communication. Concern is raised when these public health arenas also serve as retailers for addictive and harmful products. The sale of tobacco, alcohol, and lottery products in pharmacies serves as a contradiction in the health promotion role that pharmacies usually play. Tobacco products are associated with 438,000 deaths per year in the United States and $167 billion in annual health-related costs and loss of labor productivity (American Cancer Society, 2007; Centers for Disease Control and Prevention, 2005). Alcohol abuse is linked with $68 billion in lost productivity and $26 billion in health costs annually (National Institute on Alcohol Abuse and Alcoholism, 2000). Additionally, lottery ticket sales represent another threat to individual health in terms of addiction and financial loss. Most pharmacists are decidedly against the sale of tobacco and alcohol products on their shelves (Hudmon, Fenlon, Corelli, Prokhorov, & Schroeder, 2006; Kotecki, Fowler, German, Stephenson, & Warnick, 2000). The sale of these products in pharmacies is incongruous because the image projected by pharmacies' status as health care institutions collides with the destructive and unhealthy nature of these products. Freudenberg (2005) referred to such activities as "disease promotion" (p. 299) practices, and we refer to community pharmacies that sell the previously mentioned three products as *disease-promoting pharmacies*. This GIS application investigated predictors of the density of community pharmacies that choose to stock these products.

The focus of the GIS application here was geocoding, or the ability to assign an address specific spatial coordinates to place it on a map. We achieved this using ArcGIS software available from Environmental Systems Research Institute. However, there are many platforms that perform geocoding, such as Geolytics, USC Web GIS geocoder, and Batch Geocode, among others. Data sourcing for this analysis was achieved through secondary sources and was obtained either for free or for a nominal fee for mailing (these data are available for analysis in this chapter's web appendix). This is representative of much information that may be obtained for GIS purposes, although such data do not necessarily come in a form that is ready for interpretation through GIS.

Before the process of geocoding begins, the information must be rendered usable. The goal of the present analysis was to differentiate pharmacies that carry products of disease promotion from those that do not. A first step was to cross-reference the pharmacy data with the tobacco, alcohol, and lottery outlet data to create one table of address and attribute information that identified the presence of disease-promoting products. From this table we were ready to begin the process of geocoding. Before beginning the geocoding process, one must carefully look at the quality of information contained in a table. Because GIS data come from a wide variety of sources, the quality of data also varies widely. The quality of the data will affect the success in matching addresses to a position on the map, so the user should look carefully for irregularities in the data, including spelling errors, missing data, and incomplete data. There should be no empty rows in the address table because this will interrupt and compromise the geocoding process. The necessary minimum fields for completing the geocoding operation are an address and a zip code, although more information is generally included, which will inform analysis and visual representation. Finally, the table should be saved in .dbf IV format. There are several options for completing this transformation. For example, using SPSS, one can save the table as .dbf IV format for interpretation by geocoding services.

The process of geocoding uses a table of street lines and reference data to place the address correctly on a map. In the United States this reference table is created by the Census Bureau and called TIGER/Line files (topographically integrated geographic encoding and reference system). These files are digital representations of geographic features, including roads, railways, official boundaries, lakes, and more, and require the use of a GIS program to interpret them for representation (U.S. Census Bureau, 2005).

At the close of the geocoding process, the physical locations of the pharmacies were placed on a map (as in Online Figure 12.2 in which the stars and crosses represent pharmacies). This map uses the vector model of data representation that was discussed earlier, relying on points to visually convey information. Here, the locations of pharmacies are indicated by a point on the map in Online Figure 12.2. The locations of pharmacies were then used in the creation of a tract-level data file, which served as the basis for our subsequent analyses. Using GIS, we counted the number of pharmacies located in each census tract. Ultimately, data from five different sources (i.e., pharmacy licenses, tobacco licenses, alcohol licenses, lottery licenses, and U.S. Census data) were combined in this analysis. The first data set included the names and addresses of all licensed pharmacies in the study area (i.e., Passaic County, New Jersey) for the year 2008. This data set was obtained from New Jersey's Department of Law & Public Safety, Division of Consumer Affairs, Board of Pharmacy, which licenses and regulates pharmacies in the state. The second data set included the names and addresses of all retailers that had obtained licenses to sell cigarettes in the study county for the year 2008. This data set was obtained from New Jersey's Department of the Treasury. The third data set contained names and addresses of all retailers licensed to sell alcohol in the study county in 2008. These data were obtained from New Jersey's Division of Alcoholic Beverage Control. The fourth data set included the names and addresses of all retailers that had licenses to sell lottery tickets in the study county in 2008. These were obtained from the New Jersey Lottery Commission (see the web appendix to this chapter).

The pharmacy-level data set was created by adding alcohol license status, tobacco license status, and lottery license status to the data set containing all community pharmacies in the study county. For purposes of this study, if a retail outlet, such as a mass merchandiser, had a pharmacy located in it and also sold tobacco, then the pharmacy was defined as selling tobacco. Addresses of all 108 community pharmacies were geocoded using the 2000 TIGER/line street data for the county. Consistent with prior research in this area (Hickey, Farris, Peterson, & Aquilino, 2006; Morton et al., 2010), we excluded from our analysis those pharmacies located in hospitals. The use of GIS allowed us to export the data from the geocoding process discussed earlier to our final data set. Each pharmacy was assigned a spatial locator (here the census tract) that would be used as the grouping variable in our multivariate analysis. Data from the pharmacy-level data file were then added to the census tract-level file that included the dependent variable and the demographic predictors used in this study.

Density of disease-promoting pharmacies, the dependent variable, was operationalized as the number of pharmacies selling tobacco, alcohol, or lottery tickets per 10 kilometers of roadway in a census tract in the year 2008. Demographics (i.e., percentage of Latino residents, percentage of African American residents, and median household income) were obtained using 2000 census data for the tract in which the pharmacies were located. We expected that census tracts with higher percentages of Latino and African American residents and census tracts with lower median household income would have greater densities of disease-promoting pharmacies than census tracts with lower percentages of Latino and African American residents and census tracts with higher median household income.

Of the 108 community pharmacies in the county, the majority (69.4%) sold tobacco, alcohol, and/or lottery tickets. To test our main research question, we performed analyses of variance to examine differences in the density of disease-promoting pharmacies across quartile categories for each demographic predictor. We achieved this by exporting the density information from GIS and using SPSS for the statistical analysis. Analysis of variance was used to align our analysis with previous research (Hyland et al., 2003; Schneider, Reid, Peterson, & Hughey, 2005). The findings are presented in Table 12.1. The analysis of variance results indicated statistically significant effects for percentage of Latino residents, $F(3, 81) = 6.23, p < .001$, percentage of African American residents, $F(3, 81) = 3.22, p < .05$, and median income, $F(3, 81) = 4.33, p < .01$. As can be seen in Table 12.1, census tracts with the highest proportions of Latino residents and the highest proportions of African American residents had significantly greater density of disease-promoting pharmacies per 10 kilometers of roadway than did the lowest ethnic and race quartiles. Relative differences among the quartiles were similar for median household income, with census tracts with the lowest median household income having significantly greater density of disease-promoting pharmacies per 10 kilometers of roadway than tracts with higher income. (See Online Figure 12.6 in this chapter's web appendix for a map created in GIS depicting the relationship between disease-promoting pharmacies and median income.)

Thus, neighborhoods with higher concentrations of minority and low-income households may be exposed to these toxic products at significantly greater rates than neighborhoods with higher concentrations of Whites and upper income households. Living in such neighborhoods provides a combination of opportunities and constraints that limit or constrict the choices available to residents.

There are critical reasons to be concerned about increased density of disease-promoting pharmacies in minority and lower income communities. First, outlet density can increase the use of a particular product. Pokorny, Jason, and Schoeny (2003), for example, demonstrated a relationship between retail density and tobacco use. In our analysis, outlet density can be considered as representing greater physical access to tobacco, alcohol, and/or lottery products sold by pharmacies. From an economic perspective, greater outlet density is likely to lower the average travel distance between potential consumers and outlets and the pharmacies' products. These costs (i.e., travel time and money), which are often referred to as *search costs*, are an important part of the net price faced by consumers and have been known for some time to be negatively associated with the quantity of products consumed (e.g., Chaloupka & Warner, 2000; Ohsfeldt, Boyle, & Capilouto, 1997). Search costs are expected to be reduced in communities with higher densities of outlets, and consumption would therefore be expected to increase. In addition, higher densities of storefront advertising and lower prices associated

TABLE 12.1
Density of Disease-Promoting Pharmacies by Percentage of Latino Residents, Percentage of African American Residents, and Median Household Income Quartiles

% Latino (quartiles)	Disease-promoting pharmacies per 10 km of roadway	% Latino, mean differences	% African American (quartiles)	Disease-promoting pharmacies per 10 km of roadway	% African American, mean differences	Median household income (quartiles)	Disease-promoting pharmacies per 10 km of roadway	Median household income, mean differences
(1) > 48.3	.89	1 > 3,4	(1) > 20.1	.57	1,2 > 4	(1) < $31,672	.71	1,2 > 4
(2) > 26.3	.70	2 > 3,4	(2) > 4.8	.78		(2) < $44,375	.77	2 > 3
(3) > 6.0	.23		(3) > 0.75	.44		(3) < $62,600	.32	
(4) ≤ 2.4	.12		(4) ≤ 0.74	.13		(4) ≥ $62,601	.11	

Note. $p < .05$, analysis of variance for all three predictors.

with higher levels of competition among sellers are important potential drivers of the relationship between higher outlet density and demand (Jason, Pokorny, Mikulski, & Schoeny, 2004).

Structural interventions, such as the use of state and local zoning ordinances to control the density and type of retail venues, offer a potential approach for addressing the issue of high densities of disease-promoting pharmacies in communities. A promising approach to limiting access to tobacco is the enforcement of economic penalties on retailers that illegally sell their products to minors (Gemson et al., 1998; Jason, Ji, Anes, & Birkhead, 1991). This approach has been shown to be effective in controlling alcohol consumption and as a means of controlling the sale of tobacco to minors but has not yet been applied to lottery outlets, nor has it been applied across domains. Future research should test the generalizability of our findings and evaluate the effects of interventions that constrain the density of disease-promoting pharmacies in communities.

BENEFITS AND DRAWBACKS OF GEOGRAPHIC INFORMATION SYSTEMS

In this chapter, we have provided an overview of GIS, a concrete description of how to conduct a GIS analysis, and a case study analyzing outlet densities in low-income and minority neighborhoods. The case study presented a direct example of the utility of GIS and demonstrated how community researchers can apply methods consistent with their theoretical conceptualizations of community phenomena. As Luke (2005) noted, researchers' disciplinary methods often fall short of the field's theoretical understandings. GIS represents a valuable tool that can assist community-based practitioners and researchers in their attempts to bridge the gap between their conceptual orientation and practice with communities.

Uncovering relationships such as those reported in the case study creates opportunities for intervening with respect to various social issues. For example, Speer et al. (2003) described a community-organizing intervention that used GIS to understand the association between vacant housing and violent crime rates. The intervention described in their study, which focused on closing access to vacant housing, was implemented by community residents against the prevailing wisdom of some local officials who sought only to strengthen law enforcement. The intervention resulted in reduced violent crime rates, which were achieved not by targeting criminals but by intervening on the environments that allowed violent crimes to flourish.

There are some drawbacks to be aware of when considering implementation of GIS. First, the cost in terms of software and training remains an obstacle for many; however, there are limited freeware GIS applications that may help to reduce the financial burden. Another potential shortcoming can involve measurement. The use of GIS often relies on archival or secondary data sources, which can be limited. Thus, data quality can be an issue with GIS, especially for address data as used in the case study. Often these data are taken from administrative sources, so the user must be careful to assure that the information is reliable and valid before proceeding with analysis. A direct observation research tool similar to that described by Heinrich et al. (2010) might be used by citizen groups and local governments to scan local environments and provide better data for GIS analyses.

Efforts to apply GIS to the analysis of community-level phenomena can have crucial implications for future research and community interventions. Community-based initiatives that attempt to build healthy environments often target sociopolitical, economic, or physical environmental conditions that can promote or constrain lifestyle choices. By applying GIS in the identification of environmental factors that can be targeted for change, community researchers can have a potentially powerful impact in effecting positive individual and community growth and development.

REFERENCES

American Cancer Society. (2007). *Tobacco related cancers fact sheet*. Retrieved from http://www.cancer.org/docroot/PED/content/PED_10_2x_Tobacco-Related_Cancers_Fact_Sheet.asp?sitearea=PED

Burrough, P. A., & McDonnell, R. A. (1998). *Principles of geographical information systems*. New York, NY: Oxford University Press.

Centers for Disease Control and Prevention. (2005). *Annual deaths attributable to cigarette smoking—United States, 1997–2001*. Retrieved from http://www.cdc.gov/tobacco/data_statistics/tables/health/attrdeaths/

Chaloupka, G. J., & Warner, K. E. (2000). The economics of smoking. In A. J. Culyer & J. P. Newhouse (Eds.), *Handbook of health economics* (Vol. 1B, pp. 1539–1612). New York, NY: Elsevier.

Clarke, K. C. (1999). *Getting started with geographic information systems*. Upper Saddle River, NJ: Prentice Hall.

Coombes, E., Jones, A. P., & Hillsdon, M. (2010). The relationship of physical activity and overweight to objectively measured green space accessibility and use. *Social Science & Medicine, 70*, 816–822. doi:10.1016/j.socscimed.2009.11.020

Coulton, C. J., Crampton, D. S., Irwin, M., Spilsbury, J. C., & Korbin, J. E. (2007). How neighborhoods influence child maltreatment: A review of the literature and alternative pathways. *Child Abuse & Neglect, 31*, 1117–1142. doi:10.1016/j.chiabu.2007.03.023

DeMers, M. N. (1997). *Fundamentals of geographic information systems*. New York, NY: Wiley.

Environmental Systems Research Institute. (2001). *Dictionary of GIS terminology*. Redlands, CA: ESRI Press.

Freudenberg, N. (2005). Public health advocacy to change corporate practices: Implications for health education practice and research. *Health Education & Behavior, 32*, 298–319. doi:10.1177/1090198105275044

Galati, S. R. (2006). *Geographic information systems demystified*. Boston, MA: Artech House.

Gemson, D. H., Moats, H. L., Watkins, B. X., Ganz, M. L., Robinson, S., & Healton, E. (1998). Laying down the law: Reducing illegal tobacco sales to minors in central Harlem. *American Journal of Public Health, 88*, 936–939. doi:10.2105/AJPH.88.6.936

Heinrich, K. M., Hughey, J., Randles, A., Wall, D., Peterson, N. A., Jitnarin, N., . . . Poston, W. S. C. (2010). The census of social institutions (CSI): A public health direct observation measure of local land use. *Journal of Urban Health, 87*, 410–415. doi:10.1007/s11524-010-9443-7

Hickey, L. M., Farris, K. B., Peterson, N. A., & Aquilino, M. L. (2006). Predicting tobacco sales in pharmacies using population demographics and pharmacy types. *Journal of the American Pharmacists Association, 45*, 385–390.

Hudmon, K. S., Fenlon, C. M., Corelli, R. L., Prokhorov, A. V., & Schroeder, S. A. (2006). Tobacco sales in pharmacies: Time to quit. *Tobacco Control, 15*, 35–38. doi:10.1136/tc.2005.012278

Hyland, A., Travers, M. J., Cummings, M., Bauer, J., Alford, T., & Wieczorek, W. F. (2003). Tobacco outlet density and demographics in Erie County, New York. *American Journal of Public Health, 93*, 1075–1076. doi:10.2105/AJPH.93.7.1075

Jason, L. A., Ji, P. V., Anes, M. D., & Birkhead, S. H. (1991). Active enforcement of cigarette control laws in the prevention of cigarette sales to minors. *JAMA, 266*, 3159–3161. doi:10.1001/jama.266.22.3159

Jason, L. A., Pokorny, S. B., Mikulski, K., & Schoeny, M. E. (2004). Assessing storefront tobacco advertising after the billboard ban. *Evaluation & the Health Professions, 27*, 22–33. doi:10.1177/0163278703261211

Kotecki, J. E., Fowler, J. B., German, T. C., Stephenson, S. L., & Warnick, T. (2000). Kentucky pharmacists' opinions and practices related to the sale of cigarettes and alcohol in pharmacies. *Journal of Community Health: The Publication for Health Promotion and Disease Prevention, 25*, 343–355. doi:10.1023/A:1005168528085

Lee, J., & Wong, D. W. S. (2001). *Statistical analysis with ArcView GIS*. New York, NY: Wiley.

Luke, D. A. (2005). Getting the big picture in community science: Methods that capture context. *American Journal of Community Psychology, 35*, 185–200. doi:10.1007/s10464-005-3397-z

Luke, D. A., Esmundo, E., & Bloom, Y. (2000). Smoke signs: Patterns of tobacco billboard advertising in a metropolitan region. *Tobacco Control, 9*(1), 16–23.

Maantay, J., & Ziegler, J. (2006). *GIS for the urban environment*. Redlands, CA: ESRI Press.

Martin, D. (1991). *Geographic information systems and their socioeconomic applications*. London, England: Routledge.

Mason, M., Cheung, I., & Walker, L. (2004). Substance use, social networks, and the geography of urban adolescents. *Substance Use & Misuse, 39*, 1751–1777. doi:10.1081/JA-200033222

Morton, C. M., Peterson, N. A., Schneider, J. E., Smith, B. J., & Armstead, T. L. (2010). Tobacco sales in community pharmacies: Remote decisions and demographic targets. *Journal of Community Psychology, 38*, 39–48. doi:10.1002/jcop.20350

National Institute on Alcohol Abuse and Alcoholism. (2000). *Updating estimates of the economic costs of alcohol abuse in the United States*. Retrieved from http://pubs.niaaa.nih.gov/publications/economic-2000/#updated

Ohsfeldt, R. L., Boyle, R. G., & Capilouto, E. (1997). Effects of tobacco excise taxes on the use of smokeless tobacco products in the USA. *Health Economics, 6*, 525–531. doi:10.1002/(SICI)1099-1050(199709)6:5<525::AID-HEC300>3.0.CO;2-Y

Pearce, J., Witter, K., & Bartie, P. (2006). Neighborhoods and health: A GIS approach to measuring community resource accessibility. *Journal of Epidemiology and Community Health, 60*, 389–395. doi:10.1136/jech.2005.043281

Pokorny, S. B., Jason, L. A., & Schoeny, M. E. (2003). The relation of retail tobacco availability to initiation and continued smoking. *Journal of Clinical Child and Adolescent Psychology, 32*, 193–204. doi:10.1207/S15374424JCCP3202_4

Schneider, J. E., Reid, R. J., Peterson, N. A., & Hughey, J. (2005). Tobacco outlet density and demographics at the tract level of analysis in Iowa: Implications for environmentally based prevention initiatives. *Prevention Science, 6*, 319–325. doi:10.1007/s11121-005-0016-z

Society for Community Research and Action. (n.d.). *About SCRA*. Retrieved from http://www.scra27.org/about

Speer, P. W., Ontkush, M., Schmitt, B., Raman, P., Jackson, C., Rengert, K. M., & Peterson, N. A. (2003). The intentional exercise of power: Community organizing in Camden, New Jersey. *Journal of Community & Applied Social Psychology, 13*, 399–408. doi:10.1002/casp.745

Steinberg, S. J., & Steinberg, S. L. (2006). *Geographic information systems for the social sciences: Investigating space and place*. Thousand Oaks, CA: Sage.

U.S. Census Bureau. (2005). *TIGER overview*. Retrieved from http://www.census.gov/geo/www/tiger/overview.html

Verhasselt, Y. (1993). Geography of health services: Some trends and perspectives. *Social Science & Medicine, 36*, 119–123. doi:10.1016/0277-9536(93)90203-G

Weitzman, E. R., Folkman, A., Folkman, K. Z., & Wechsler, H. (2003). The relationship of alcohol outlet density to heavy and frequent drinking and drinking-related problems among college students at eight universities. *Health & Place, 9*, 1–6. doi:10.1016/S1353-8292(02)00014-X

13

ECONOMIC COST ANALYSIS FOR COMMUNITY-BASED INTERVENTIONS

ANTHONY T. LO SASSO AND LEONARD A. JASON

Community-based interventions frequently deal with such issues of public policy significance as HIV/AIDS risk mitigation, nutritional awareness and improvement, substance abuse prevention, and violence reduction (Jason et al., 2004). As such, support from policymakers or private foundations for implementation of creative solutions to social problems depends critically not only on the benefits of a given program but also on the program's costs. The ability to demonstrate that the value of a program's benefits to

We appreciate the support of Paul Molloy and Leon Venable and the many Oxford House members who have collaborated with our team for the past 15 years, including Bertel Williams, Kathy Sledge, Robin Miller, Bill Kmeck, Makeba Casey, Lester Fleming, Ron Blake, Stephanie Marez, Rory Murray, Carolyn Ellis, LaRonda Stalling, Randy Ramirez, Richard Albert, and Gilberto Padilla. In addition, our thanks to other colleagues and graduate students for helping us with the studies mentioned in this article including (in alphabetical order): Josefina Alvarez, Christopher Beasley, Peter Bishop, Blake Bowden, Richard Contreras, Carmen Curtis, Lucia D'Arlach, Meg Davis, Joseph Ferrari, David Groh, Annie Flynn, Gwen Grams, Ron Harvey, Elizabeth Horin, Bronwyn Hunter, Elias Kinoti, Eve Kot, John Majer, David Mueller, Megan Murphy, Brad Olson, Olya Rabin-Belyaev, Ed Stevens, Ed Taylor, Judah Viola, and Lisa Walt. We appreciate the financial support from the National Institute on Alcohol Abuse and Alcoholism (NIAAA Grants AA12218 and AA16973), the National Institute on Drug Abuse (NIDA Grants DA13231 and DA19935), and the National Center on Minority Health and Health Disparities (Grant MD002748).

proportion minority grants

221

society exceeds its costs is clearly not the only criterion on which program funding (private or public) will be judged, but it is certainly an important one. Moreover, community interventions must be judged not in isolation but relative to existing and competing alternatives. A better social and community intervention can be developed, but at what cost relative to the available or possible alternatives?

The purpose of this chapter is to discuss the essential ingredients necessary to provide useful information to policymakers on the relative costs and benefits of community-based interventions, with an eye toward the unique challenges researchers face in collecting such data in a community research setting. Although these types of data are often either not reported in community-based interventions or are dealt with in a cursory manner, we argue that economic analyses should play a more prominent role in such work.

BACKGROUND AND BASIC TERMINOLOGY

Cost analysis was formally recognized by the federal government as a necessary component of policy analysis during the Reagan administration and later reaffirmed during the Clinton administration. Although at times controversial, the use of economic cost analysis has become an important part of federal review of new regulations and a critical tool for policy planning and resource allocation. The critical guiding principle behind cost analysis is that all activities, from the most mundane to the most intricate and involved, have costs. (metrics)

right

The term *cost* is not simply to be thought of in terms of dollars but more broadly with respect to resources in general. Resources can be material, human, or time. The common thread to resources is that many are inherently scarce. When a scarce resource is used for one purpose, it cannot simultaneously be used for another purpose. For example, an individual can perform only so many tasks in a given day. As another example, when a building or structure houses one production process or provides shelter to one group of individuals, it cannot serve another purpose at the same time. As a third example, when time is spent doing one activity, that time in most cases cannot be spent engaged in another activity. Hence economists view the value of a resource, be it labor, machinery and equipment, or land, relative to the *next best alternative use* of the resource, which is defined as the *opportunity cost*. Opportunity cost is relevant because it explicitly measures the value of what society must forgo to devote a resource to a given purpose.

def.

The notion of defining cost according to opportunity cost is what differentiates economic cost analysis from accounting cost analysis. Accounting *pluralism → policy dev. Bookends*

costs typically are frequently backward looking and depend on prior expenses (often in the context of a firm), for example, previous purchases and the book-keeping costs associated with the purchase price (possibly altered by depreciation adjustments based on accounting rules or tax law).

Economists maintain that scarcity combined with demand for resources is what imparts value to them, which in competitive markets is represented by their price or wage. A good or service that nobody desires (regardless of the price) is in economic analyses inherently without value. The essential role of competitive markets is a recurring theme both in economics and in cost analysis because competitive markets are believed to yield prices that represent the full social costs and societal values of the good or service. Competitive markets are characterized by homogeneous goods (e.g., agricultural products); many fully informed, utility-maximizing consumers; and many profit-maximizing producers operating in unfettered markets. Although not all markets and goods and services meet this standard, the assumption of competitive markets is usually a reasonable approximation. The benefit of the assumption is that market prices and wages can then be used to estimate social costs. There are, however, a number of important exceptions and limitations to this assumption that may need to be recognized, which we discuss in the section that follows.

TYPES OF COST ANALYSIS

There are several types of cost analyses, including cost-minimization, cost–benefit, cost-effectiveness, and cost-utility analyses. They provide policymakers with metrics that allow them to evaluate what gain is derived from a given program at what cost. Ideally, hypothetical policymakers could evaluate all consequences of competing treatments or interventions to make the best choice for maximizing outcomes given budgetary constraints.

The most basic type of cost analysis is *cost-minimization analysis,* in which the goal is to estimate the costs associated with one or more interventions to identify the intervention having the minimum cost. Gains are not considered in this approach. Although seemingly lacking in practical use and inherently limited in its scope, cost minimization is used surprisingly often in economic studies. It is particularly useful in cases for which the outcome of several interventions is the same, for example, accomplishing a given objective, or in cases in which the outcomes are yet unknown. In addition, cost ✓ *are* minimization can be helpful in determining how the *distribution* of the costs might differ between treatment alternatives. For example, patients might bear a greater burden in one case than in another, and this information might be of use to policymakers.

used to compare benefits of prog, serv, treats.

inform resource allocatn. &

Cost–benefit analysis involves the comparison of costs and benefits, all measured in dollar value terms, of at least one new treatment or policy with existing or alternative treatments or policies. The approach usually is best when the outcomes potentially affected by the intervention are manifold, and thus not easily aggregated, or when the outcomes are different across the interventions in question. In community research, cost–benefit analysis is typically the most appropriate technique. For example, one type of intervention aimed at the treatment of depression in the community may have a greater effect on reducing employment turnover, whereas another might reduce use of non-mental-health-care services. In these (quite common instances) the need for a common denominator becomes essential. Dollars become the common denominator for the purposes of comparing costs and benefits. The typical output generated from a cost–benefit analysis is the *net benefit* of each intervention in question, that is, the dollar value of benefits less the dollar value of costs for each intervention.

Cost-effectiveness analysis compares the costs and effectiveness of at least one new treatment to an existing treatment or to no treatment. Cost-effectiveness analysis is usually appropriate when comparing interventions with different expected costs and effectiveness. Importantly, though, effectiveness can be generally encapsulated in one unambiguous outcome measure, typically *life years saved*. The typical output generated from a cost-effectiveness analysis is the *incremental cost-effectiveness ratio* (ICER), which is calculated as the ratio of the incremental costs of the new treatment relative to the established treatment divided by the incremental effectiveness of the new treatment relative to the old treatment. Specifically, the ICER is calculated as follows:

$$\text{ICER} = (\text{cost}_{new} - \text{cost}_{old}) / (\text{life years saved}_{new} - \text{life years saved}_{old}) \quad (1)$$

Because effectiveness is measured in life years, the ICER produces a measure of cost per life year saved. Should a new program cost less than the old program and result in more life years saved, economists maintain that it dominates the old program, and the intervention is worth doing. The gray area usually faced by decision makers is an intervention that increases costs but leads to improved outcomes. In this instance the ratio produces a value of cost per life year saved that does not say in isolation whether the intervention is worth doing; the decision to implement the program or intervention requires an additional step to compare the cost per life year saved against some threshold. The value of the threshold is inherently controversial because any threshold implies that some life-saving interventions are too costly to implement from a societal perspective. It should be noted, however, that cost–benefit studies subsume the issue of valuing life within the analysis, with such improvements in well-being converted into dollar value terms in the course of the study; in this respect cost–benefit analysis must wrestle with the same ethically challenging issues as does cost-effectiveness analysis.

Cost-utility analysis is nearly identical to cost-effectiveness analysis, but the outcome, life years saved, is adjusted by quality of life (or utility) to produce quality adjusted life years saved. The quality of life adjustment involves the assignment of a scale between 0 and 1 in which 0 represents *immediate death* and 1 represents *perfect health* to each life year gained. This modification of cost-effectiveness analysis represents an attempt to incorporate morbidity into the analysis. For example, an intervention for diabetic patients to improve diet and physical activity could have effects on the rate of blindness as well as on mortality rates. Although living with blindness is still living, some might argue that it is living with a lower quality of life than living life not being blind. Thus, the impact of improved diet and exercise among diabetics could lead to increases in the quantity of life (life years saved) but also could lead to reductions in the rate of blindness, which implies fewer life years with blindness. It is intuitively appealing to consider quality of life in the context of life-extending interventions because not all years saved are of the same quality, depending on symptoms, pain, and numerous intangibles. However, the practical measurement of quality of life is not without considerable controversy.

A common theme of cost-effectiveness and cost-utility analysis is the need to compare directly one or more policies, programs, drugs, or interventions with another approach, often the current standard of care. By contrast, cost–benefit analysis allows the analyst to determine whether a program has a positive net social benefit relative to an implicit "do nothing" option. Thus, at least in principle, a program with a positive net social benefit is worth doing. Because cost-effectiveness studies produce a cost value for a given increment in a health outcome (e.g., life years saved) associated with doing one intervention versus another, in situations in which there is not a standard treatment option the approach may be less applicable.

VALUING BENEFITS AND COSTS

In this section, we examine a number of important questions that should be addressed in any cost analysis, including whose perspective is appropriate in cost analysis, what type of costs should be tabulated and for how long, and difficult issues regarding how one arrives at monetary values for health outcomes.

Whose Benefits and Costs?

A key issue in any cost analysis is defining the perspective of the study. That is, from whose perspective are the costs and gains being measured?

Possible perspectives include patient, provider, employer, insurance company, and government, but the most preferred perspective for the purposes of public policy decisions is that of society as a whole (Drummond, O'Brien, Stoddart, & Torrance, 1997; Gold, Siegel, Russell, & Weinstein, 1996). The societal perspective is the only approach that does not count as a gain, something that comes as a cost to someone else.

Although all good and credible cost studies should provide an estimate of the societal perspective if for no other reason than as a reference point, it can be useful in particular contexts to provide estimates from other perspectives. For example, corporations often argue that they should not be expected to consider the societal perspective in decisions that must be made; they often claim that their fiduciary duty is to act solely in the interests of their shareholders. In public policy settings, elected representatives, based on their voters' preferences, sometimes focus on the public payer perspective versus the full societal perspective; such a decision criterion would tend to yield policies that lead to costs being shifted to affected groups or beneficiaries of interventions rather than tax payers. The key point is that in all cases the analyst needs to make explicit the study's perspective.

Types of Costs

Accurate and consistent measurement of economic costs requires distinguishing among several types of costs. Monetary costs are the most straightforward because they involve the actual purchase of goods or services, whereas nonmonetary costs do not involve the actual purchase of goods and services and frequently involve opportunity costs. For example, if goods and services are donated, that does not imply that they are free; goods and services are valued by their opportunity cost, which typically would represent their market value or price. Likewise, if unpaid volunteers are used in an intervention, economists believe that they too are not free. Because the goal is to measure social costs, their time is valued on the basis of the opportunity cost of their time, which is typically estimated by using the full wage (cash wages plus the value of any fringe benefits) that individuals with similar human capital would need to be paid to induce them to do the same type of work. As is evident, there are many values that underlie these types of practices and analyses, and being explicit about such values when making computations is critical.

It is also important to distinguish conceptually between the direct and indirect costs associated with an intervention. Direct costs are those immediately related to the intervention or illness, such as hospital charges. By contrast, indirect costs are not immediately related to the intervention or illness and are "downstream." Indirect costs might involve the value of time spent getting to an intervention site, for example. Indirect costs are no less important than direct costs and, in many instances, can be greater in magnitude, but they are frequently more difficult to measure and thus easier to forget or ignore by researchers.

Other general principles in the estimation of costs are important to note. As noted previously, market-determined prices are generally preferred when imputing a value to a good or service. Nonmarket items pose a measurement challenge. For example, valuing lost leisure time is difficult, but in general the individual's wages can be used as a proxy. If the individual is not employed, it does not mean that the individual's time is valued at zero. Typically either a statistical algorithm is used by economists or a "quick and dirty" assumption such as the minimum wage is used as an estimate. With respect specifically to health care interventions, it is important to note that in economic analyses, medical provider charges are rarely equated with costs. The reason offered is that charges are often not determined through a competitive process; however, contract rates with payers are likely to have a closer resemblance to actual costs. Whenever it is feasible, paid or allowed amounts are to be preferred to charges. Similarly, a flat per diem cost for inpatient days is likely not an accurate reflection of economic cost because the 1st day is probably a high cost, but the 7th day is likely lower.

How Long to Track Costs and Benefits?

A common challenge to analysts is how long to collect both cost and benefit data. As a general rule, it is important to collect cost and benefit data for as long as relevant effects associated with the intervention can occur. This might be 6 months or a lifetime depending on the nature of the intervention. The time frame must be chosen with a critical eye on not selecting a time period that might bias decision makers. For example, when evaluating a therapeutic intervention, it may not be advisable to choose a 24-month follow-up period when there is a risk of subsequent complications 5 years in the future. There are examples of very long-term follow-ups, such as Vaillant's (2003) 60-year study of men who were dealing with alcohol abuse. However, it is obviously often impractical to collect cost and benefit information for a lifetime, but it is incumbent on the analyst to argue credibly why such future costs and benefits are safely ignored. An alternative is to use estimates from other studies to impute the likely lifetime effects of an intervention. For example, an intervention to increase healthy activity among senior citizens might result in weight loss among participants; using population-based epidemiological estimates of the relationship between weight loss or body mass index and life years saved or risk of heart disease and the like, a credible estimate of these longer term outcomes can be constructed.

When confronting future costs and benefits, economists believe that it is essential to recognize the time value of money; therefore, all future costs and benefits are discounted. In other words, a dollar today is more valuable than a dollar next year or in 10 years. The reason for this is not solely because of inflation (although that is certainly a factor). The most fundamental reason for economists is the notion of opportunity cost: The dollar could be spent and enjoyed today on a good or service, and consumption today is preferable to waiting for a future date (a costly activity). Moreover, the future itself is uncertain; put simply, one could be either disabled or not alive in a year or at some time in the future.

The formula for deriving the present value (PV) of future costs and benefits is as follows:

$$PV = X / (1 + r)^t, \tag{2}$$

where PV represents the discounted present value of the amount X t years in the future; r is the discount rate. More generally, a stream of costs or benefits accrued over a future period of time would be dealt with using the following formula:

$$PV = \sum_{t=0 \text{ to } n} X_t / (1 + r)^t, \tag{3}$$

where $\sum$ represents the summation operator and the other terms are as shown in the previous equation. The appropriate discount rate, r, should conceptually represent the societal discount rate (i.e., the rate at which society should discount future benefits). Although there is little dispute regarding the need to discount, the value of the societal discount rate is the subject of considerable academic and policy debate. In general, a rate of 3% to 5% is used in practice.

Some might argue that discounting biases decision makers toward more short-term (and potentially less ambitious) interventions, but there are several key points to consider in favor of discounting. For example, it is easy to consider scenarios in which community interventions with small (but persistent) gains into the future are worth doing no matter what the cost. For example, Jason, Ji, Anes, and Birkhead (1991) developed procedures for reducing the illegal sale of tobacco to minors. These procedures were controversial because it was expensive to nationally monitor and provide consequences to merchants who illegally sold minors tobacco; questions were raised as to whether these types of strategies were either effective or a good use of resources. However, DiFranza, Savageau, and Fletcher (2009) found that a 25% increase in compliance of laws prohibiting cigarette sales to minors had a deterrent effect that was similar to increasing the price of a pack of cigarettes by $2.00. Even more concretely, it was estimated that for every 1%

increase in the rate of merchant compliance with the laws, daily smoking rates among 10th graders fell by 2%.

Valuation of Health Outcomes

Undoubtedly, one of the most challenging (and often controversial) aspects of economic cost analysis is the assignment of dollar values for health outcomes and human life. There are two broad categories of methodologies for arriving at such values. The first involves the use of observed behaviors to infer the value of health outcomes, and the second involves the use of surveys and questionnaires to estimate the value of health outcomes. We briefly describe both of these approaches in turn.

In estimation based on observed behavior, the goal is to use a consistent and theoretically justified methodology rooted in economic principles to arrive at a dollar valuation of health outcomes. A common strategy is rooted in the human capital model from labor economics. Broadly speaking, the human capital approach values individual lives by the summing the total of their earning potential, which is influenced among other things by their education, training, experience, intelligence, and health. Consequently, interventions aimed at improving health can make individuals more productive and thus increase earnings. (Of course, interventionists are also often very interested in other outcomes, such as quality of life indicators.) Effects are then measured by estimating changes in hours worked or earnings; such strategies are extremely common in cost analyses.

The implicit assumption of economists is that earnings or wages represent the societal value of what the worker produces. However, there are a few problems with this assumption. First, labor market imperfections can cause earnings or wages not to accurately reflect the value of what the worker produces. The broader problem with the human capital approach is what to do with individuals who are not employed because they are too young, too old, disabled, or otherwise out of the labor force. Strategies that have been used in prior work to deal with such situations include assigning all nonemployed individuals the minimum wage and imputing an earning change or simply assigning them a zero; neither approach, however, is theoretically satisfactory. As an alternative, regression-based estimation techniques are available to impute wages for the nonemployed.

Another approach based on observed behavior is known as *revealed preference*. The basic idea is to study the trade-offs that individuals make between some (generally difficult to value) good and money wages to impute a value of the good. A common example is the notion of a worker accepting a higher wage job for which there is a higher risk of injury or death. If an individual is willing to accept a job that pays $2,000 more per year but comes with

1-in-1,000 higher risk of death per year, the implied value of life revealed by the individual's choice is $2,000,000. This revealed preference valuation is frequently referred to as the value of a *statistical* life. Similar calculations can be made to value the risks of specific injuries.

The clear benefit of the revealed preference approach is that it is based on actual individual choices. However, the approach has several potential shortcomings. First, individuals may not be able to fully grasp very small risks, such as the hypothetical 1-in-1,000 higher risk of death per year above. Also, individuals are not homogeneous with respect to their degree of risk aversion. There is also a very strong information requirement implicit in this approach. That is, there needs to be very good and widely disseminated information about the injury and mortality risks associated with different activities, and this is certainly not always the case.

The other broad category of methods designed to estimate the value of health outcomes involves the use of questionnaires and other approaches to directly elicit responses from individuals. The primary approach is the contingent valuation study, which uses surveys to present respondents with a hypothetical scenario or set of scenarios. Respondents are often asked to choose the maximum they are willing to pay for the good, service, or intervention in question. In this type of study, rather than estimating the value of the benefits from each individual component potentially affected by a community intervention, representative members of the community might be selected and asked what their maximum willingness to pay is for the service or set of services (or health outcomes) that the intervention comprises. The approach has the advantage of frequently being cheaper to conduct than other methods for assessing the value of the manifold outcomes associated with an intervention.

Among the limitations with this approach, there is a distinct difference between stating that you would be willing to pay a given sum for a service and actually paying a given sum for a service. Economists as a rule tend to believe what people do over what they say. Also, the willingness to pay an estimate tends to be quite sensitive to the method used to elicit the value.

Sensitivity Analyses

No economic cost analysis is complete without a thorough battery of sensitivity analyses. The goal of a sensitivity analysis is to test the robustness of the results to alternative model assumptions, that is, how sensitive the results are to each component of the costs and benefits. For example, it could be that a particular community intervention affects drug use, drug treatment service use, and criminal justice encounters. In such a case the cost associated with the criminal justice system could be large relative to the other components and thus potentially quite influential in the overall net benefit calculation. A reasonable sensitivity analysis in this instance might be to consider lower estimates of the cost of criminal justice interactions to see how the net benefit changes. More formally, sensitivity analyses recognize that every measured component of the costs and benefits is typically measured with error. Sensitivity analysis is an attempt to incorporate the sampling error into the analysis. If standard errors are available for each component of the analysis, it is possible to use simulation methods to generate a distribution of the net benefit calculation.

A SPECIFIC EXAMPLE OF ECONOMIC COST ANALYSIS: OXFORD HOUSE RECOVERY HOMES

Each year 600,000 inmates are released back into communities, often without receiving substance abuse or mental health treatment during their incarceration (National Institute on Drug Abuse, 2002). Many ex-offenders are released from prison with ongoing drug addictions, and studies indicate that substance abuse within correctional facilities occurs at roughly the same rate as substance abuse before incarceration, with estimates ranging from 74% to 82% (Keene, 1997). Although many factors contribute to criminal recidivism, such as lack of employment or housing, the strongest predictor of recidivism is substance use (National Center on Addiction and Substance Abuse at Columbia University, 1998). One of the most effective ways of reducing recidivism is through substance abuse treatment (Broome, Knight, Hiller, & Simpson, 1996). Some intensive prison-based drug treatment programs have contributed to reduced recidivism rates (Wexler, 1995; Wexler, Williams, Early, & Trotman, 1996), but these tend to be expensive and are available only for relatively brief periods of time.

Therapeutic communities with professional staff are one effective way of creating a stable abstinence support system. However, in contrast to therapeutic communities, another model—recovery homes—might have advantages with respect to both cost and the availability of these supports for longer periods of time. Researchers have long maintained that recovery homes are an essential component of the solution for a wide range of offenders (Steadman, Morris, & Dennis, 1995). Oxford Houses are one type of recovery home setting for individuals dealing with substance abuse problems. In the United States there are more than 1,440 Oxford Houses in 387 cities and 46 states serving more than 11,000 people, thus making this organization the largest self-help recovery residential program in the country (Oxford House, 2010). No professional staff are involved with the houses; the residents live together in a democratic, moderately sized (from seven to 10 individuals), single-sex, single-family home and provide each other with a supportive abstinent social support network. The residents must follow Oxford House guidelines, which include paying rent, abstaining from alcohol and drug use, and avoiding disruptive behavior. Oxford House residents are free to choose whether to seek psychological or drug treatment by professionals or Narcotics Anonymous or Alcoholics Anonymous affiliation. In short, Oxford House residents have the freedom to decide whether to seek the treatment of their choice while they receive constant support and guidance.

The expansion of Oxford Houses was in part due to a provision within the Anti-Drug Abuse Act of 1988, which required all states to begin a revolving loan fund of $100,000. These loans were made available to anyone in recovery who wanted to open a recovery house. The $4,000 loans provided the funding to rent and furnish the houses, but the loans would have to be repaid by the house members over the subsequent 2 years.

In addition to these loan funds that each state was required to set up, some states also paid for Oxford House recruiters to help establish homes. To examine the impact of this policy on the nationwide growth of Oxford Houses, that is, the diffusion of this innovation, we looked at house growth in a state-level multiple baseline framework. The use of this operant research design is most compatible with Kelly's (2003) recommendation for pluralistic inquiry in community research. We therefore essentially treated the policy as a behavioral intervention, tracing the growth of houses in 13 states. In Figure 13.1, the x-axis represents years, starting in 1975, and the y-axis represents the number of Oxford Houses. The y-axis shows the number of houses, starting at 0 and going up to 100. There are two groups of states, with the intervention occurring at different times for these two groups of states (this is called a multiple baseline design). For the top of the figure, each line represents one of 10 states.

In the top part of the figure, the low number of houses in each state is called a baseline, and it represents what occurred when there were neither loan programs nor recruiters in the 13 states. In 1988 and 1989, there was dramatic growth in each of these states. This is the date the Anti-Drug Abuse Act of 1988 went into effect, and these 10 states were among those that had both the loan funds and technical assistance involving hiring recruiters. In the bottom part of the figure, one can see that when three other states did not use the loan fund and technical assistance in 1988 and 1989, very few Oxford Houses emerged; however, a few years later, when these three states used the loan fund and the technical assistance associated with it, the growth of Oxford Houses increased with this policy initiative (Jason, Braciszewski, Olson, & Ferrari, 2005). These findings indicate that supportive economic policies, such as a loan fund and technical assistance, can help increase the number of residential abstinence-supportive settings in states. From a policy point of view, though, a critical question is whether these recovery homes are effective in helping individuals remain abstinent and out of the criminal justice system.

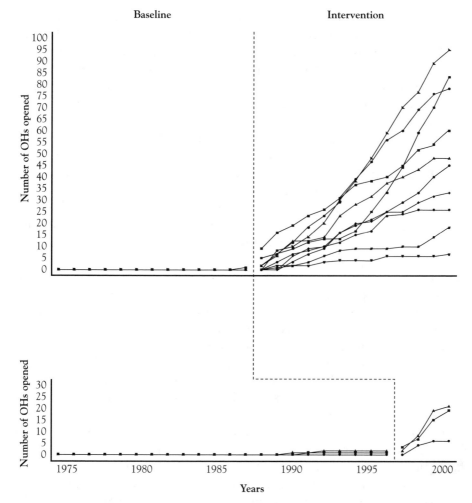

Figure 13.1. The growth of Oxford Houses (OHs) over time. From "Increasing the Number of Mutual Help Recovery Homes for Substance Abusers: Effects of Government Policy and Funding Assistance," by L. A. Jason, J. Braciszewski, B. D. Olson, and J. R. Ferrari, 2005, *Behavior and Social Issues, 14,* p. 76. Copyright 2005 by L. A. Jason, J. Braciszewski, B. D. Olson, and J. R. Ferrari. Reprinted with permission.

Oxford House Outcomes

Jason, Olson, Ferrari, and Lo Sasso (2006) evaluated the evidence surrounding the costs and benefits of the Oxford House program. In Jason et al.'s study, which was supported by a National Institute of Alcohol Abuse and Alcoholism grant, 150 individuals who completed treatment at alcohol and drug abuse facilities in the Chicago metropolitan area were recruited, with half being randomly assigned to live in an Oxford House and the other half receiving community-based aftercare services (i.e., usual care). A 24-month follow-up found that 31.3% of the participants assigned to the Oxford House condition reported substance use, compared with 64.8% of the usual care participants, and 76.1% of the Oxford House participants were employed, versus 48.6% of the usual care participants. During the 30 days prior to the final assessment, the mean number of days engaged in illegal activity was 0.9 for the Oxford House participants and 1.8 for the usual care participants. The Oxford House participants earned roughly $550 more per month than did the participants in the usual care group.

Next, Lo Sasso, Byro, Jason, Ferrari, and Olson (2011) used a cost–benefit approach to study the relative effects of Oxford House versus usual care. Their results suggest that Oxford House compares quite favorably with usual care. Specifically, costs were obtained by summing the estimated costs associated with treatment, including inpatient and outpatient substance use treatment, the opportunity cost of time spent in self-help programs such as Alcoholics Anonymous and Narcotics Anonymous, and the costs associated with Oxford House. The benefits were estimated by estimating dollar values associated with differences in alcohol and drug use, illegal activity, and incarceration rates. When these estimates were combined, the net average benefit of Oxford House stay was estimated to be more than $23,000 per person. The positive net benefit for Oxford House was primarily driven by a large difference in illegal activity between the Oxford House and the usual care participants. Using a sensitivity analysis, Lo Sasso et al. estimated the net benefits under a more conservative approach and still arrived at a net benefit favorable to Oxford House of $13,136 per person. Conversely, when adopting the public payer perspective rather than the societal perspective, given that Oxford House residents pay the rent and expenses associated with the treatment modality out of their own pockets, the net benefit would be an even more favorable $31,043 per person.

These findings have important implications because they point to the potential savings that could be had by supporting self-organized aftercare treatment options. At a time when many states are looking for ways to reduce spending, community-based programs such as Oxford House could provide an appealing and effective alternative.

As discussed, economic cost analysis is a powerful tool that allows the analyst to compare the dollar value of a given program or programs, in this case Oxford House and potentially staff-managed treatment settings like therapeutic communities, with respect to the dollar-valued economic costs associated with the programs (Cartwright, 1998, 2000; French, 1995, 2000). In an ongoing study supported by a grant from the National Institute on Drug Abuse, we are currently evaluating the differential effectiveness of three conditions (an Oxford House, a staff-managed therapeutic community, and usual aftercare) for people leaving prison or jail. The advantage of cost–benefit analysis over cost-effectiveness analysis in this case is that there are a multitude of benefits that could result from complex interventions such as Oxford House and therapeutic communities. Had we been, for example, primarily focused on a single outcome such as drug or alcohol use, we could have used the methods of cost-effectiveness analysis formulated for the study to measure the cost per drug or alcohol relapse averted. If we had had a measure of quality of life, we could have likewise incorporated methods from cost-utility analysis.

Although the appropriate perspective of a study of Oxford House (vs. other care modalities) is the societal perspective, because the majority of substance abuse treatment is financed through the public sector and such programs are increasingly scrutinized by state and federal policymakers looking to save money, it is also of interest to estimate the costs and benefits accruing to the public sector. A potentially interesting secondary analysis could examine a policy-relevant aspect of Oxford House, namely, its self-funded and largely self-governing nature, which has the ability to reduce government expenditures (in part through shifting the costs, such as rent, to the client) with potentially equivalent benefits relative to government-funded treatment.

Economic Costs of Treatment

Measuring the bulk of the economic costs of Oxford House treatment can be accomplished by administering the Drug Abuse Treatment Cost Analysis Program (DATCAP) instrument (French, 2001; French, Salome, Sindelar, & McLellan, 2002). DATCAP has been used successfully to estimate economic costs associated with therapeutic communities (French, Sacks, De Leon, Staines, & McKendrick, 1999). DATCAP allows researchers to obtain measures of the economic or opportunity costs, which as discussed previously are distinct from the accounting costs representing the actual expenditures and depreciation of those resources used by the treatment program. Economic costs represent the full value of all resources regardless of whether a direct expenditure is involved (French, 2000). DATCAP is flexible enough to generate total cost estimates for individual cost categories and for the program as a whole. With client case flow data, that is, the length of time clients are actually in the treatment program, DATCAP also generates average cost estimates of providing uninterrupted treatment services to a single client for a given time period (French, 2001).

DATCAP generates economic cost estimates for Oxford House, therapeutic communities, and similar programs by surveying relevant contact persons at the program sites. Economic costs are estimated by measuring any revenue derived from client fees and the costs of personnel, contracted services, buildings and facilities, equipment, supplies and materials, and other economic costs, including the value of donated goods and services. Where appropriate, one attempts to use local-level prices to arrive at a value of goods and services. By calculating the program-level costs on a per person basis, one can ascertain the economic costs associated with treatment. This provides a useful first step in understanding an important portion of the costs associated with Oxford House, for example, and can be useful in comparisons with published estimates of alternative treatment modalities for ex-offenders, such therapeutic communities (see, e.g., French, McCollister, Sacks, McKendrick, & De Leon, 2002). One is also able to examine how the cost analysis differs when one considers only those costs accountable by the public sector to address the policy-relevant issue of whether government costs are indeed lower with a self-governed and self-funded program such as Oxford House. Completed DATCAP surveys for three representative Oxford Houses in the Chicago area can be found in the web appendix to this chapter (http://pubs.apa.org/books/supp/Jason-Glenwick).

CONCLUSION

As mentioned earlier, community research frequently deals with issues of high public policy significance, and as such, support from policymakers for the implementation of creative solutions depends critically not only on the benefits of a given program but also on the program's costs. In addition, new community interventions are often judged relative to existing (competing) alternatives. Cost analysis has an important role for community research because it can provide a critical link between research and policy when the goal is to provide a well-reasoned and economically justified pathway to implementation. In this chapter, we have provided an overview of the general economic considerations involved in cost analysis as well as an example of how such an approach has been carried out in the context of an ongoing study of the residential treatment of ex-offenders with a substance use history.

REFERENCES

Anti-Drug Abuse Act of 1988, Pub. L. No. 100–690, Stat. 4181 (1988).

Broome, K. M., Knight, K., Hiller, M. L., & Simpson, D. D. (1996). Drug treatment process indicators for probationers and prediction of recidivism. *Journal of Substance Abuse Treatment, 13*, 487–491. doi:10.1016/S0740–5472(96)00097–9

Cartwright, W. S. (1998). Cost–benefit and cost-effectiveness analysis of drug abuse treatment services. *Evaluation Review, 22,* 609–636. doi:10.1177/0193841X9802200503

Cartwright, W. S. (2000). Cost–benefit analysis of drug treatment services: Review of the literature. *The Journal of Mental Health Policy and Economics, 3,* 11–26. doi:10.1002/1099-176X(200003)3:1<11::AID-MHP66>3.0.CO;2-0

DiFranza, J. R., Savageau, J. A., & Fletcher, K. E. (2009). Enforcement of underage sales laws as a predictor of daily smoking among adolescents—A national study. *BMC Public Health, 9,* 107. Retrieved from http://www.biomedcentral.com/1471-2458/9/107 doi:10.1186/1471-2458-9-107

Drummond, M. F., O'Brien, B., Stoddart, G. L., & Torrance, G. W. (1997). *Methods for the economic evaluation of health care programmes.* New York, NY: Oxford University Press.

French, M. T. (1995). Economic evaluation of drug abuse treatment programs: Methodology and findings. *The American Journal of Drug and Alcohol Abuse, 21,* 111–135. doi:10.3109/00952999509095233

French, M. T. (2000). Economic evaluation of alcohol treatment services. *Evaluation and Program Planning, 23,* 27–39. doi:10.1016/S0149-7189(99)00035-X

French, M. T. (2001). *Drug abuse treatment cost analysis program (DATCAP): Program version* (7th ed.). Coral Gables, FL: University of Miami.

French, M. T., McCollister, K. E., Sacks, S., McKendrick, K., & De Leon, G. (2002). Benefit–cost analysis of a modified therapeutic community for mentally ill chemical abusers. *Evaluation and Program Planning, 25,* 137–148. doi:10.1016/S0149-7189(02)00006-X

French, M. T., Sacks, S., De Leon, G., Staines, G., & McKendrick, K. (1999). Modified therapeutic community for mentally ill chemical abusers: Outcomes and costs. *Evaluation & the Health Professions, 22,* 60–85.

French, M. T., Salome, H. J., Sindelar, J. L., & McLellan, A. T. (2002). Benefit–cost analysis of addiction treatment: Methodological guidelines and empirical application using the DATCAP and ASI. *Health Services Research, 37,* 433–455. doi:10.1111/1475-6773.031

Gold, M. R., Siegel, J. E., Russell, L. B., & Weinstein, M. C. (1996). *Cost-effectiveness in health and medicine.* New York, NY: Oxford University Press.

Jason, L. A., Braciszewski, J. M., Olson, B. D., & Ferrari, J. R. (2005). Increasing the number of mutual help recovery homes for substance abusers: Effects of government policy and funding assistance. *Behavior and Social Issues, 14,* 71–79.

Jason, L. A., Ji, P. Y., Anes, M., & Birkhead, S. H. (1991). Active enforcement of cigarette control laws in the prevention of cigarette sales to minors. *JAMA, 266,* 3159–3161. doi:10.1001/jama.266.22.3159

Jason, L. A., Keys, C. B., Suarez-Balcazar, Y., Taylor, R. R., Davis, M., Durlak, J., & Isenberg, D. (2004). (Eds.). *Participatory community research: Theories and methods in action.* Washington, DC: American Psychological Association.

Jason, L. A., Olson, B. D., Ferrari, J. R., & Lo Sasso, A. T. (2006). Communal housing settings enhance substance abuse recovery. *American Journal of Public Health*, 96, 1727–1729. doi:10.2105/AJPH.2005.070839

Keene, J. (1997). Drug use among prisoners before, during and after custody. *Addiction Research*, 4, 343–353. doi:10.3109/16066359709002968

Kelly, J. G. (2003). Science and community psychology: Social norms for pluralistic inquiry. *American Journal of Community Psychology*, 31, 213–217. doi:10.1023/A:1023998318268

Lo Sasso, A. T., Byro, E., Jason, L. A., Ferrari, J. R., & Olson, B. (2011). Benefits and costs associated with mutual-help community-based recovery homes: The Oxford House model. *Evaluation and Program Planning*. Advance online publication. doi:10.1016/j.evalprogplan.2011.06.006

National Center on Addiction and Substance Abuse at Columbia University. (1998). *Behind bars: Substance abuse and America's prison population*. New York, NY: Author.

National Institute on Drug Abuse. (2002). *NIDA and other agencies establish research network to improve substance abuse treatment services in criminal justice settings*. Retrieved from http://archives.drugabuse.gov/newsroom/02/NS-11-5.html

Oxford House. (2010). *Oxford House—Celebrating 35 years*. Silver Spring, MD: Oxford House World Services.

Steadman, H. J., Morris, S. M., & Dennis, D. L. (1995). The diversion of mentally ill persons from jails to community-based services: A profile of programs. *American Journal of Public Health*, 85, 1630–1635. doi:10.2105/AJPH.85.12.1630

Vaillant, G. E. (2003). A 60-year follow-up of alcoholic men. *Addiction*, 98, 1043–1051. doi:10.1046/j.1360-0443.2003.00422.x

Wexler, H. K. (1995). The success of therapeutic communities for substance abusers in American prisons. *Journal of Psychoactive Drugs*, 27, 57–66.

Wexler, H. K., Williams, R. A., Early, K. E., & Trotman, C. D. (1996). Prison treatment for substance abusers: Stay 'n out revisited. In K. E. Early (Ed.), *Drug treatment behind bars: Prison-based strategies for change* (pp. 101–108). Westport, CT: Praeger.

AFTERWORD

JAMES G. KELLY

The contributions to this important volume present a variety of methods available to the community psychology discipline that can clarify with some precision community-based preventive interventions and social policy innovations. What underlies these presentations is the spirit of improvisation, discovery, and serendipity that is so pivotal when generating inquiry, especially outside the confines of an academic research laboratory. ✓

Over the years community psychology has represented the potential and, increasingly, the reality for understanding community and organizational processes. Especially pertinent has been knowledge about the ways in which community-generated inquiries contribute new understandings and insights. These methods increase the options for grounded understandings of community systems, especially methods that can illuminate positive processes, events, and efforts to improve the quality of life of a particular community.

In this book, the authors illustrate how methods in community psychology can address the interdependence between social and contextual topics and the everyday lives of individuals. Such multimethod efforts can contribute to the selection of those methods to best illuminate the complexity within a specific community. With the availabilty of a variety of methods, more explicit connections can be offered to contribute to public policies for that locale.

Big picture

CHAPTER APPRAISALS

As Jason and Glenwick assert in their Introduction (see Chapter 1, this volume), the increasing interdisciplinary activities of community psychology represent a shift in how the choice of methods is considered. In this volume are examples of research that includes more than just one method assumed to be apt for a variety occasions. There is an emerging view that interventions need to be understood from different vantage points. The operating premise is that the presence and applications of varied methods can express different facets of a topic. This value can encourage the participation of different disciplines, which with their own traditions and choices of methods can add to the dialogue between researchers and citizens about the interpretation of findings.

Tebes (see Chapter 2) anchors the presentation of this variety through a review of past philosophical efforts to move beyond the tenets of logical positivism. Instead, there is an emerging openness about those philosophical tenets that give legitimacy to the values and aspirations of the field of community psychology. As Tebes asserts, perspectivism is one current resource for these trenchant inquiries.

Chp3

Barker and Pistrang (see Chapter 3, this volume) appraise the use of pluralistic methods, as presented in this volume, as a resource for community psychologists doing community-based research. One major point they make is that inquiry should be question driven and not method driven. For me, that assertion is the key to the use of multiple methods: So goes the question, so goes the method. This means that doctoral education, journal editors, and granting agencies can support proposals and submissions that make an effort to break new ground and let the choice of difficult complex topics set in motion the choice of method, even though the method may be outside the focus of convenience of contemporary thought. The authors present a compelling list of criteria, such as sensitivity to people's contexts. Researchers are improving, but more could be done to illustrate the compelling use of novel methods. Whether the investigator thinks from a realist or constructivist epistemology, as the authors point out, the field should give itself "periodic methodological health checks." Each of the chapters in this book gets investigators started.

MM

Campbell, Gregory, Patterson, and Bybee (see Chapter 4) illustrate that the timing of the use of multiple methods is salient for both the processes of the inquiry and communication with the various audiences of the research reports. They present how a sequential design with various methods and successive new questions can stimulate inquiry with direct policy implications for organizational changes in service delivery systems. A potential side benefit is the range of new collaborations between the research staff and community organizations.

Dymnicki and Henry (see Chapter 5) illustrate how cluster analysis, a variety of methods to delineate natural groupings, can be an unexpected resource to understand block groups in neighborhoods. One of the side benefits of using such methods is the use of graphical methods in contrast to statistical tables. This way to illustrate findings is a potential asset in communicating results with citizens. It also allows the researcher to provide data that dissipate stereotypes about class, race, and qualities of neighborhoods and is, therefore, a welcome resource for public policy discussions.

Bogat, Zarrett, Peck, and von Eye (see Chapter 6) point out that quantitative approaches are salient for examining a small group of participants when there are observations and data over several hundred times. The rhythm of episodes can be pinpointed to illustrate another meaning of the ecology of individual behavior. In one example, one of the coauthors, von Eye, clarified risk factors related to mothers experiencing partner violence. Out of eight risk factors only maternal depression and easy child temperament were significant predictors of adaptation, especially for children who were exposed to only one or two time periods. This work not only informs research on intimate partner violence and the effect on children in such relationships but also stimulates increased efforts on the family impacts of maternal depression and the protective factors in child temperament.

Durlak and Pachan (see Chapter 7) remind readers that the American Psychological Association now offers guidelines for the use of meta-analysis as a method for critically evaluating a body of research. This contribution can encourage community researchers to take advantage of a method that can clarify just what the impacts have been in community-based interventions. Standardized mean differences can help community psychologists evaluate the impact and utility of community programs. Meta-analysis also has implications for how literature reviews are conducted, how research is described, and the differences in criteria used when reporting results in conference reports, dissertations, and unpublished papers. The authors present a clear example of using meta-analysis methods to assess the outcomes of after-school programs for school-age youth.

One of the themes that each of the contributions points to is that most of the methods depend on accurate measures. This is especially so with time-series analysis (TSA) when accurately modeling serial dependence. Hoeppner and Proeschold-Bell (see Chapter 8) point to a unique resource that TSA provides community-based research, namely, the analysis of archival data.

Anecdotal observations can be tested by TSA. Community psychologists can rely on these methods to identify at regular intervals the impact of health and welfare policies as well as worldwide events. Another attractive feature of TSA is the focus on cyclical or seasonal contextual patterns so that data collection procedures can adapt to such patterns. As Hoeppner and Proeschold-Bell point out, using TSA requires a very supportive relationship with those persons providing data at regular intervals—another hallmark of community psychology!

Connell (see Chapter 9) orients the reader to a method that can illuminate social conditions, such as returning home from out-of-home placement or negative events like injurious behavior to self or others. Here the challenge is to select a target event, identify plausible starting points for observations, and select metrics to assess duration of the event. As Connell points out, these decisions require some informed judgment as to which point in time all individuals still at risk will experience the target event. Becoming informed about community conditions prior to the selected event again means that the more the investigator knows about the local community and its culture, the more such informed choices can enhance the use of this method.

Todd, Allen, and Javdani (see Chapter 10) present a description of multilevel modeling as a powerful resource for community researchers who have large data sets and want to examine differences among groups in different organizations. With many community researchers examining how schools enhance or limit the learning of students, this method can illuminate contextual effects.

Another topic salient for multilevel modeling is the investigation of neighborhood effects on personal coping and styles of living. Jason, Porter, and Rademaker (see Chapter 11) orient the reader to methods of public health involving establishing the prevalence and incidence of particular conditions. Although they concentrate on the measurement of prevalence as a resource for community researchers, they also point to future connections between the use of these methods and panels of persons who might serve as informants in future Internet and social media inquiries. The authors point to the value of accessing information not only from selected individuals but also from their friends and family members.Such steps can better help clinicians evaluate subjective experiences such as pain, fatigue, or feeling subdued. Friends and family, not usually considered as research informants, can be significant resources for interpretations of prevalence data by noting the personal ecology of the primary informant.

Morton, Peterson, Speer, Reid, and Hughey (see Chapter 12) introduce the reader to a set of methods not as familiar to psychologists, even community psychologists, geographic information systems. This method is a potentially compelling resource for those community psychologists and community researchers who will be asked to present information to public and elected officials and community organizations about large social forces active in a community. This method also can help to validate public policies that are now working. A pertinent example is the connection between the availability of green space and positive exercise activity.

Lo Sasso and Jason (see Chapter 13) point to a class of methods that are apt for evaluating self-governing efforts to reduce the incidence, for example, of new episodes of abusing drugs. Such programs as DATCAP, as they point out, can specify the economic costs of the elements of a multifaceted program such as 1,400 Oxford Houses located in 400 cities. Such economic methods have multiple benefits because they speak to the interests of residents, administrators, and potential new hosts of these recovery programs. As a bonus, such methods are an incentive to establish intensive multiple case studies for the unique program elements in each of the Oxford Houses. This process, in turn, can celebrate the Oxford participants' commitment to recovery as well as an evaluation of their efforts to recover.

SOME AFTERTHOUGHTS

Reading these contributions reminded me of how far the field has matured since the days of the Swampscott Conference in 1965, which gave rise to the field of community psychology. The richness and variety of methodological opportunities now available is energizing. These achievements suggest that the field is continuing to understand the connections among people, their various living conditions, and those ever-present historical forces.

There is increasingly palpable evidence that community researchers who are proponents of varied methods can openly and frankly present, analyze, and reflect on ways in which knowledge can be generated to better understand the ecology of individuals and social systems. During the next period of deveopment, increased attention can be devoted to understanding more about how these various research methods affect the processes of creating partnerships with citizens. Related is the issue of the calender time required in applying these methods over time periods expected—by researchers and citizens—to carry out these community-based methodological enterprises.

Some 30 years ago, Elliot Mishler (1979) noted that there was increasing evidence that research findings appeared to be context dependent. Nowadays there are scholars, such as the contributors to this volume, who develop exemplary examples to keep on the journey to create knowledge and to probe the complexities of people living in both geographical and self-defined communities. Multiple methods are resources to keep reaching toward this goal.

With increasing interdisciplinary activity in the social and health sciences, I hope that there will be increased connections between community psychologists and those who study history and philosophy and those who carry out oral histories and do narrative research. These colleagues offer community researchers potentially deep insights about living and coping in various circumstances. Julian Rappaport and his colleagues, for example, have been paving the way for narrative inquiry for some time (Aber, Maton, & Seidman, 2010). Another recent example is the work of Arthur W. Frank, who has illustrated how stories shape human experience (Frank, 2010). As Frank observed, "From stories we humans learn whom to trust and distrust, what to hope for and what to fear. We are always guessing, and we learn to guess by hearing stories" (p. 144).

In this vein, I have been personally impressed with how oral histories of six community leaders can enlarge the meaning of empirical findings about community leadership. My experience of videotaping these personal stories was enlightening and formed a validating memoir of the very reasons why 10 years of work were carried out. These videotaped statements by a sample of six community leaders were very gratifying to create and see. (Kelly, 1999b). Their personal statements made the work cited in the following publications even more significant for me because they were authentic and expressed personal and private values for each individual's commitment to being a community leader. (Kelly, 1999a; Kelly, Mock, & Tandon, 2000; Tandon, Azelton, Kelly, & Strickland, 1998).

As a future prospect, there may be collaborations with neuroscientists. A finding reported by Hruschka (2010, pp. 215–216) is that parts of the brain activate differently when seeing a close friend than when seeing an acquaintance. I hope that psychologists' collaborations with citizens and researchers in other professions develops to the point that those collaborating with psychologists respond to each other as close friends rather than neutral or aversive contacts!

Another asset for appreciating these contributions is the increasing awareness of how the research process works. Mythologies and genuflections are put aside. The authors of these chapters assert that inquiry, especially inquiry accomplished by community researchers, is more open, more accessible, more public, and demystified.

Increasingly, there are more presentations of how science "really" works. The writings of Stuart Shapin (1994, 2010) have done much to get psychologists' attention. In his earlier work he illustrated how the code of gentleman civility in 17th-century England was a major context for the response to Boyle's research on the use of the air pump (often referred to as *Boyle's law*—that the volume of a gas varies inversely with the pressure of the gas).

At the time, the philosopher–scientist was both free and knowledgeable, whereas his technician was dependent and merely skilled.

In contemporary scientific exploration within the social sciences there is less homage paid to the hard sciences. Schapin (2010) pointed out, "there is not now, and never has been, a consensus about what such a scientific method is" (p. 386). In closing his treatise, he wrote, "The place of science in the modern world is just the problem of describing the way we live now: what to believe, who to trust, what to do" (p. 391).

With the critical examination of varied approaches to method, psychologists can be exemplars for how discovery embedded in community contexts can be an enlightening demonstration that inquiry is congruent with a collaborative community and not confined to prior histories and paradigms of past research traditions.

Psychologists can be creditable because their thinking is deep and their curiosity prevails across time; their conversations can continue to point to how in their field their personally selected method is connected to other sources of information from other disciplines and, most assuredly, with their informants and collaborative partners. This way of doing inquiry suggests that psychologists know that their work is time bound, place located, and influenced by the limits of funding as well those ever-present local opportunities and constraints.

It seems to me that psychologists are on the cusp of realizing that in their chosen field there is a continuous, inevitable challenge to be conscious of the multiple milieus of where they work and with whom they work, including informants who are now colleagues. Psychologists can now admit that there is a grounded common sense about research. The proof is in the pudding, and the pudding varies from place to place. When the pudding varies, the contexts vary, and the choice of methods can vary.

There are rites of passage for the new community investigator, especially when there is a contrast among the researcher, the proposed method, and the style of the researcher in responding to differences in gender, ethnicity, and cultural modes of living within the collaborating group. These topics are germane, if not paramount, when there is an overture by a community investigator to participate in research with informants when the heritage of the potential collaborators varies from that of the researcher.

There is no longer any reason for a disconnect between psychologists' values for collaborative inquiry and the possible heritage of "high science." Psychological science is rooted in psychologists' own personal values, their collaborative style, and their willingness to really fit the method to the situation. This means time will tell, as opinion makers can see and value the economic return of having a field that is pluralistic in methods, responsive to informants' life situations, and informed about the complexities and subtleties of locales. There will continue to be, no doubt, eventful expeditions to report. This book sets a tone for these continued adventures.

Words from philosopher Stephen Toulmin (2001) form the coda for the comments in this Afterword, "The future belongs not so much to the pure thinkers who are content—at best—with optimistic or pessimistic slogans; it is a province, rather, for reflective practitioners who are ready to act on their ideals" (p. 214).

Onward!

REFERENCES

Aber, M. S., Maton, K. I., & Seidman, E. (2010). *Empowering settings and voices for social change*. New York, NY: Oxford University Press. doi:10.1093/acprof:oso/9780195380576.001.0001

Frank, A. W. (2010). *Letting stories breathe*. Chicago, IL: University of Chicago Press.

Hruschka, D. J. (2010). *Friendship: Development, ecology, and evolution of a relationship*. Berkeley, CA: University of California Press.

Kelly, J. G. (1999a). Contexts and community leadership: Inquiry as an ecological expedition. *American Psychologist, 54*, 953–961. doi:10.1037/h0088205

Kelly, J. G. (Producer/Director). (1999b). *Developing communities project exemplary leadership series. Oral history videos of six community leaders*. Available from Lynne C. Mock, PhD, c/o Developing Communities Project, 11300 South Halsted, Chicago, IL 60628.

Kelly, J. G., Mock, L. O., & Tandon, D. S. (2000). Collaborative inquiry with-African-American community leaders: Comments on a participatory action research process. In P. Reason & H. Bradbury (Eds.), *Handbook of action research* (pp. 348–355). London, England: Sage.

Mishler, E. G. (1979). Meaning in context: Is there any other kind? *Harvard Educational Review, 49*, 1–19.

Shapin, S. (1994). *A social history of truth: Civility and science in seventeenth-century England*. Chicago, IL: University of Chicago Press.

Shapin, S. (2010). *Never pure: Historical studies of science as if it was produced by people with bodies, situated in time, space, culture, and society, and struggling for credibility and authority*. Baltimore, MD: Johns Hopkins University Press.

Tandon, S. D., Azelton, S., Kelly, J. G., & Strickland, D. A. (1998). Constructing a tree for community leadership: Contexts and processes in collaborative inquiry. *American Journal of Community Psychology, 26*, 669–696. doi:10.1023/A:1022149123739

Toulmin, S. (2001). *Return to reason*. Cambridge, MA: Harvard University Press.

INDEX

ABOUT THE EDITORS

Leonard A. Jason, PhD, is a professor of psychology at DePaul University, Chicago, Illinois, where he heads the Center for Community Research. He has authored over 550 articles and 77 book chapters on recovery homes for the prevention of alcohol, tobacco, and drug abuse; preventive school-based interventions; media interventions; chronic fatigue syndrome; and program evaluation. He has been on the editorial boards of seven peer-reviewed psychology journals and has edited or written 23 books. He has served on review committees of the National Institute of Drug Abuse and the National Institute of Mental Health and has received more than $26 million in federal grants to support his research. He is a former president of the Division of Community Psychology of the American Psychological Association (APA) and a past editor of *The Community Psychologist*. He has received three media awards from the APA, and he is frequently asked to comment on policy issues for the media. Dr. Jason is the recipient of the 2011 Perpich Award from the International Association for CFS/ME (chronic fatigue syndrome/myalgic encephalomyelitis) for distinguished service to the CFS/ME community.

David S. Glenwick, PhD, is a professor of psychology at Fordham University, New York, NY, where he also has been the director of the graduate program in clinical psychology and co-coordinator of its specialization in clinical child and family psychology. He has authored more than 110 articles and edited four books, primarily in the areas of community and preventive psychology, clinical child psychology and developmental disabilities, and the teaching of psychology. Dr. Glenwick is a former president of the American Association of Correctional Psychology and a former editor of the journal *Criminal Justice and Behavior*. He is a fellow of seven divisions of the American Psychological Association (APA) and has been a member of the APA Continuing Education Committee. Dr. Glenwick has been on the editorial boards of four professional journals and is currently the chair of the New York State Psychological Association's Continuing Education Committee.

Notes

23 quote

4   M M
5   & MMR
p 4   Pluralism ; why not chapter 4, 3, 2

p148 def. operationalization
p 142 text who looking in detail
      TSA